HOLY TREES
and other ecological surprises

Lucy Goodison, PhD, specialises in the study of the religion of Minoan Crete. She has been an Honorary Research Fellow of University College London and a Leverhulme Research Fellow, and is the author of several books on archaeology, culture, psychotherapy, spirituality and the history of symbolism. She started work as a maker of historical documentary films for BBC TV. Then, influenced by libertarian politics and the women's liberation movement, she left the BBC to become involved in community-based politics. She helped start the Red Therapy group, trained in therapeutic massage, and is a Registered Dance Movement Therapist. As a freelance journalist she has specialised in learning difficulties and mental health issues. She has a daughter and a son and lives in Dorset.

By the same author:

(With Sheila Ernst) *In Our Own Hands: A Book of Self-Help Therapy*, The Women's Press, London, 1981

Death, Women and the Sun: Symbolism of Regeneration in Early Aegean Religion, Institute of Classical Studies, London, 1989

Moving Heaven and Earth: Sexuality, Spirituality and Social Change, The Women's Press, London, 1990; abridged, Pandora, London, 1993

The Dreams of Women, The Women's Press, London, 1995; W W Norton & Company, New York and London, 1996

(With Christine Morris, eds) *Ancient Goddesses: The Myths and the Evidence*, British Museum Press, London, 1998

The author wishes to express her gratitude to The Women's Press

HOLY TREES
and other ecological surprises

Lucy Goodison

Published in Great Britain by
Just Press
www.justpress.co.uk

British Library Cataloguing in Publication Data
A catalogue record for this book is available from the British Library

Library of Congress Cataloging in Publication Data
A catalog record for this book is available from the Library of Congress

Just Press offers books, DVDs, art works and lectures/exhibitions
that provide a platform for exchange between different generations
and interests. In areas including history, religion, theatre, health,
politics, art, poetry and fiction, we honour unsung aspects of human
experience and celebrate the unorthodox.

ISBN 978-1-907352-00-3

Typeset by FiSH Books, London, with additional typesetting and
design by The Running Head Limited, Cambridge,
www.therunninghead.com

Printed and bound in Great Britain by
TJ International Ltd, Padstow, Cornwall

CONTENTS

In memory of the trees
that used to stand
at 37 Coldharbour Lane
climbed on by young Goodisons,
Robinsons, Smiths, Wilkinsons and Colleys

ACKNOWLEDGEMENTS

My thanks are due to the Leverhulme Trust for a Research Fellowship facilitating archaeological work in Crete, in the course of which my interest in holy trees first developed; to the British School at Athens for accommodation in Crete during that work; to Portugal 600 for a 'Go and See' grant; and to the Ashmolean Museum, Oxford, and the Somerset Rural Life Museum, Glastonbury, for access to objects in their collection.

I would also like to thank the many people who contributed to the project by providing thoughts, information or practical help, including Mario Alves, Manolis Apostolakis, Pedro Baptista, Michael Collins, Michael L Collins, Henri Couturier, Luciano Cristino, Inga Czudnochowski, Diana Dantes, the late Linda Dove, Tony Dowmunt, Sheila Ernst, Geraldine Farrell, M Fossard, Claudine Frigère, Ruth Goodison, Judith Griffies, Firmo and Jacinta Guarita, V Guerin, Suki Harrison, Patti Howe, Danae Tsoukala Konidari, Yannis Konidaris, Georgios and Eusevia Koutenthakis, Guylène Lebon, José Alves Lopes, Colin Macdonald, Heather McDougall, José Moita, Will Parfitt, Lynne Prather, Maria Psilakis, Nikos Psilakis, Gwyan Rhabyt, M Richer, Ana Robinson, Nancy Robinson, Claire Ropers, Marialba Russo, Joanna Ryan, Nick Schofield, Beth Shaw, Gillian Spraggs, Di Steeds, John Steeds, Jonathan Trustram, Antonis Vasilakis, Michael Vickers, Marie Noelle Vivier, David Walker, Peter Warren and Briar Wood.

It was not possible to become a specialist in each of the areas touched on in this book, so I have been very grateful for the help of librarians, especially at the libraries of the Institute of Classical Studies; Warburg Institute; University College London; University of Glasgow; Le Service Communications (Vie Locale) de la Mairie de Cerizay; Institut Français; The Folk-Lore Society; and Biblioteca Nacional de Lisboa.

The book benefited from the calmness, efficiency and clarity of Charlotte Cole as editor. I am also grateful to Liz Puttick for the inspiration and encouragement she gave to an earlier project, from which this one grew. David Williams gave much-valued wide-ranging help and support in the final stages of preparation for publication. For giving their time to read parts of the book and offering valuable and constructive criticism, I would like to thank Caroline Cole, Jane Foot, Alan Griffiths, Carlos Guarita, Christine Morris, Beth Shaw and Tom Weld. Any mistakes are of course my own. I appreciated the generosity of Hilary Armitage in reading the whole manuscript and making thoughtful comments on language and content. Stef Pixner has watched over and nourished the project from the start, playing a crucial role in shaping it and giving staunchly from her reserves of empathy, writing skill and intellectual understanding.

The work would not have been possible without the good will and support of family and friends, especially Hilary Armitage, Jane Foot, Corey Goodison, Julio Guarita, Barbara Morrison, Paul Morrison, Stef Pixner, Ana Robinson and Helen Schafer. On hillsides and in libraries, on the road and at the computer, the photographer Carlos Guarita has given indefatigably of his companionship, originality and enthusiasm. Thank you.

Grateful acknowledgements are made to the following for use of picture material: Bibliothèque Municipale de Caen; Biblioteca Nacional de Lisboa; Editions Heimdel; Carlos Guarita; Hansmann und Vogeser in Munich; Museu Nacional de Arquelogia e Etnologia in Lisbon; Ingo Pini at the Corpus der Minoischen und Mykenischen Siegel; Marialba Russo; Stitchting Mens en Kultuur in Gent. Every effort has been made to contact the holders of copyright material, and if any have been omitted the author regreats this fact and apologises for it.

INTRODUCTION:
IF GOD WERE A TREE

W e found the first holy tree by chance. It was high summer and we were in Crete doing archaeological fieldwork on prehistoric Minoan remains. Sitting in a café in Ayii Deka, a little town at the western end of the Mesara Plain, two elderly women had been eyeing us and we struck up a conversation. It was only 10 a.m., but they had finished their shopping and asked if we could give them a lift back to their village in the foothills. It was on the way to a prehistoric tomb we hoped to find, a circular grave built by early Cretans – usually called 'Minoans' – during the Middle Bronze Age. The small hired car sank under the weight of the black-clad women and their bags of shopping as we set out on the road south. The smooth asphalt was broken by occasional cavernous potholes which appeared without warning; it led through an idyllic landscape of fields and olive groves shimmering in the morning sun. It was straight and utterly flat. Ahead the blue-grey wall of the Asterousia mountain range filled the windscreen.

As the road started to climb we asked if they could show us the site of the prehistoric tomb. So we drove straight through the village's main street, past waiting relatives who apparently – as we learned later – thought we might be kidnappers. After the next village, as the asphalt surface gave way to stones, and an argument started between them as to which roadside mound concealed the tomb, one of our passengers suddenly asked, 'Have you seen the holy tree?'

Following her finger we cast our eyes far, far across a deep valley to a small white speck at the foot of a towering sheer mountain face. One could make out a white building, and a white wall with a fir tree inside it. Was that the tree? No, they said, that was just the church, the tree was next to it. In what way was it holy? It healed ailments, especially of the eyes and stomach. Its qualities were miraculous, they said.

After we had found the Bronze Age tomb, and returned our passengers to their village, we headed for the tree. We followed their directions onto a dirt track leading into a landscape of ever greater desolation, over the sides of the dry brown mountains. Signs of human life became fewer until we arrived suddenly at a pair of iron gates skirted by low whitewashed buildings. We did not know that this was the entrance to a monastery. All this time the sun had been rising, and the heat made one want to run for cover. The place seemed deserted, but from the beaded curtain of a doorway a young man eventually emerged, surprised to see us or dazzled by the glare of sunlight, it was hard to tell which. He directed us onwards, past a graveyard, down a steep rutted track. As the car climbed down into the bottom of the valley we were surrounded by large boulders and strange spiky bushes with pink flowers, which looked like plant life on the floor of a dried-out ocean.

The tree itself was an aged holm oak, very wide in girth with a diameter of about 1.5 metres, but severely damaged on one side – apparently by fire. It was ringed by a white wall with railings on top, entered through a gate (Fig. 1). Outside stood a little wayside shrine or 'saint-box' on legs, painted in red and green, which held icons of the female saint Ayia Paraskevi (St Friday) along with candles, charcoal for incense-burning, oil in a plastic mineral water bottle, and a cigarette lighter. The icons inside the glass box showed the saint holding the cross in her right hand, and in her left hand an oval plate with a pair of eyes on it, emphasising her link with healing the power of sight. Beyond the tree was a little stone drinking-trough with a mountain spring running into it, and around it a herd of sheep grazed. Their quiet movements and occasional bleating were the only interruption of the intense midday silence and the sense of stillness and isolation in this hollow surrounded by sheer mountain slopes. I felt I was waiting for something to happen. I remembered reading about ancient Greek traditions of 'panic' – fear of the god Pan inspired by the wildness of certain places – but here the atmosphere was not frightening so much as strange and self-enclosed, as if we were the first people ever to set foot in it.

Clearly we were not. There was an empty shepherd's hut, and nearby was the little white Greek Orthodox chapel with a trim cypress tree growing in its forecourt – perhaps intended as a rival attraction. In the branches of the holy oak itself, people had hung ribbons, a baby's rattle, a corset. Thinking of a knee problem which had troubled me for several months, and wondering if the tree could help with legs as well as eyes and stomachs, I entered the gate and leant my back against the tree trunk. Shaded from the paralysing heat of the sun, I closed my eyes and let my body relax into its support. The word 'comfort' instantly came to mind, and I imagined myself engulfed in cradling arms. I stood still for what seemed a long time. The after-effects were to make a deep impression and would bring me to question everything I had previously thought about trees.

This was the beginning of an interest which became a fascination lasting more than 17 years. Whether pursuing archaeological research in Greece with my partner, the photographer Carlos Guarita, or visiting family in Portugal, or friends in Germany, or simply travelling in different parts of Europe, the project became a hobby, a puzzle, sometimes an obsession. We were led on a trail through Europe and across the centuries to find glimpses of an untold history of magical trees.

Worldwide there is far more material than we were able to chart. I am aware of examples from pre-Columbian Mexico to the Scandinavian world tree Yggdrasil, the Kalpadruma of the Vedas and the sacred tree of Buddhism (the 'Tree of Wisdom'). They would not all fit into one book. Moreover, we cannot assume they are all the same. To me they seem quite different, and I would want to acknowledge that cultural diversity. My imagination had been captured by one particular tree whose path I had crossed: a Cretan tree associated with a female saint and with healing. The discovery resonated with years of visiting Greece for the sake of archaeology and friendship; also with years of practising in the field of therapeutic bodywork, which made me curious to find out how healing procedures might be constructed around a tree. I plucked that one specific strand out of a complex tapestry of practice and belief, to see where it might lead. This book is not a comprehensive survey but an account of our travels following that lead. I have tried to throw a spotlight on those times and places which we could study first hand, and to investigate links between them. Many people helped us along the way; I have respected the privacy of those whom we met in the field, and have named in the text only those who came forward in a professional capacity to assist us.

Because of my archaeological work I knew that branches and trees were ritually touched in Minoan Crete; but our investigations led us to find unexpected examples of tree trunks allegedly providing healing in medieval Portugal, miracles in the fields and villages of Normandy, and priests' visions and peasant practices in early England. This long overlooked material suggested a link between sacred trees across Europe, not through the action of a disembodied 'archetypal' force but through living connections between peoples whose work was on the land and whose spiritual beliefs encompassed the natural world in a way not found in the mainstream of the Judaeo-Christian tradition. Tracing the journeys across Europe of some other folklore themes and stories suggested possible routes of passage of this little-known tradition of holy trees. Recurrently it involved a centred and often female tree which integrates the physical and the divine and which has been believed to be the source of visions and healing.

The surprise was to find that – despite centuries of repression and appropriation by the Church – there are still so many places in Europe where traces of holy trees continue to survive, from the Cretan countryside to an unlikely ceremony just off an English motorway and the famous apparition of the Virgin Mary at Fatima in Portugal. We were pursuing the answers to two questions. One was about the past: where do the origins of this phenomenon lie? In other words, are there pre-Christian precursors? Was it possible to trace a link between the modern and medieval holy trees back to the clearly documented sacred trees of prehistory? Greece seemed important: the trees and leaves used for prophecy and inspiration in classical Greece provided a clue which eventually enabled us to trace a curious history for this phenomenon of the miracle-working spirit of the tree trunk. The other question was about the future: how can one understand this intriguing visionary tradition and how is it reframed in contemporary experiences? In the context of ecological crisis, what has it to teach contemporary Western culture about different attitudes and new forms of consciousness that might become possible in our interactions with trees and the natural world?

Trees have been used centrally as symbols in the history of religion in the West. As symbols of nature they have been celebrated, imitated and worshipped; as symbols of nature they have also been blamed and execrated, from the tree of knowledge in the Garden of Eden to the crucifixion cross. My studies impressed me with a sense not only of the practical importance of plants to human life over the centuries, but also of the deep physical and spiritual connection between people and the green world, which institutionalised religion has tried to reframe, yet has not been able to destroy.

Amidst the realisation that consideration for the natural world is vital for our survival on the planet, we are now aware that trees in particular play a crucial role in preserving ecological balance. Scientifically we know that they are the lungs of the earth. Spiritually they have become a symbol of respect for the values which are being destroyed in the exploitation of the environment, a symbol of protest against the damage being wreaked on the earth.

However, I came to believe that no radical change in our culture's relationship to the natural world – and consequently no effective action against the vested interests responsible for global pollution – could be achieved without questioning certain assumptions basic to Western thought. These cultural norms set 'man' above – and separate from – 'nature', and privilege 'mind' over 'body'. The project became not just a story about holy trees and the goddess or female saint who occupied them, but a search for alternatives to the prevailing dualistic way of seeing the world. The female-oriented tradition which our researches revealed seemed to embody a world view which was not polarised but circular, inclusive, and focused on inspiration and healing. The veneration of a tree was an affirmation that the divine could be embodied in the physical. However, it was people's concrete experience which shaped such perceptions of the natural world in the past. To draw the spirit of such alternative traditions into the present seemed to demand, therefore, a radical renewing not just of our mythologies, beliefs and attitudes but also of our everyday life. Throughout the book the stories about 'visions' and 'miracles' at holy trees have raised questions about the physical and material context which generated those phenomena. This led me to explore alternative – non-Western and non-consensual – ways of constructing body experience, which draw the spiritual into the practical, resacralising the physical itself and allowing the possibility of new ways of coexisting.

1

SACRED TREES OF EARLY GREECE

We returned many times to the holy tree in the Asterousia mountains. We descended again to the strange stillness of that seabed valley, and slowly began to piece together an understanding of the tree's significance for the people in the scattered mountainside communities around. We stumbled on clues and themes which were to crop up again and again during later travels.

In a village some miles away an old man told us that 30 years ago he had visited the tree with his baby son, who was crying a lot and whose belly button had come out. At the tree they cut and dressed the belly button, and it healed within a month. In the village nearest to the tree we were told another story of a remarkable recovery. A self-professed sceptic, a tall man with a thick moustache, told me that his sister's son had problems with his stomach (in Greek 'to koili', often accompanied by a gesture to the right side of the abdomen) which the doctor said could be remedied only by surgery. They took the boy to the tree and performed a 'twig-splicing' ritual for him; the boy stopped crying from that point on, and surgery was not necessary. 'I am not religious, and I don't believe any of that stuff, but I believe what I saw with my own eyes,' the man concluded. Perched on the barren mountainside, his village evidently offered a hard living to its inhabitants. We could appreciate the importance of health for the survival of families working the land in remote areas without accessible medical provision. The tree seemed to fill a practical as well as a spiritual need.

We learned more about this 'twig-splicing' ceremony when we were invited into one of the low whitewashed houses by the gates of the monastery which overlooked the valley of the tree. We met the family of a shepherd, who lives there with his wife and his young daughter as well as his three brothers and grandmother. The television, which was showing an interview with a coiffured celebrity, was switched off and over a black coffee served Greek-style with a glass of cold water, we learned that they were tenants of the monastery, and that the sheep grazing by the tree belonged to them. It was they who had seen and put out the fire which threatened to destroy the tree a few years previously. No one seemed sure whether the fire was started by a cigarette or candle used at the site, or whether it was an act of deliberate vandalism by someone who disapproved of the tree on religious grounds. The fire was fuelled by many dead branches in the tree which had not been cleared because tradition maintained that anyone climbing into the tree's branches would not come back. There was also a story that if you put icons inside the trunk, the tree takes them into itself and they disappear. On a later visit we saw a big rectangular swelling of the bark on one side of the tree trunk which we were told had been one such icon.

The family described themselves as Orthodox Christians who believed in the tree as a matter of faith. They had no sense of contradiction about this. For them the healing ritual of 'twig-splicing' required a priest to be present ('a monk will not do'), although in the village I heard the ritual described with no mention of any religious personnel. It goes as follows: the child ailing with stomach problems is taken to the tree where a cut is made into one of the tree's twigs. A piece of material is placed into the spliced twig and bound around tightly. Then the child is walked three times under the tree, with a woman named Maria on one side and a man named Manolis on the other (signifying the Virgin Mary and Jesus Emmanuel – the latter name gets shortened to Manolis in Greek). This is the part, according to some versions, where the priest says prayers. If the twig heals over, so will the child.

All our informants were adamant that the tree belongs to the monastery, which is dedicated to St Antonis and overlooks the steep valley where the tree stands. However, the exact nature of the links between tree and monastery remains unclear. Many fabulous stories describe the choice of site for the monastery's founding. One of them tells that it was started by a monk given the land by a rich Turk whose eyesight he had cured. Another tells that the icon of St Antonis fell off the back of the monk's donkey to mark the spot. A monk was also apparently later guided by a dream to miraculously find water at the site. We met one present-day monk: a small elderly man perspiring in a white vest with a long grey beard. We were told that he was one of the very few left, since the economic pressures which used to drive poor families to pack one of their sons off to a monastic life had eased. Few written records have survived, but oral tradition dates the founding of the monastery to 1443. In his guidebook on Crete, Antonis Vasilakis mentions its heyday in the 16th and 17th centuries when it was a brilliant centre of education, and its sacking by the Turks in 1827. As for the history of the tree, the oldest local inhabitant, an 89-year-old, remembers the oak as long as he has been alive. Its age and origin remain uncertain, but the shepherd's family believe it might be as much as 1000 years old. This would be an exceptional age for an oak, which normally lives no more than 700 or 800 years.

Like other remote sacred places in Greece, the tree has an annual festival when people travel out for a special service. We waited six years before we had the chance to attend.

A Modern Cretan Tree Festival

It was a shock to see people at that lonely spot. The night before the festival about two dozen vehicles made the steep drive down to attend an evening service at the chapel. There were about 100 visitors in all, and as they arrived almost all of them went first to the tree to pay their respects. They entered the enclosure to look at it, discuss its health, take a twig. Many also carefully took water from the spring before joining the crowd in the low-walled forecourt of the small whitewashed Greek Orthodox church.

On the morning of the festival itself people started arriving before dawn. When the sun hit the church, the morning service started. As is customary, many of those attending poured an offering of olive oil into a big plastic container by the entrance. By 9 a.m. there were over 50 vehicles parked and roasting in the sunshine, with more arriving all the time and the service continuing. At one point the visitors numbered over 300. Some went to cross themselves in front of the tree, looking in at the icon inside the trunk. A group of taxi drivers sat on some boulders, swinging their car keys, smoking, discussing the turnout, their families and the afterlife. One of them had driven two men over from a place near Mallia on the other side of Crete. There were always a dozen or more people standing around in the shade of the tree, inside or outside the enclosure, as the sun kept rising and the service was still in progress.

Then, soon after 10 a.m., I was surprised to see the priest and congregation themselves move *en masse* from the chapel to the tree. Outside the enclosure, on the slope above the tree, the priest faced it with the congregation behind him doing the same. I found the fast liturgical delivery hard to follow, but at one point he seemed to be reading out names of people to be healed. Inside the enclosure a woman joined in, also looking towards the branches. I was aware it might be the first and last time in my life I would witness a Christian service like this, with a tree receiving the words of prayer addressed towards it.

Perhaps we had leant a little too hard on the famous Cretan hospitality to arrive at such a remote spot as obvious strangers to observe this ceremony. We were befriended by a Cretan woman who now lived in Yonkers, New York, and was back visiting family; also by a young Cretan man with learning difficulties. Many people, including the priest, presented us with portions of the specially blessed bread. No one was unfriendly, but no one was over-friendly. With the yearly invasion of holidaymakers, it may be hard for Cretans to feel that anything is private. But perhaps there was also some embarrassment about the nature of the festival and its primitive-seeming object of veneration, the battered oak tree.

Resonances with antiquity there certainly were. As an archaeologist I already knew about what has been described as 'tree cult' in prehistoric Crete within the Bronze Age period (usually dated approx. 3000 BC–1100 BC). Seeing this modern holy tree, I wondered if it were possible that some practices and beliefs could have survived the millennia of war, population movements, conversion, natural disasters, invasions and occupations, let alone the 20th century's technological developments and the growing impact of global capitalism. It made me want to look again at the prehistoric evidence, to ask afresh what can be learned about the ceremonies which the Bronze Age Cretans – the Minoans – held around trees. Archaeologists and others have written about 'ecstatic vegetation ritual' and a great 'Nature Goddess'. But there are no written records until nearly the end of the Bronze Age, and all anyone has to go by are pictures. I wanted to look with new eyes at those pictures to try to decipher the story they tell about trees in the Aegean over 3000 years ago.

Tree Worship in Bronze Age Greece?

A little bronze plaque which lay for centuries in a Cretan cave, like a time capsule from the Bronze Age, gives one of the fullest and most detailed scenes of something special happening around a tree (Fig. 2).

The Psychro or 'Diktaean' cave in the Lasithi Plain was excavated by Arthur Evans in 1896. According to an agreement with the Greek government of the time, he was allowed to bring a certain number of his Cretan finds back to England where they made their way onto the shelves of Oxford's Ashmolean Museum. That is how I had the chance to hold this 3500-year-old bronze plaque in my hand.

I had seen photos and drawings of it, read about it, even written a little about it, but as I waited behind the scenes at the museum, in a back room full of papers, boxes and a caseful of ancient vessels in store, nothing prepared me for the tininess of the actual object when it emerged from its case. The Senior Assistant Keeper of Antiquities Michael Vickers carried it in, cradled in tissue paper on a cardboard lid. It was hard to believe that something so important could be so small and look so fragile. A scrap of greening bronze, it could rest in my palm and – like a piece of old parchment – had a tear down the centre from top to bottom.

John Boardman, who published the plaque, suggests that it can probably be dated no later than the first phase of the Late Bronze Age, the 'Late Minoan I' period. (In Crete the Late Bronze Age started about 1600 BC – all dates are debatable – and was divided by Arthur Evans into the three phases: Late Minoan I, Late Minoan II and Late Minoan III.) The design lacks the smooth lines of some other Late Minoan artworks. It is vigorous, but not crude. It is boldly drawn and explicit, yet remains in some ways mysterious. Like Egyptian hieroglyphics, it carries a coded message telling us what people believed and how they worshipped at that time. The three horn-shaped objects, the 'horns of consecration', are well known from many other Minoan finds and sites as a sacred symbol; they make it clear that this is a religious scene. But perhaps words like 'religious' and 'worship' are not appropriate, for they carry ideas developed over 2000 years by the dominant religion of the Western world, Christianity. Can we imagine 'religion' or 'worship' separate from the associations of Father, Son and Mother, with their parental role and moral precepts? We need to. For at the centre of this plaque the object of religious veneration is not a figure in human form – with a white beard, on the cross, or in a blue robe – but simply a tree.

Some would argue that this is magic rather than religion, but for the communities living in Crete at this time, the design reflects their practices, beliefs and preoccupations, and that modern distinction would make no sense.

No one knows for sure what the 'horns of consecration' mean, but on the basis of the Bronze Age evidence – including numerous seal designs – archaeologists agree that they appear on altars and with sacred objects between them. Here each of the 'horns' carries a plant or bough with short, upturned branches or twigs. On the ground at the centre of the scene is a larger plant looking like a leafless Christmas tree. Its long branches are drooping downwards. Next to it stands a figure, by his clothes and shape a man, roughly drawn and wearing a loin cloth. Behind him are two squiggles which Arthur Evans thought might be the man's name in the early, undeciphered Linear A script. In front he has an arm outstretched with the lower half raised – like a gesture which indicates worship in other scenes. The object of worship, directly in front of him, appears to be the leafless tree. But the scene is not all trees. At the other side, on the bough between the 'horns of consecration', perches a large bird.

So far the scene could be a realistic picture of a religious rite. But next to the bird, hovering in midair, is a fish. Suddenly one's understanding of the picture changes. This is not a literal scene, a descriptive account of a place, but rather a collection of symbols which belong together according to some thought patterns of the early Cretans, now hidden from us. The symbols start to become indecipherable when we focus on a third object close by the bird and fish: shaped like a heart or a kidney, it could equally be a seed or a stone. At the top centre of the picture two dart-shaped graphics are equally hard to decode.

There is no difficulty, however, in recognising two further symbols at the top corners of the scene: on one side a clear radiant sun, on the other a crescent moon. Here again is a reminder that this is not a literal scene. Sun and moon are shown in this way not because they regularly – or indeed ever – appear side by side in the sky but because, for the artist, they both have some special significance. They are both important occupants of the heavens – as trees are of the earth, birds of the air, and fish of the sea. So the picture perhaps shows a cosmology: not just a picture of a tree ritual but of the world view surrounding it.

This is just one of many fascinating objects showing vegetation at the centre of ritual in Bronze Age Crete. Here at the beginning of the story of the holy tree in the Western world, a series of other designs on sealstones, gems and rings from the Bronze Age – illustrated in my book *Death, Women and the Sun* – suggest that animals and heavenly bodies were also honoured in ritual actions. Simple designs from the Early and Middle Minoan periods show people – sometimes in bird costume – doing things with trees and branches, as on Figs. 3 and 4. In the Late Minoan period more complex scenes are shown, often on gold rings. These tiny pictures are usually interpreted as showing religious activity. Surviving clay sealings stamped with impressions of some designs from rings and stones show they had a practical use, apparently to seal containers and mark property; but archaeologists have suggested that a sealstone could also have served as a sort of magic talisman or amulet.

The fullness of the scene on the bronze plaque from Psychro provides evidence from a different medium, and confirms that we are finding numerous scenes of ritual activity, although they are not of the form we might have expected. Such scenes have sometimes been described as showing 'nature cult', while the term 'religion' is reserved for divinities in anthropomorphic form. However, these scenes show reverence or communion, or perhaps actions and experiences of a spiritual nature which our language cannot accurately describe, in which personified deities apparently play no part.

The idea of sacred trees seems to have been familiar to people on the Greek mainland too. A tree ceremony is shown – for example – on a gold ring from the Peloponnese now in the Nemea Museum (Fig. 5), engraved with the graceful flowing lines typical of the skill of Late Bronze Age craftspeople. On this ring, three women in flounced skirts face, and seem to approach, a structure which is identifiable from other seal and ring engravings as a shrine. In front of the shrine is a tree, towards which the women seem to be addressing their gestures. Did such rituals actually happen at the little-known place where it was found? Or was the ring, so Minoan in style and theme, imported to the mainland Mycenaean culture as a luxury object whose decoration had little meaning to the locals? Does it show a ritual in Crete or one which the Mycenaeans also took up? We went to visit the site where it was unearthed: a Late Bronze Age cemetery excavated in the late 1970s at a village called Aidonia. The ring was found together with two others – one of which showed a similar scene with lily and papyrus flowers rather than a tree – in a small shaft grave containing the remains of two women and their grave gifts. These women were apparently the owners of the rings. Did they take part in such rituals when they were alive? To possess such luxury objects, they must have had wealth or status; were they priestesses?

Approaching Aidonia today, it is hard to believe that its people would have been wealthy enough to own such gold rings over 3000 years ago. It is an out-of-the-way village nestling at the foot of the mountains, a few kilometres drive along the flat of a valley from Nemea. On directions from the main road, we climbed by foot one January day up a steep path to the ancient site and found a group of families busy with tarpaulins, sticks and ladders, harvesting the olives from the trees beside the prehistoric cemetery. The grass on the high hillside was tossed by strong gusts of wind. The graves were mostly of a late type of 'tholos' tomb, circular like the ones in the Mesara region of Crete but differently constructed, with a long passage sloping down into a domed underground chamber. The protective sheets of corrugated iron left by the excavators were falling away, and some tombs were interconnected. While their parents worked, the children chased into one hole in the ground and out of another, disappearing into the past and popping out into the present somewhere else. Higher up on the hill, the terrain was rocky, as depicted on the ring. The leaves of the trees rippled, the shouts of the children carried on the breeze, and down in the valley the wintry sunshine picked out every edge in silver. It was a magical scene, and I found it easy to imagine that the prehistoric Greeks might have experienced the whole landscape as alive.

Down by the olive trees, one of the women complained that 'They've taken away all the relics they found'. Were they not on display in the museum at Nemea? Not much, she replied, they had taken it all away; a familiar refrain in the Greek countryside. They seemed to make little distinction between the excavators and the thieves whose looting prompted the legal dig to start in 1978. Many fingers were itching for the hillside's treasures, and in 1993 the Greek government filed suit in the US Federal Court to recover valuables from the tombs – including this ring – which had been removed before excavation began and had turned up for sale in New York.

The woman was interested in our picture of the ring showing a tree ritual. 'That's a fig tree,' she volunteered, pointing to the big tree in front of the shrine, 'and that's an olive' (the small tree – or is it a branch? – behind). Her friend was consulted and agreed. Since they see the trees all the time, I took their interpretation seriously. Even today the mountain slopes above Aidonia are covered with woods, including oak and plane trees. Perhaps similar forests made it a suitable location for tree worship in the Bronze Age. Studies of landscape history suggest that the prehistoric Aegean was wetter and probably less strongly seasonal than now, and there were types of tree such as lime which died out as the climate became more arid. Oliver Rackham and Jennifer Moody suggest that 'The change to a "Mediterranean" climate seems to have developed gradually during the Bronze Age, being completed by the middle of the first millennium BC.' At his excavation of an Early Bronze Age settlement at Myrtos in south Crete, Peter Warren found an olive stone of dimensions suggesting that olive trees were cultivated there.

Practical Prayer?

Fig. 6 shows the design on a lens-shaped Cretan stone of dark green steatite which has been dated to a late phase of the Late Bronze Age (Late Minoan IIIA, ie 14th century BC), and is now in the Metropolitan Museum in New York. It represents a figure who seems to be naked and – judging by her breasts – female. She is dancing energetically and her arms are raised into the branches of a tree, as if she were shaking it. The tree is growing out of a little structure. Other similar scenes have identified this structure as a shrine. The fact that the figure is naked and is making such exuberant gestures suggests some special occasion or ritual rather than an everyday scene. Some scholars have suggested that this action, which is repeated in other engravings, is intended to attract the attention of the 'divinity' who inhabits the tree either temporarily or permanently.

It was when we happened to be in Greece at midwinter that we noticed the similarity to olive-harvesting, when the branches of the trees are shaken to help the olives drop. The contemporary Greeks we saw were not naked, but it was an occasion with a festive quality: the whole family turned out, and related families helped each other, with breaks for picnics and wine. Contemporary Western culture separates work (something active which you do on weekdays) from religion (something inactive which you do in work breaks or on Sundays). We cannot assume that the people of prehistoric Crete made the same distinction. We cannot even be sure what kinds of trees are shown on the seals and rings, but it is possible that ritual actions grew out of practical work activities, and religious ceremonies out of times of harvest and celebration in the agricultural year.

The importance of water in agriculture may also have been acknowledged in ritual. Asking the way when you are off the main road in Greece today, you often get directions located in relation to a water cistern or a well. You are told that the place you want is just after it, or the well is where you turn off. These landmarks, and the long black hose pipes snaking from them far into the fields and orchards, are a reminder of how important it is to local farmers to get water to the plants on which their livelihood depends. As the climate became more Mediterranean during the Bronze Age, this may have been a growing preoccupation then too. So perhaps it is not surprising to find pictures of Bronze Age plant rituals involving jugs: like Fig. 7, a sealstone from Crete which shows two imaginary creatures known as 'genii', each holding a jug. The other name these creatures are sometimes given by archaeologists is the ancient Greek term 'daimones', the origin of our word 'demons', although these Minoan creatures seem to be benign spirits.

Jugs like these on seals may mean that there were rituals which involved pouring water, or symbolically some other liquid, over plants. The seal engraving on Fig. 7 may be an imaginary scene, like a picture of the three bears of the Grimms' fairy tale sitting down to eat their porridge; or it may be a scene which people dressed up to act out, like the dance of the dragon at the Chinese New Year. The muzzles of the 'genii' are elegant, their waists stylishly accentuated like people in Minoan drawings. Could they be human beings in costume?

While we were in the Ashmolean Museum I held this same richly coloured brown cornelian stone of the 'genii' in my fingers and pondered it at length, and found no answers. It had seen wear: there was a hole through it lengthwise as if for threading on a necklace, and at one end the opening was damaged. What struck me was how curved the surface of the stone was, the design sloping away at each side. When we tried to photograph it, the camera lens could not focus on the whole design at once, and I could barely read it all in focus at one time even by eye: the stone had to be moved, the eye had to travel round it. The bold brown and white lines in the pattern of the stone itself also disguised the subtle lines of the engraving. It seemed that the design was not meant to be read directly from the stone, that it was like a message in transit, a letter in a sealed envelope. Impressed on a clay sealing it could have been read, but embodied in the stone itself the message was not to the eye but to another dimension. Remembering that Arthur Evans described some of these amuletic seals as 'rain charms', I wondered if what I was holding was a prayer for rain.

Some of the Bronze Age scenes of tree ritual seem much further from the utilitarian relationship of human to plant, and from processes like watering. For example, on a haematite seal from Midea on the Greek mainland two figures with what look like bird heads are holding branches while walking or dancing (Fig. 8). On a seal said to be from Knossos, a female figure raises her right arm in a gesture of adoration before an altar topped with horns of consecration and standing next to a palm tree (Fig. 9). There are many other examples which show people holding or touching boughs at altars, dancing, wearing bird heads and perhaps other costumes, saluting trees, shaking branches and taking part in processions: the activities of the Minoans in the pursuit of their religion were many and various. Perhaps some were ritualisations of agrarian tasks; some may have celebrated the seasons or harvests; it is possible that some were alcohol- or drug-induced scenes of excitement or possession whereby the participants hoped to communicate with something beyond themselves, obtain healing, or learn about the future. We cannot tell for sure. The pictures I show here are a tiny sample from the hundreds of seals and dozens of rings that have survived. Despite this wealth of material, archaeologists are still at a loss as to how to understand the meaning and beliefs underlying these Bronze Age activities around trees because of the lack of translatable written texts for most of the period.

Over the years I have begun to wonder whether archaeology has been using the wrong tools.

Looking For a New Vocabulary

The intellect, the prime tool of the academic, is an excellent instrument for investigating past technologies, wars, logistics, population growth, legal structures and power relations. In any type of study it is crucial for assessing sources, for grasping the complexity of a wide picture, for checking details and for self-reflection. However, for investigating past emotions, spirituality, passion, ecstasy, sensual and physical experience, perhaps the intellect on its own is inadequate – like trying to write about swimming without getting wet. Understanding any religion calls for a vocabulary and a quality of response which is not within the academic repertoire, and in the case of prehistoric Crete we have in addition to allow for the millennia of distance. Ideas, feelings, beliefs, and consciousness itself, change with time and circumstance, and we may need to stretch our sense of the possible if we want to come close to the experience of human beings in prehistory.

Scientific developments of the 20th century undermined the notion that there could be such a thing as a neutral observer, since the act of perception changes what is observed. In questioning the 'grand narratives' of academic discourse, the post-modernist view has affirmed the validity of many diverse voices, each speaking from a different position and each therefore able to select and describe different aspects of the same material. The notion of 'objective analysis' has long been challenged by the sociology of knowledge, deriving from the work of Marx, Durkheim and others, and has now had to be abandoned. The authority of academic knowledge has also been undercut by a growing awareness that everyone has something to hide. Each individual (consciously or unconsciously) has an investment in certain versions of the past which validate what they hold dear in the present. In any historical project, this affects what that person looks for, and what they are able to see. In this light, it becomes crucial that we try to extend our sense of what we are looking for beyond the bounds of our personal intellectual and experiential limitations, and also that we are vigilant about checking our interpretations and expectations against the first-hand material which has survived from the past.

My own view, influenced by my experience with therapeutic bodywork (massage) as well as with archaeology, is as follows. I have an idea that people in the past – specifically Minoan Crete – had a very different attitude to, and experience of, the physical world from ours today. By this, I mean their experience of their own bodies as well as of the physical world around them. Writers like Michel Foucault have highlighted how society's attitudes to the body vary in different places and historical periods; this affects humans' lived experience of their own bodies, which changes accordingly over time. So what were the current attitudes towards, and experience of, the physical world in the prehistoric Aegean? What happens if, as students of the past, we try to extend our sense of the possible by exploring how some non-archaeologists with different perspectives on the physical world have pictured prehistoric consciousness? I will take two examples.

Jane Roberts produced a series of books – the 'Seth' books – which she dictated in trance; at various points her text discusses the development of human consciousness. Thus, in *The Nature of the Psyche: Its Human Expression*, she proposes that:

> In ... early times, ... consciousness was more mobile. Identity was more democratic ... A person, then, looking out into the world of trees, waters and rock, wildlife and vegetation, literally felt that he or she was looking at the larger, materialized, subjective areas of personal selfhood ... You [the modern reader] can imagine atoms and molecules forming objects with little difficulty. In the same way, however, portions of identified consciousness can also mix and merge, forming alliances.

Roberts suggests that words and images, as symbols of emotions or intents, were not involved in early language, which dealt with a free flow of directly cognitive material. While we are taught to perceive the world in separate and distinct categories, in a very different culture 'A man, wondering what a tree was like, *became* one, and let his own consciousness flow into the tree. Man's consciousness mixed and merged with other kinds of consciousness with the great curiosity of love.'

No dates or places are mentioned and no evidence offered beyond the claim to be channelling knowledge which comes from outside herself. And yet Roberts' proposition is not very different from that of scholars who have in the past described the Minoan ritual scenes as showing 'mystical communion', also offering no evidence beyond their subjective interpretation of the pictures. If anything, Roberts' text adds detail, texture and a sense of structure which flesh out the notion of 'communion'. It becomes less 'mystical', and more a specific process within human consciousness.

From the very different tradition of rationally argued historical theory, Karl Marx speculated as to how the different economic basis of early peoples might have affected their relationship with the natural world. Thus, in a passage in his *Pre-Capitalist Economic Formations* which has interested me for a long time, he suggests that because of the processes of survival in a community organised by kinship and based on farming, so different from the processes of survival in present-day advanced industrial societies, 'work' would not be separable from the individual's entire relationship to the community and to the land. Where the purpose of labour is not 'the acquiring of wealth' but 'self-sustenance' or a person's 'own reproduction as a member of the community', then there is a 'natural unity of labour with its material requisites'. By this he means that human beings' relationship with the material source of their sustenance, the natural world, is comparable to their relationship with their own bodies:

> The *attitude* to the land...means that a man...has an *objective mode of existence* in his ownership of the earth, which is *antecedent* to his activity and does not appear as its mere consequence, and is as much a precondition of his activity as his skin, his senses, for while skin and sense organs are also developed, reproduced, etc, in the process of life, they are also presupposed by it. [his emphases]

Living in the natural world as one lives in one's body is a far cry from the 'man/nature' polarisation prevalent in contemporary patterns of thought. Marx is proposing the possibility of past cultures in which humans did not exist in a landscape of separate objects but where they inhabited the natural world like another skin, so that their work on it and exchanges with it need not have been purely mechanical or manipulative but rather characterised by a sense of participation. Again, there is no evidence that this was so, although Marx has reached this proposition through a process of deduction following his hypothesis that the economic base of a society will always influence – and interact with – its social, cultural and spiritual life.

Thus from diverse perspectives both Marx and Roberts are speaking about a closer identification with the natural world in early human societies which did not have a developed division of labour and large economic surpluses. Although not archaeologists, both are offering new frameworks which might help to understand prehistoric experience. The Aegean seal and ring designs – showing religious scenes where sometimes naked bodies are engaged in energetic physical activities involving plants and animals – do seem to suggest that the body, the natural world and what we (for want of a better word) would call spirituality were closely linked in a way hard to imagine from our viewpoint in the contemporary Western world. Mircea Éliade in *The Sacred and the Profane* has written about an attitude or consciousness which sees 'sacrality... revealed through the very structures of the world'; and 'participation' is a word which has been used by classical scholars as they have groped towards understanding the mentality of early societies. The suggestion of a 'participation mystique' between early man and the natural world is evocative. However, the word 'mystical' can be used to claim truths which are presented as being beyond questioning. I prefer to think more specifically in terms of different material relationships – such as the economic and work relationships which Marx considers, or the use of different physical human faculties now fallen into disuse, such as those to which Roberts alludes – possibly contributing to a different lived experience in prehistory. Ultimately all interpretations are speculative, but it can be useful to try out new models of understanding to see if they fit the evidence.

However we are to understand the Minoan pictures, their representations of various forms of respectful interaction between people and trees suggest that the divide between human beings and 'nature' was less sharp then than now. The same was perhaps true of the divide between life and death.

The Tree of Life and Death

The cemetery of Phourni rises up the hill away from the village of Kato Archanes with funerary buildings of different shapes and sizes wall to wall along much of the slope. Some Minoan cemeteries contain one, two or three tombs, but this place is an entire city of the dead which was used for over 1000 years. Often at grave sites my main impression is of the architecture, the peaceful atmosphere, the view. But here, although all the human remains excavated have been taken away, a heavy atmosphere seems to linger on and the dead seem a stronger presence than the living.

Such gloomy thoughts may be inappropriate at a prehistoric Cretan cemetery. Some of the pictures of rituals on seals and rings suggest that the Minoans' attitude to dying was different from ours: that tree rituals were part of a belief system which viewed the dead without fear, incorporating death and regeneration as part of the cycle of nature. A striking example is a gold ring from this site at Phourni (Fig. 10).

The ring was found in one of Phourni's later tombs, Tomb A, from the Late Minoan IIIA period. During the Bronze Age, the cemetery buildings gradually spread uphill, and Tomb A is almost at the top. It had a long entrance passage, or 'dromos', sloping down into a beehive-shaped chamber. An opening from this led to an inner chamber where the excavators Yannis and Efi Sakellarakis found the skeleton of a woman of apparently great wealth and importance, whom they described as a princess or priestess. They found the chopped-up bones of a horse, perhaps sacrificed in her honour. Among her luxurious grave goods were numerous jewels, including this gold ring.

One end of the design shows a familiar activity: a near-naked male figure dancing energetically and grasping the boughs of a bush or tree which grows from a shrine building. In the centre stands a large female figure in the flounced skirt familiar from other ritual scenes. She has a wiggle in her body, one arm raised from the elbow, and a disappearing head, a convention which Christine Morris and Alan Peatfield have suggested may indicate an altered state of consciousness: she has perhaps 'blown her mind'. Beneath their feet is a paved floor. Floating in the air are five indecipherable little symbols, one resembling an eye and two of them rather like insects (butterflies?). At the other end of the design there is a different element: a figure – again almost naked – is kneeling to bend over what looks like a jar or 'pithos'. There are many examples of engravings showing people leaning and bending in this way. Sometimes the object they lean over looks like a jar, sometimes a rock or boulder; sometimes plant life is growing out of it. Burial in a 'pithos' was a custom in the Bronze Age, and sometimes what is bent over looks more like a tomb. Axel Persson interpreted such scenes as showing 'sorrow over death', with these bending figures in an 'attitude of mourning'.

With the repetition of these two themes – the tree-shaking and the bending – appearing together, several scholars have suggested that scenes like the one on this ring show two aspects of an ecstatic vegetation cult: on the one hand mourning the death or loss of plant life, leaves or fruit, and on the other celebrating its return by dancing and shaking the branches. If this is so, what seems unusual is the integration in the same scene of elements which we might regard as opposite or contrasting: grief and joy, death and life.

Persson suggests that the tree-shaking was to attract the attention of the deity associated with the tree, and he tries to fit various gold rings into a seasonal vegetation cycle in which barrenness (the leafless tree in winter) is followed by fertility. He also writes of 'the well-known symbolism, as for example in the cult of Adonis, where the dead is first wept over before his later ecstatic and joyful resurrection'.

The quote from Persson illustrates how strongly earlier generations of archaeologists were affected in their thinking by parallels from the near East of ecstatic vegetation cults, like those of Adonis, Tammuz and Attis, in which sacred trees were linked with animals, as on Fig. 11, and with the death and resurrection of a young male god. These scholars tended to back-project such Eastern religious influences, well-evidenced for later periods of classical antiquity, back in time on to the Aegean Bronze Age where the evidence is not so clear. The tree in Fig. 11 is centuries later than, and decorated in a way quite unlike, the Minoan trees. However, there is local and contemporary Bronze Age Cretan evidence for a circular scheme of belief involving regeneration, in the tombs in the Mesara region whose doorways were almost all built to face east towards the rising sun at specific times of the year. This could suggest, as Keith Branigan has noted, 'a belief in the revival of the body after death'. The pattern of orientation indicates that the sun's cycles – especially sunrise – were important, and combined with the evidence for plant rituals suggests that both dead vegetation and dead people may have been imagined as being regenerated like the daily resurgence of the sun. Other evidence from the Mesara tombs, such as the extensive handling of the bones of the dead, also creates the impression that the dead were not held at the same fearful distance as in our culture. What we regard as a polarised divide between life and death was perhaps felt by them to be different stages of a circular process, moving from life to death and life again, just as the sun returns every morning and plant life returns annually. The arguments and extensive evidence for this view are presented fully in my archaeological book *Death, Women and the Sun* and, more accessibly, in *Moving Heaven and Earth*.

We cannot prove that the early Cretans had such a belief system about death, but there is plenty of evidence that their Mediterranean neighbours the Egyptians did, since they have left not only pictures but poems, prayers and other texts. In different ways at different times over the centuries, we find in Egyptian religion the belief that the soul of the dead person could join the setting sun to travel in its boat through the underworld, become regenerated like the seed of vegetation or the god Osiris, and be reborn with the sunrise. As early as the third millennium BC Egyptian religion knew the goddess Nut as the sky who swallowed and gave birth to the sun. Egyptian beliefs encompassed several distinct ideas about the fate of the dead: one fate was to join your ancestors in living happily in the cemetery, as long as the tomb was properly attended. The soul could return in the form of a bird. Another idea, which became more widespread around the end of the third millennium BC, was that the soul soared up to join the sun and moon and stars in their round. The 'rebirth' imagined in the cult of Osiris is not a literal rebirth: he is reborn not in his old form but as the vegetation of the new year. If proper observances were followed, the dead king could become one with the soul of the original Osiris; over time, the idea became democratised and was seen as a possibility for ordinary people. As RT Rundle Clark explains, one version of the underworld is that it lies in the waters under the earth. The sun, travelling through the underworld on a boat, then rises to sail across the sea of the sky; to be able to join that boat of the sun god Ra was one of the ambitions of the dead soul. The goddess Hathor was associated with the sycamore tree, and CJ Bleeker in his study of the goddess points out that since the time of the Coffin Texts in the third millennium BC the boat is one of her sacral attributes, reflected in her epithet 'mistress of the ship'. Texts tell us that she travelled in the sun god's boat through the realm of the dead; her voyage was reflected in festive rituals symbolising victory over chaos and death.

From the surviving evidence, there are several parallels between Egyptian and Minoan religion during the formative years of the Early and Middle Bronze Ages in Crete (dating approx. 3000–2100 BC and 2100–1600 BC respectively), and there are also intermittently artefacts suggesting influence and contact with the Egyptians. Whether or not these scraps of evidence add up to what one could call a close relationship between the two cultures is much debated by Minoan archaeologists. However there is again relevant independent evidence from Crete in a series of Minoan representations of boats, often with trees in them. These are not practical boats for fishing or trade, but boats linked with the dead and with religious gestures and ritual. The Cretan evidence suggests that for the Minoans – as for the Egyptians – the boat was the vehicle for the journey of the dead. We find boats painted on coffins, and on one famous sarcophagus from Ayia Triadha in south Crete a boat is apparently being offered to the deceased. On seals and rings, boats are shown in scenes which are clearly religious: they carry on board variously a tree, a shrine, and a female figure who is sometimes taking a posture of mourning, and sometimes seated in pride of place under the tree and next to the shrine as in Fig. 12.

So while the sacred barque of the Egyptian sun god Ra has many occupants as it sets off for the underworld, the ritual boats in Minoan pictures usually have only one occupant, and she is female. Rarely a male figure appears too, as on the gold ring from Crete shown on Fig. 13. Here a boat is leaving shore, with a figure steering and rowers in place, dolphins underneath and in the air above it a female figure and a tree. On the shore a scantily clad man holds a woman by the wrist. Persson concludes that 'the goddess is leaving the sanctuary, voluntarily or not, to betake herself over the sea'. Some scholars have suggested that scenes like these show an early representation of later myths about the flight of Theseus and Ariadne after she had helped him to defeat the Minotaur, or the kidnapping of Helen by Paris which started the Trojan War.

Boat, death, tree and an important female figure appear to be linked in these pictures; there may also have been some involvement with the sun which seems to have been associated with the female gender, as I have suggested in *Death, Women and the Sun* and *Moving Heaven and Earth*. For the Minoans the symbolic boat journey of the female figure may have been based on the departure of a season, the disappearance of vegetation, the passing on of the dead, the setting of the sun, or some blend of those elements. Perhaps those elements were also the raw materials of stories which at some point developed into myths like those about Ariadne and Helen.

A fuller symbolic picture of the role of the boat, and of a circular journey, emerges from the design on a large and controversial gold ring (Fig. 14). At one time it was thought to be a forgery, but recently Ingo Pini and Peter Warren have argued strongly that this so-called 'Ring of Minos' is genuine. Not that it ever belonged to Minos: although he has given his name to a myth and, via Arthur Evans, to the whole dating system of Bronze Age Crete (Early Minoan, Middle Minoan, etc), there is no firm evidence that King Minos ever existed. But the ring is real, and the scene on it is real – not as a picture of anything that actually happened as such, but as a portrayal of what the Bronze Age Cretans believed or imagined: it was real to them.

The ring shows four scenes combined in one picture. At the centre top and on the right are familiar scenes of scantily clad figures (one male, one female) dancing and touching foliage at tree shrines surrounded by boulders. The centre of the picture is occupied by what looks like a hill with a pattern on it. This may reflect the importance in Minoan religion of the peak sanctuaries; these were shrines located on (often precipitous) hill and mountain tops where fires were lit and ceremonies held, mostly from the Middle Minoan period onwards. On this ring, the base of the hill seems to turn into running water, for in the middle of it, at the bottom, is an animal-headed boat travelling through. On board at the front is a shrine bearing the 'horns of consecration', reaffirming the boat's religious significance. At its rear a female figure, with naked top half and flounced skirt or pantaloons, is punting with a long pole. Here the shrine-carrying boat, with its female occupant, is clearly placed in a context. It is shown as belonging to a set of ritual actions involving rocks, built shrines, trees and ecstatic dance. It belongs to a cycle of religious belief.

The scene on the far left seems to be the boat's destination. Sitting on a shrine, with hand apparently touching the horns of consecration, is a large female figure in the familiar flounced skirt, which looks more like flounced pantaloons in this instance. She is evidently an important figure: her position next to the horns of consecration places her in direct contact with the divine. Who is she and what is she doing? And what is the little figure in the air in front of her?

To address these questions, we need to step back briefly to take a wider view. It is important to bear in mind that Minoan religion, like Minoan civilisation, is not one homogenous entity. The clusters of symbols used by the Minoans, and their associated beliefs, were specific to time and place. The early phases of the Bronze Age in Crete saw a development from a society composed mostly of small agricultural settlements to one which included larger complexes – the 'proto-palaces'. In this early period, burial customs and styles of pottery manufacture vary between different parts of Crete; there is evidence for contact and exchange but not for centralisation or standardisation of culture. Religious beliefs and practices were therefore perhaps unlikely to be identical all over the island. There was also change over time. By the Late Bronze Age the 'palaces' – the best known are Knossos, Mallia, Phaistos and Zakro but others have quite recently been discovered at Galatas and Petras – were sophisticated centres whose functions variously included manufacture, storage and administration as well as ceremonial or ritual activities. Alongside these social developments, the pictures and symbols the Minoans used – and therefore probably their beliefs – also changed.

During the Late Minoan period, Mycenaean influence in Crete grew; most archaeologists now think that this reflects some sort of occupation of Crete by the mainland Mycenaeans. The clay administrative tablets inscribed with 'Linear B' script, which have survived from the last stages of the Bronze Age (Late Minoan III), belong to this period. Their exact date is debated, but many archaeologists now place them in the 13th century BC. They list names showing that by this time there were a large number of individual deities, male and female. Some of them carry the names of later classical Greek divinities such as Athena, Artemis, Hera, Hermes and Poseidon. (There are similar tablets from the mainland listing the names of different deities, with some overlap.) The Cretan tablets record offerings made to a number of deities, and transactions involving specialised personnel apparently involved in running their shrines. The dozens of divine names suggest a multiplicity of divinities rather than the monotheism which some early archaeologists assumed. Some of the terms suggest special functions, descriptive epithets or place names, and may refer to local cults. We can only guess when these deities first emerged; we have to assume that they did not make their appearance overnight.

It is therefore interesting that, considerably earlier than the tablets, a series of minute figures start to appear in the designs of the gold rings, which are generally dated to the 15th century BC. These tiny figures are on a different scale from the others in the designs, and are airborne; this indicates that they are divine, and could be taken as suggesting that all other, earthbound, figures – whatever their size and apparent importance – are human. At the top left of the illustration of the 'Ring of Minos' on Fig. 14, it is possible to make out one such tiny hovering figure. She is floating just in front of the face of the large female figure seated at the shrine at the left of the design. This flying figure too is wearing a flounced skirt; one arm reaches down towards the seated figure, and a long braid of hair is suspended horizontally as if in mid-flight. What words of divine wisdom, what gifts of divine strength, what knowledge of the future or what spirit of possession she might be imagined as imparting to the seated figure, we cannot tell. Certainly she is supernatural, and the seated figure looking towards her may thus be taken as human, perhaps a priestess. How the tree-touching, the dancing, the netherworld boat journey, or the touching of the horns of consecration, might have contributed to creating the apparition of the little figure, we also do not know. But it seems clear that when various gold rings show these little flying figures – who look rather like fairies – we have the first conclusive engraved evidence that the people of the Aegean Bronze Age imagined their divinities in human form. And in some cases the context suggests that what we are seeing is the visualisation of the spirit of a tree.

The Spirit Leaves the Tree

There has been a lot of debate about the sacredness of trees themselves. 'The sacred tree might itself be regarded as permanently filled with divine life as manifested by its fruit and foliage', wrote Arthur Evans in his book *The Earlier Religion of Greece in the Light of Cretan Discoveries*. Peter Warren has noted that the gesture of salutation used towards the trees in cult is 'a standard Minoan gesture of "adoration" or "worship" often used before anthropomorphically rendered divinities'. Other scholars have been less happy to accept the idea that trees were seen as sacred in themselves. Martin Nilsson, the Swedish scholar whose classic book *The Minoan-Mycenaean Religion and its Survival in Greek Religion* is still the best overall guide, comments that '. . . we cannot always decide with certainty whether the tree is holy on its own account, or as the embodiment of a deity, or simply because it belongs to a sacred grove inhabited by the god or containing his temple'. Quoting him with approval, the Greek archaeologist Nanno Marinatos rejects the idea of 'tree cults' as being part of the Victorian notion of 'primitive religion'. She argues that the tree was never worshipped in itself: '. . . the tree is sacred in Minoan religion not because it is inhabited by a vegetation spirit, nor because it is an object of worship in itself. Its function is to mark the sacredness of the spot and to be the focus of cultic activities which cluster around the worship of the gods.'

As this example shows, the idea of people venerating a tree which lives and regenerates itself and provides for human survival is regarded by some scholars as more 'primitive' than people worshipping an invisible imagined deity in human form, and tree veneration is therefore dismissed as a possibility. Scholars also sometimes look for a set of religious beliefs and practices which are fixed and static, rather than practices which change over time.

It is not only that Crete and the mainland have produced evidence of two very different cultures: the Minoan and the Mycenaean. It is also that the evidence for Bronze Age religion comes from a period which stretches over nearly two millennia, and from a civilisation which developed from the small farming settlements of the Early Bronze Age to the Late Bronze Age's complex palaces in Crete and imposing citadels on the Greek mainland. Cretan society may also have shifted from a more collective way of life – as suggested by the early communal graves – to hierarchical organisation in the palaces and the bureaucratic administration recorded in the Linear B tablets. It is hardly surprising that the evidence for religion also changes over time.

Some people have looked to find a 'Great Mother Goddess' in Neolithic and Early Bronze Age Crete. However, as Christine Morris and I have argued more fully in *Ancient Goddesses*, the evidence for such a figure is slender and inconclusive. Evans was influenced by near-Eastern religious schemes of a goddess and son/consort, and as a result he interpreted as goddesses female figurines whose use has been debated without resolution. Later archaeologists have picked on other female representations to identify an original goddess, such as the so-called 'vessel goddesses' (pots in human shape) which are found at a few sites, or the large female figures on gold rings which could be priestesses. My own view is that in the early seal engravings, and in scenes such as those showing saluting a tree (eg Figs. 2 and 9) or dancing at a shrine (eg Fig. 5), where there is no conclusive evidence for any kind of personified divinity, we cannot assume that there was one. Nor – without evidence – should we assume that it was the place rather than the tree which was sacred. Aspects of the natural world, including trees, are clearly shown receiving veneration as if they were holy in themselves. In those scenes we have no evidence to suggest otherwise, and a modern desire to find a primal divinity should not be back-projected on to the ancient material.

However, one of the main changes in religion over the course of the Bronze Age seems to be a shift of focus away from the natural world and towards personified divinities. Arthur Evans commented on the process whereby 'The old baetylic [sacred stone] and pillar forms, and the sacred trees that overshadowed them, fall into the background to make way for the anthropomorphic image of the divinity.' And when, in the Late Bronze Age, we begin to see the little flying divinities appearing at scenes of ritual involving trees, here for the first time I believe we may say that there is an abstract notion of a divinity which is perhaps linked with, or living in, the tree, rather than being the tree itself. The tiny hovering figure on the 'Ring of Minos' (Fig. 14) is an example. A Cretan bronze ring from Kavousi (Fig. 15) again shows a little airborne figure next to a tree, here being saluted by a female worshipper or priestess. This airborne figure is hard to interpret in any other way than as a vision of an anthropomorphic divinity associated with the setting. The spirit seems to have left the tree. Or perhaps, rather, the spirits have left the trees, for we may have several tree goddesses rather than just one.

There seems to be widespread agreement with Robin Hägg's analysis of developed Minoan religion as centring on epiphany (the appearance of the deity), which could be either visionary (an apparition of the divinity) or enacted (with someone acting the part of the divinity). Attention was shifting away from the physical tree towards the envisioned deities and towards the priestesses or priests who could claim to represent them, a process recognisable on a number of Cretan rings and sealstones. The mainland material has some affinities, for example the scene on a famous gold ring from Mycenae (Fig. 16), where a powerful female figure – enacting the divinity? – receives a procession bringing her offerings. The natural world is still in evidence, with sun and moon shown above, flowers being carried, poppy heads being flourished, and the leaves of the tree being touched; but it seems to be the seated figure beneath the tree, and not the tree itself, who is receiving honour here. Persson believes she is 'the epiphany of the Tree Goddess receiving homage' and cites Spyridon Marinatos' idea that, because of the medicinal uses of opium, the poppy suggests she was also the 'Goddess of Healing'. Wolf-Dietrich Niemeier thinks that the ring shows a Mycenaean artist cramming in Minoan motifs like the double axe as symbols rather than as real objects. He suggests that the Mycenaeans borrowed design elements which fitted their own beliefs but did not adopt Minoan beliefs, and points out that the ecstatic element of epiphany so important in Crete is almost entirely missing on the mainland.

In Crete the religious changes reflected in the seal and ring designs may have been related to social changes and the centralisation of power in the hands of secular and religious officials. During this Late Bronze Age period male deities also start to appear for the first time at scenes of vegetation ritual, similarly floating in the air, sometimes with hair flying and often adopting a typical 'striking' pose or gesture of command, as on Fig. 17. The growing importance of male figures and of postures of authority in the pictures might be the result of the influence of the Mycenaeans, as the growing power of the mainlanders resulted in them having some sort of dominion in Crete before the end of the Bronze Age. Alternatively those changes in priorities may pre-date Mycenaean incursions and may have resulted from long-term processes of change within Cretan society itself. We cannot tell for sure.

After a series of destructions caused by natural disasters and perhaps also human violence, Knossos and other settlements throughout Crete were laid low in about 1450 BC, and many sites were afterwards abandoned. The occupation – in whatever form – by the mainlanders is taken as part of the picture. The palace of Knossos was re-used during the following centuries – and its ruins have survived and been reconstructed to become one of Greece's major contemporary tourist attractions – but this is the end of the Minoan story.

From the closing years of the Bronze Age there are many examples of sculptures of deities in human form. A divine gesture of 'upraised arms' often identifies them. Some of the sculptures are almost life size. All this is different from the earlier religious representations. But there are also some consistent themes which seem to have survived, and which continued to survive throughout the 'dark age' following the final collapse of Minoan and Mycenaean civilisation. One such theme is the continuing importance of the female, and the other is the continuing importance of trees.

The First Trees in Greek Literature

We can be sure that the sun shone as brightly on Greece throughout the 'dark age' as it shone before and since. It is only the modern scholar who is relatively in the dark about what went on during the centuries after the end of the Bronze Age (very approx. 1100 BC) and before the beginning of the historical period (usually placed at about 900 BC). The evidence that has survived from those intervening centuries is sparser and technologically simpler than what went before. The art of writing was lost, buildings and artefacts were less impressive. Contact between different regions of Greece, and international travel, seem to have been drastically reduced. But when signs of renewal emerged with the beginning of the Early Iron Age, or so-called 'Geometric' period (usually dated approx. 900–700 BC), it is apparent that many ideas and traditions had survived. There was a new stiffness in the drawings and designs, as if in some ways artists were starting again. The art of this period had a formality typically seen in the repetitive geometric patterns on pottery. Buildings and texts suggest that social organisation was hierarchical, with women in a secondary role in the home, and feudalistic working relationships on the land. There were also signs of fresh input from renewed contacts with the near East, which gave an oriental flavour to some of the artworks. But the preoccupations were similar to those of the Bronze Age.

So the female figure on a funerary urn from Arkades in central Crete (Fig. 18) has Egyptian-looking hair, adopts a rigid frontal pose, and takes her place in an antithetical design typical of oriental art. Her head was originally modelled in relief, and the archaeologists looked in vain in the tomb to recover the piece or pieces which had broken off. She is framed by lines of geometric designs. But in each hand she holds a plant, the 'trees of life' according to the excavator Doro Levi, while the Greek archaeologist Stylianos Alexiou describes her as 'the goddess of vegetation with a sacred tree in each of her hands'. This linking of vegetation with a female figure, birds and death is familiar from the pictures of the Bronze Age. Despite many social and religious changes apparent in Early Iron Age culture, the holy tree of the Minoans had not died altogether. The Geometric period offers many other pictures and stories which maintained the memory that plant life had once been sacred.

Thus vase paintings show branches in use in ritual and burial scenes. Fig. 19, the design on a bowl in the Archaeological Museum in Athens, shows a procession of women carrying branches as they approach an enthroned female figure, evidently someone of religious significance. Sadly, with the random damages of the centuries her top half has been lost and it is not certain who she is. Fig. 20, a vase fragment in the same museum, shows a common motif: the 'prothesis' or laying out of the dead. Here the body of the deceased lies on a high table draped with branches. On either side people raise their hands to their heads in the gesture of mourning, and two central figures hold out long branches over the body. What practical, symbolic or magical purpose this gesture may have served is uncertain, but it recurs on vase paintings and was evidently an important part of funerary ritual.

There are also curious innovations in the visual arts. The sanctuary of Hermes and Aphrodite at Kato Symi in south central Crete, excavated by Angeliki Lembessi for the Greek Archaeological Service, was a place of worship continuously from the Middle Minoan period through to the 3rd century AD. From the Archaic period (straight after the Geometric) the site yielded a bronze plaque of the god Hermes appearing in the branches of a tree (Fig. 21); later inscriptions refering to 'Hermes Dendrites' (Hermes of the Tree) confirm the association. The plaque is on display in the Heraklion Museum. The tree theme, and the element of divine epiphany, recall the art of the Bronze Age, but there are important differences: here it is a male divinity linked to a tree, unlike the predominant females of the Bronze Age. Moreover, his position in relation to the tree is different. In the Bronze Age significant figures sat underneath trees or floated in the air beside them; they did not sit in the branches like this figure. This is a new element in the repertoire and I am curious where it came from. The stiff frontal pose of the upper body looks near-Eastern, while the profiled legs look Egyptian. This may give a clue to the source of the motif. Perhaps the plaque reflects the influence of Egyptian models such as the picture of the goddess Nut in the branches of the sycamore tree on Fig. 22? Both Hathor and Nut were believed to inhabit the sacred sycamores, and were venerated and presented with offerings in that capacity. Vignettes in the *Book of the Dead* often show the soul on its journey to the next world coming to one of these sycamores and receiving a supply of bread, fruit or water from the goddess of the tree. Perhaps with the cultural contacts of the period the goddess's place in the tree, if not her role as helper of the dead, influenced the Cretan material.

While pictures can still present a puzzle, now an additional new source of evidence is available: literature. With the rediscovery of writing, this period has left us texts from the earliest surviving Greek poets, 'Homer' and 'Hesiod'. Homer is the name given to the author, or rather collator, of two traditional epic tales spun by generations of anonymous poet-singers and written down perhaps not much before 700 BC. His story, like a historical novel, is set in the past: his heroes purport to live in the Bronze Age, but elements from intervening centuries slipped in before it was written down. The result is a mixture, but it is a cultural mix which we know was in the mindset of his audience. Hesiod is the name given to the working owner-farmer who wrote two poems covering a range of topics from the origin of the universe to the best date for sowing crops. He is placed later than Homer, perhaps soon after 700 BC. Some of the 'Homeric Hymns' dedicated to various deities, though written down in the centuries following the Geometric period at various dates between the 8th and 6th centuries BC, have a style and language similar to Homer and Hesiod, and were probably also composed in a traditional way, so they can be looked at here. For the Bronze Age, apart from Linear B's bureaucratic notes at the very end of the period, there are only pictures to go by. Now, for the first time, we have words woven into sentences and stories; those words spell out clearly that the traditional sanctity of plants was not just a thing of the past.

In the Homeric poems the references to sacred trees seem to slip into the interstices of the main narrative as if they had become marginal but had not gone away. They are often tantalisingly brief. Thus in *The Iliad* we find a mention of the 'shining grove' of the god Poseidon, and references to the oak tree being sacred to the god Zeus. Athena's sacred grove (with a spring in the middle of it) is mentioned in passing in some street directions, and on reaching the underworld an important landmark for Odysseus is the grove of Persephone, where poplars and willows grow at the ends of the earth. In one passage in *The Odyssey* (Book 6) the shipwrecked hero tells the princess Nausikaa, whose help he needs, that he worships her perfection, and has seen the like only in the beautiful palm tree by the altar of Apollo at Delos which he visited on his travels: 'I remember how long I stood spellbound at the sight, for no lovelier sapling ever sprang from the ground. And it is with just the same wonder and veneration that I look at you, my lady; with such awe...' (Rieu's translation). I wonder whether it was a similar veneration to that shown towards a palm tree by the saluting figure at the altar on the Bronze Age sealstone shown on Fig. 9.

In the Homeric poems, trees often provide a suitable setting for a ritual, as when in *The Iliad* the Greeks, before departure for Troy, sacrifice to the gods at Aulis on altars beside a spring under a plane tree. But the natural world, and human beings' dealings with it, also had sacred significance not just as a background to ritual but in itself. Homer describes how the goddess Demeter helps the wind to separate the grain from the chaff on the 'sacred' threshing floor. Hesiod writes about the 'holy grain' and gives instructions always to pray before ploughing. Hesiod and Homer both make it clear that it was important to pray before crossing or swimming in a river. Interaction with the divine was still very physical, including practical activities like singing, dancing, processions, sacrifice, possession, and taking part in athletic games. Listing some of these different ways of honouring the gods in this period, the ancient historian Moses Finley pointed out that 'Religion ... was not set aside in a separate compartment but was meshed into every aspect of personal and social behaviour'.

Certain themes emerge in myths which give clues about the symbolic meaning trees seem to have carried for these early Greeks. One recurrent theme is the idea that trees were inhabited by spirits or 'nymphs'. The *Homeric Hymn to Aphrodite* refers to mountain nymphs who are neither mortal nor immortals, although they live long and dance with the gods: '... at their birth pines or lofty oaks grow up with them on the fertile earth – fine, flourishing trees ... People call them the holy places of the immortals, and never cut them with the axe. But when their allotted time of death draws near, first those lovely trees wither as they stand, and the bark around them shrivels, and the twigs fall, and in the end the spirit of the nymph and of the tree leave the light of the sun together.' As with the hovering figures of deities on Minoan rings, we have here female spirits who are separate from, but still closely identified with, the trees they inhabit. Those deities, and these nymphs, may be part of the same tradition. Ash trees are mentioned too, and in a passage in his *Theogony* Hesiod tells about nymphs called Meliae or 'ash nymphs' who were born from Earth near the beginning of time – perhaps reflecting a sense that they were linked with beliefs of the past. There are also several mentions in the texts of caves sacred to the nymphs, and these early poets give the impression that the countryside was peopled by nature spirits. From snippets like these a picture builds up of a scheme of ideas which was still current at the margins of organised religion.

Another tradition reflects what may be a continuing link between trees and cycles of life and death. The *Homeric Hymn to Apollo*, describing how Leto gave birth to Apollo next to a palm tree, throwing her arms around the tree during her labour, gives an independent corroboration of the importance of this particular tree as mentioned in *The Odyssey*. In another passage of *The Odyssey*, Penelope refers to an ancient notion of humans born 'from oak or stone'. And generations of classical scholars have been enthralled by a beautiful passage in *The Iliad* (Book 6), where the warrior Glaukos compares the generations of human life to the leaves of a tree: 'For the wind showers the leaves onto the ground, but the budding timber grows fresh ones when spring comes round again. So one generation of people is born while the other passes away.' Perhaps waving branches over the dead as on Fig. 20 was intended to encourage the rebirth of life by a similar analogy. The scholar Christiane Sourvinou-Inwood linked this symbolism of regeneration with a traditional 'accepting' attitude towards death as a familiar and necessary event, in the context of a community with a continuity which offsets the brevity of individual lives.

Again scavenging through the Homeric poems for evidence of an alternative culture beyond the epic heroes and Olympian deities who fill the main narrative, we find that these early Greeks also knew of the healing properties of some plants. A passage in *The Iliad* refers to a woman Agamede who knew all the 'pharmaka' (root of the modern 'pharmacy') which the broad earth grows. From healing to magic has been a short leap in many cultures, and in *The Odyssey* (Book 10) the sorceress Circe uses 'pharmaka' to transform Odysseus's companions into animals. To help Odysseus counteract her potion, the god Hermes picks him another plant with magical properties, a herb with a black root and a white flower. The other magical tool that both Circe and Hermes use is also of plant origin: they both have a wand. The ancient Greek word, *rabdos* or *rapis*, can also mean a staff or sceptre and this leads us to the function of branches which is referred to most frequently and most strikingly in these early poems: their power to transmit superhuman knowledge.

Thus in Book 1 of *The Iliad*, the hero Achilles has a huge row with King Agamemnon in front of the Greek army. In the course of the row Achilles swears a major oath, which is more like a curse. He swears that the day will come when all the Greeks will bitterly rue the day when they treated him – the best man in the expedition – so contemptuously. He swears that they will tear their hearts out in remorse, and he swears it on a sceptre: 'this sceptre, which never again will grow leaf or branch since it was cut in the mountains...this sceptre, which now rests in the hands of our lawgivers'. So the branch, its woody origin not forgotten, played a role in the making of laws and was a powerful object to swear on. Again, at the start of Book 2, when Agamemnon goes down to summon his troops, he dresses and arms himself carefully and then takes up the 'immortal sceptre of his fathers' as an essential piece of equipment; here it also seems to have a hereditary significance. In another scene later in the poem, the elders sitting in court are each in turn given the speaker's rod and come forward to give judgment with staff in hand.

The source of the staff or sceptre's power is spelled out at the start of the *Theogony*, when Hesiod tells how the Muses taught him the gift of song: 'They picked a branch of fertile laurel and gave it to me as a sceptre, a wonder to behold, and they breathed into me a sacred voice, to tell of the past and what is to come.' So the branch was seen as the path to inspiration, to divine wisdom. This was why it needed to be in the hands of kings and lawgivers, this was why it was a powerful object to swear an oath on. It was also believed to connect its holder with the secrets of the future. When in Book 11 of his adventures Odysseus visits the underworld, he finds the prophet Teiresias holding a golden sceptre while he warns what lies ahead.

If a branch was so powerful, how much more powerful could a tree be? These early literary sources give intriguing references to two particular trees which were to become household names throughout the period of Greek antiquity: the oracular laurel at Delphi and the oracular oak at Dodona.

By the time of Homer, Delphi was probably already a wealthy oracle centre, since a passage in *The Iliad* (Book 9) refers to 'all the treasures that the stone threshold of the Archer keeps within, the threshold of Phoebus Apollo at rocky Pytho'. A passage in *The Odyssey* (Book 8) mentions a Delphic prophecy given to Agamemnon, leader of the Greeks, before the Trojan War: HW Parke points out that since it refers to Apollo himself 'speaking', it is clear that the advice was given by a medium inspired or possessed by the god, parallel to a prophetic outburst by a traveller Theoclymenus in Book 20, 'the one passage where the poet represents ecstatic prophecy'. The *Homeric Hymn to Apollo* states that after his first arrival at Delphi, the god prophesied 'from the laurel tree'; so the evidence suggests inspired prophecy associated with a tree. In this, the earliest, account of the oracle's origins, Apollo took the site forceably by humbling a stream (he pushed her over a crag) and killing a resident she-serpent, whom the sun then rotted away. The verb *pytho* (I make to rot) is given in the poem as the derivation of the oracle's place name, Pytho, whence the title of Delphi's prophetess, the Pythia. The hymn recounts – interestingly – that it was Knossians travelling by ship from Crete whom Apollo chose to keep his oracle at the site. Taking the shape of a dolphin, he landed on their ship and steered it to harbour near Delphi, where he leaped out of it like a star at midday before adopting human form to give them their instructions on running the establishment. So here we have an oracle based on a laurel tree, associated with a stream, using inspired prophecy and run by Cretans. It is however occupied by a male god; moreover, the female prophetess – the Pythia – seems to have been a later arrival at Delphi, and Parke makes it clear that Apollo's oracles usually had male prophets.

Dodona had no stated connections with Crete, but the classical Greeks regarded it as the oldest oracle of all. I will cite the early references, since they are short and each adds another small piece to the puzzle. At one point in *The Odyssey* (Book 14), Odysseus in disguised identity makes up a story that Odysseus has 'gone to Dodona to learn the will of Zeus from the huge oak tree sacred to the god', and to get advice on how to plan his return. He repeats the same fabricated story in Book 19. A Hesiodic fragment refers to the oak tree site at Dodona as the 'home of the Pelasgi' (regarded as an early pre-Greek people). Another fragment gives more detail, saying that Zeus loved Dodona and established it to be his oracle, to be honoured by humans: 'And they... [the doves?] ... lived in the hollow of the oak. From there mortals carry away all kinds of prophecy, any mortal who, bringing gifts with good omens, travels there and puts a question to the immortal god.' The most revealing reference is in *The Iliad* (Book 16) when Achilles takes out a special cup, puts wine in it, and goes into the forecourt to look up into the sky and pray as he pours a libation: 'Lord Zeus of Dodona, Pelasgian Zeus, you who live far away and rule over wintry Dodona, surrounded by your interpreters the Selli, who keep their feet unwashed and sleep on the ground...'

So here there is a well-known oracle tree, associated in texts with the earliest inhabitants of Greece, giving prophecies through attendants who are strongly connected to the earth. If, as scholars like Parke suggest, the incomplete Hesiodic fragment refers to the doves described by later sources as living in the holy tree, there is also an early link with birds, which were important in Minoan religion (for example, Fig. 2). This reminds me of a curious passage in *The Iliad* (Book 7) where Athena and Apollo sit on an oak tree sacred to Zeus 'in the shape of birds of prey' – evidently the bird was one form in which deities could occupy trees. Homer has no problem either with divine apparitions in human shape: gods and goddesses frequently get involved in the action, taking part in fighting in *The Iliad*, or materialising – like Athena so often in *The Odyssey* – in glowing form to give advice at sticky moments. In *The Odyssey* (Book 13) Athena actually appears under a 'holy olive tree'.

However, there is no hint of apparition or even of ecstatic prophecy in any of the early evidence about Dodona. It is in the north-west of mainland Greece near Ioannina, a long way from Crete, and, as at Delphi, the patron deity is male. Parke, who links Minoan tree cults with near-Eastern religion, suggests that the Dodona oracle with its sky-god and unwashed attendants has more affinities with tree cults in Prussia and Italy. So, from a first look at the evidence, possible connections with Crete are tenuous at Delphi, non-existent at Dodona, and the gender of the tree deities has changed. The only female supernatural figures identified with trees in this Early Iron Age period are the lesser beings known as nymphs.

The pictures from the Bronze Age showed that during that period people saluted, touched, shook, sat under and had visions at trees, activities involving both males and females with female figures predominating. From the surviving material we can see their actions, and even their visions, but in the lack of texts we cannot fill in the content and the meaning for those prehistoric people of their interactions with the trees. In the earliest historical period, the Early Iron Age, pictures show – as we have seen – that at that time people certainly did things with branches in religious and funerary rituals, while the first literary texts reveal that people knew of their use for magic, inspiration, wisdom and healing. Groves were associated with divinities, and a tree was a good place for a ceremony or an apparition. A god such as Hermes was pictured sitting in a tree, and gods at two oracular tree sites on the Greek mainland were known and consulted for their prophetic advice.

Thus it is clear that in the imagination and ritual practices of the new world which emerged from the 'dark age' trees still had a place. But what had become of our prehistoric tree goddess(es), linked with the ecstatic dancing and visionary appearances? Had they disappeared? Had they been irreversibly shrunk to tree nymphs? Was that tradition lost? Was the female-associated holy tree we had found in contemporary Crete a random excrescence on the surface of history? It might have seemed so, and this might have been the end of our story, had we not stumbled on another tradition of holy trees, linked with visions, miracles, healing, and a female supernatural being, which were to lead us on a fascinating winding path across the centuries. This time, however, it was in Portugal, and the apparition was of the Virgin Mary.

Book References

Aidonia, see *Hellenic Republic Ministry of Culture Press Office* press release dated 23 January 1996. See also Katie Demakopoulou, ed, *The Aidonia Treasure*, Ministry of Culture, Athens, 1996

Alexiou, Stylianos, *Guide du Musée Archéologique d'Héraklion*, Direction Générale des Antiquités et de la Restauration, Athens, 1973, 102

Bleeker, CJ, *Hathor and Thoth: Two Key Figures of the Ancient Egyptian Religion*, EJ Brill, Leiden, 1973, 60, 69–70, 73, 92–3

Boardman, John, *The Cretan Collection in Oxford*, Clarendon Press, Oxford, 1961, Pl. XV No. 217, 46 and Fig. 21

Book of the Dead, most accessible in EA Wallis Budge, ed, *The Book of the Dead* Arkana, London and New York, 1985 (first publ. 1899), eg 204 (Vignette showing Ani kneeling beside a pool of water; in the sycamore tree appears the goddess Nut pouring out water for him from a vessel and giving him cakes.) This collection of documents known as the Theban Recension of the Book of the Dead was copied between 1600 and 900 BC

Branigan, Keith, *The Tombs of Mesara: A Study of Funerary Architecture and Ritual in Southern Crete, 2800–1700 BC*, Gerald Duckworth, London, 1970, 105

Éliade, Mircea, *The Sacred and the Profane: The Nature of Religion*, trans. WR Trask, Harvest/Harcourt Brace Jovanovich, New York and London, 1959, 117

Evans, Arthur J, *The Mycenaean Tree and Pillar Cult and Its Mediterranean Relations*, Macmillan, London, 1901, 127

—, 'The Ring of Nestor', *Journal of Hellenic Studies* 45 (1925), 1–75, here 21 ('rain charms')

—, *The Earlier Religion of Greece in the Light of Cretan Discoveries*, Macmillan, London, 1931, 13

Finley, Moses, *Early Greece: The Bronze and Archaic Ages*, Chatto and Windus, London, 1981, 129

Foucault, Michel, *A History of Sexuality Vol 1*, Vintage, New York, 1980

'Genius' in Minoan religion, see Margaret AV Gill, 'The Minoan Genius', *Mitteilungen des Deutschen Archäologischen Instituts: Athenische Abteilung* 79 (1964), 1–21

Goodison, Lucy, *Death, Women and the Sun: Symbolism of Regeneration in Early Aegean Religion*, Bulletin Supplement 53, Institute of Classical Studies, London, 1989

—, *Moving Heaven and Earth: Sexuality, Spirituality and Social Change*, The Women's Press, London, 1990 (abridged, Pandora, 1993)

— and Christine Morris, eds, *Ancient Goddesses: The Myths and the Evidence*, British Museum Press, London, 1998, and University of Wisconsin Press, Madison, 1999, 113–132

Hägg, Robin, 'Epiphany in Minoan Ritual', *Bulletin of the Institute of Classical Studies* 30 (1983), 184–5

Hesiod, *Theogony*, line 30 (inspiration from laurel); 187 (ash nymphs). Hesiod, *Works and Days*, 465–7 ('holy grain' and ploughing); 737ff (praying to river). Hesiodic Fragments *Catalogues of Women* No. 97 and Unknown position No. 14 (both on Dodona). All most accessible in *Hesiod, the Homeric Hymns and Homerica*, trans. HG Evelyn-White, Loeb Classical Library, Heinemann, London and Harvard University Press, MA, 1982 (first publ. 1914)

—, *Fragments*, see R Merkelbach and ML West, eds, *Fragmenta Hesiodea*, Clarendon Press, Oxford, 1967, Nos. 240, 319 (on Dodona)

Homer, *The Iliad*, Book 1, lines 233ff (Achilles' oath on staff), 238 (staff held to administer justice); Book 2, 46 (Agamemnon's sceptre), 305–7 (Aulis), 506 (grove of Poseidon); Book 5, 499 (threshing-floor), 693 (oak sacred to Zeus); Book 6, 146–9 (Glaukos on mortality), 162ff (Delos palm tree); Book 7, 59 (deities in bird form), 60 (oak sacred to Zeus); Book 9, 404–5 (Rocky Pytho); Book 11, 740–41 (Agamede); Book 16, 233ff (Achilles prays to Dodonan Zeus); Book 18, 505 (staves held to administer justice), 557 (king holds staff). I prefer the translation of EV Rieu, *The Iliad*, Penguin Books, Harmondsworth, Middlesex, 1950

—, *The Odyssey*, Book 5, lines 445ff (praying to river); Book 6, 291–2 (Athena's grove); Book 8, 79 (Delphic prophecy); Book 10, 238, 293 and 319 (Circe's wand), 277 (Hermes' wand), 509 (Persephone's grove); Book 11, 91 (Teiresias); Book 13, 102–4, 221–2, 288–9, 372; Book 14, 328 (Dodona); Book 19, 163 ('oak or stone'), 297 (Dodona); Book 20, 351 (Theoclymenus). I prefer the translation of EV Rieu, *The Odyssey*, Penguin Books, Harmondsworth, Middlesex, 1946

Homeric Hymn to Aphrodite, lines 264ff; *Homeric Hymn to Apollo*, line 18 (his birth by palm tree), 244–544 (founding of Delphi), both most accessible in *Hesiod, the*

Homeric Hymns and Homerica, trans. HG Evelyn-White, Loeb Classical Library, Heinemann, London and Harvard University Press, MA, 1982 (first publ. 1914)

Kato Symi, most of the publications by A Lembessi are in Greek, eg *Praktika tis en Athenais Archaiologikis Etaireias* (1973), 188ff (Plate 205 has the inscription) and (1974) 222ff (Plate 167a has the plaque). In English, see A Lebessi (*sic*) and PM Muhly, 'The Sanctuary of Hermes and Aphrodite at Syme, Crete, *National Geopgraphic Research* 3 (1987), 102–13. There is the briefest mention of the plaque and the later inscription in JA Sakellarakis, *Herakleion Museum: Illustrated Guide to the Museum*, Ekdotike Athenon, Athens, 1980, 106

Levi, Doro, 'Arkades: Una Città Cretese all'alba della Civiltà Ellenica', *Annuario della R. Scuola Archeologica di Atene*, X–XII (1927–1929), 331 (on urn)

Marinatos, Nanno, 'The Tree as a Focus of Ritual Action in Minoan Glyptic Art', *Fragen und Probleme der Bronzezeitlichen Ägäischen Glyptik*, Gebr Mann Verlag, Berlin, 1989, 127–143, here 142

Marx, Karl, *Pre-Capitalist Economic Formations*, Lawrence and Wishart, London, 1964, 67–9, 74, 81

Morris, Christine and Alan Peatfield, 'Feeling Through the Body: Gesture in Cretan Bronze Age Religion', in Y Hamilakis, M Pluciennik and S Tarlow, eds, *Thinking Through the Body: Archaeologies of Corporeality*, Kluwer Academic/Plenum Publishers, New York, 2002, 105–120, here 114

Niemeier, Wolf-Dietrich, 'Cult Scenes on Gold Rings from the Argolid', in Robin Hägg and Nanno Marinatos, eds, *Death and Divinity in the Bronze Age Argolid*, Paul Åströms Förlag, Stockholm, 1990, 165–70, here 167, 169–70

Nilsson, Martin P, *The Minoan-Mycenaean Religion and its Survival in Greek Religion*, CWK Gleerup, Lund, 1950 (first publ. 1927), 264

Parke, HW, *Greek Oracles*, Hutchinson University Library, London, 1967, 15–19, 20–1, 24, 30–2, 93

Persson, AW, *The Religion of Greece in Prehistoric Times*, University of California Press, Berkeley and Los Angeles, 1942, 32, 34, 35–6, 74, 82, 104 and *passim*

Pini, Ingo, 'Zum "Ring des Minos"', in *Eilapine* (Festschrift for N Platon), Vikelaia Vivliothiki, Heraklion, 1987, 421–455

Rackham, Oliver and Jennifer Moody, *The Making of the Cretan Landscape*, Manchester University Press, 1996, 39

Roberts, Jane, *The Nature of the Psyche: Its Human Expression*, A Seth Book, Prentice-Hall, Englewood Cliffs, NJ, 1979, 96–99, 102-3

Rundle-Clark, RT, *Myth and Symbol in Ancient Egypt*, Thames and Hudson, London, 1959 (first paperback edition 1978), 74, 57, 49 and passim

Sakellarakis, Yannis and Efi Sapouna-Sakellaraki, *Archanes: Minoan Crete in a New Light*, Ammos, Athens, 1997, 158–168 (Tomb A), 655–660 (the ring)

Sourvinou-Inwood, Christiane, 'A Trauma in Flux: Death in the Eighth Century and After', in Robin Hägg, ed, *The Greek Renaissance of the Eighth Century BC*, Paul Åströms Förlag, Stockholm, 1983, 33–48, especially 34

Vassilakis (*sic*), Antonis Sp, *Crete*, I. Mathioulakis & Co, Athens, 237–8

Warren, Peter, *Myrtos: An Early Bronze Age Settlement in Crete*, British School of Archaeology at Athens/Thames and Hudson, London, 1972, 315–7 (Jane M Renfrew, 'Appendix V. The Plant Remains' on the olive stone)

—, 'The Ring of Minos', in *Eilapine* (Festschrift for N Platon), Vikelaia Vivliothiki, Heraklion, 1987, 485–500

—, 'Tree Cult in Contemporary Crete', in *Loibe: In Memory of Andrea G Kalokairinou*, Society of Historical Cretan Studies, Heraklion, 1994, 261–278, here 272

2

THE MIRACLE TREE AND THE APPARITION OF THE VIRGIN

It all started with Rodney Gallop's book *Portugal: A Book of Folk-Ways*. Written in the 1930s, this is a vivid, personal and information-packed account of the author's journeys around the country at that time. On a visit to Portugal to investigate May folk customs, we found it perfect to read aloud on long journeys, and in the section on beliefs and customs we came across an illustration which was enough to make us stop the car. It was a reproduction of an engraving showing the Virgin Mary sitting up in the branches of an oak tree, holding the body of the dead Christ, with a herdsman and an ox kneeling on the ground (Fig. 23). Gallop's text explained that at the village of Merceana in central Portugal there is a church dedicated to the Virgin, with the following story attached. A herdsman saw an ox of his, named Marceano, repeatedly kneeling by an oak tree. One day he saw in the branches a vision of Mary with the dead Christ. Queen Leonor of Portugal founded a church on the spot, and until the 18th century a herd of cattle dedicated to 'Our Lady' was kept outside. During mass the doors were flung open so that they could partake. Gallop speculated that 'this legend was invented to account for some ancient cult of the oak tree and the bull'. We decided to drive to Merceana to see if any traces could still be found there of this curious cult.

The Apparition in the Tree

Our first port of call, as usual with such researches, was the café, where an enquiry sent people to look for people who could help us. We sat outside drinking *galāo*, the delicious long milky coffee served in Portugal in a tall glass, while we were waiting. In the late afternoon sunshine in the village square, we watched the comings and goings: tractors passing or parking, motorbikes, small trucks full of tools and equipment, all the activity of what is still a peasant economy. Eventually the verger arrived with a huge key to open Merceana's big old church. There, hanging in the vestry, was the same print which Gallop had reproduced in his book, along with others showing sickbed recoveries due to the healing powers of this Mary of the oak tree. In the verger's account there was no vision, but instead the shepherd found in the branches of the tree a small idol of Our Lady of Pity. An *ermida* or small country chapel was originally built to shelter the object. Nowadays the idol is stored behind an imposing gilded baroque façade beyond the church's altar. The verger fetched it down, and from a gilt casing brought out a small gnarled-looking wooden carving. It was a strange object which gave little away about its age and history. For more information we had to turn to a local history booklet written by Father João Marques.

This said that the origin of the legend is usually dated to 1305 when records show that the shepherd's village Aldeia Galega was awarded a royal decree giving it special ecclesiastical status. The fame of the legend apparently spread throughout the region. A yearly *romaria* or religious procession was established from Lisbon to attend the festivals of the Holy Ghost in Alenquer, proceeding on to Merceana to honour 'Our Lady of Pity' a few days later. This lasted until 1431 when the plague made travel unsafe. In 1520 the present church was built to replace the primitive *ermida*. The date 1535 is carved on a pillar in the church, and the ownership of the herd of cattle is dated back to that century. In the nave, two large panels of 17th-century blue-and-white mural tiles retell the story of the man and his ox, showing the apparition of the Virgin in the branches. In the 18th century the herd numbered 71, and bulls were rented out for bullfights in nearby towns; an accounts book has survived which started in 1753. Dated by the church back to the 16th century, and by textual evidence two centuries earlier, this Merceana cult of the Virgin Mary in a tree seemed at first like an interesting oddity. I named her 'Our Lady of the Tree Trunk'. Then a chance turning at a street corner in the town of Evora, much further south in the Alentejo region of Portugal, gave events in Merceana an entirely different complexion.

We were lost, wandering through the narrow back streets of this old walled town, trying to find our way back to the gate, when we came upon a weather-worn doorway with a tiled picture above. It showed another scene of the Virgin in a tree. Details were different from Merceana: here the Christ she held was an infant, the ox or cow was not kneeling but lying on its back with legs in the air. But it was indisputably a similar scene. And the picture was titled underneath, not as a scene from Merceana, but as showing the '*Senhora das Brotas*'. After finding out that the building was several hundred years old, and that Brotas was a small village further north in the Alentejo, we were confronted by the possibility that Merceana was not an isolated case. There seemed to be a more widespread tradition linking the leading female symbol of Catholicism to a tree.

The village of Brotas sits at the foot of a steep escarpment, and its story of Mary and the tree reflects this geography. A poor man had a cow on whom he depended to support his family. When one day the cow fell from a hilltop and he found it dead, he was in despair. Taking out a knife, he started through his tears to skin the animal to save the hide and what else he could. He had cut off one of its hooves, when he found himself surrounded by a great light and a voice said: 'Do not fear or despair.' The voice told him to go to his village and call the people and 'when you return your cow will be alive'. (In another version, the Virgin appeared over a pine tree, and told him to dedicate a building to her on the site.) When he returned he found his cow alive, revived and grazing, as if nothing had happened. With no sense of contradiction, it is also said that from the bone of the hoof an image of the Lady had been fashioned in half-relief by the angels. The image is said to have had a gold crown and no child, and the story suggests that it could have been found in the trunk of one of the pine trees at the place.

Brotas now seems a rather desolate spot. When we drove into the village in the late afternoon of a May Sunday, people on the main street looked surprised to see a car. After taking the wrong road along a rushy river-bed at the foot of the ravine, we found our way back to the church and after a wait managed to meet the lady with the key. It was again a large church, built long ago for big congregations, with a slightly damp and disused feel. It was hard to believe that this had been the centre of a cult which, as our guide told us, had reached from Brotas as far as Brazil. She led us to the side of the church and showed us the holy water which still flowed in from a natural spring. Drawing water from the well, she offered us to drink from a wooden ladle and told us about its healing powers. On the ceiling of the church she pointed out paintings showing the scene of the miracle. We would have stayed longer but our guide's small grandson, whom she was minding, had taken the key and seemed intent on locking us all in the church; we decided it would be wise to beat a retreat.

The Brotas cult of the 'Lady of the Tree Trunk' is well documented through several centuries. The dead cow is a characteristic feature which distinguishes illustrations of the Brotas miracle (eg Fig. 24) from the other Marian apparitions. The earliest secure dating of the cult is from 1424, when a book of property demarcations gives a reference to 'Saint Mary of Brotas'. In 1534 a member of the clergy, one Luis Alvares de Proença, visited the chapel, and his comments and list of instructions for repairs are preserved in the Evora Public Library. From 1646 there is an extensive inventory of church furniture and artefacts, including silver lamps and a silver cross. In 1718 a long piece was written about the church by Frei Agostinho, a cleric who travelled around Portugal and wrote a classic work about the shrines of the Virgin Mary. In his section on Brotas he remarks that a small pine forest above the mountain served as a resting place for pilgrims and religious processions which could be very large in summer, coming from all over the Alentejo region.

Frei Agostinho does not mention any specific special tree still standing at the spot, but he deals at some length with the healing properties of the local plant *abroteas* (asphodel), which gave its name to the place and could apparently cure a number of ailments from snakebites to swellings, tapeworm, kidney stones, inflamed eyes, coughs and congested chests. Frei Agostinho goes to some lengths to assert the connection of the plant with the Virgin Mary, 'because she is the universal medicine in all our ills'; he also describes her as the 'holy earth' and wife of the Holy Ghost. It seems he labours almost too hard to make these connections, as if a cult centred on healing plants, earth, and perhaps animals, was still not securely anchored in the symbolism of the Church.

Later reading in Moisés Espírito Santo's book *Oriental Origins of Portuguese Popular Religion* brought to light more examples of the association of Mary with trees in Portugal. At Resende, for example, there is a tradition that some boys were throwing stones to bring down chestnuts from an old and cavernous chestnut tree; a stone fell into a hole in the tree and struck a bell, inside which was an image of the Lady and relics of some other saints. According to one version, the Lady offered one of the boys an apple. Several of Espírito Santo's accounts are drawn from the work of the same cleric Frei Agostinho. At São João da Raiva the story tells that the Virgin Mary appeared to a farmer in the trunk of a tree. She was taken to the church but fled back to the tree. When the villagers tried to chop down the tree, the first blow wounded a man. They then decided to make a chapel near the tree, but the following day she fled from the chapel back to her tree. From these miracles the villagers understood that the Lady did not want to leave the tree. Eventually they made the chapel altar out of the tree trunk; the Lady was then satisfied and did not flee again.

P Antonio Carvalho da Costa records a variation of the story, from Villa do Rei in the district of Bucellas. Here people saw a great light coming from a nearby oak wood, and when they went to investigate they found an image of the Lady with a lit torch in her hand, on an oak tree. After moving the image – with great reverence – to the parish church, they found her fled back to the tree and eventually built her a fine church next to the tree, dedicated to 'Our Lady of the Oak'. At some point over the centuries the reference to the tree was removed and the church is now dedicated to 'Our Lady of Purification'. At Varatojo near Torres Vedras the date of 1474 AD is given for the discovery, in a cavity of a holm oak, of a 70 cm image of *Nossa Senhora do Sobreiro* (Our Lady of the Holm Oak). Legend claims it was brought and hidden 300 years earlier by English soldiers come to help Don Afonso Henriques in the conquest of Lisbon, but does not suggest how or why. A convent was built at the site; engravings tend to show the Lady with flowers on her cloak seated under the tree (eg Fig. 26).

In these stories the Lady sometimes appears in the branches and sometimes from within the tree trunk itself. In several of them there is also an ambiguity between her appearing as a vision and her manifesting as an image or idol. There are several other recurrent themes, such as: the setting of the event in an isolated part of the countryside; the person who finds or experiences the Lady being a herdsman, a child or a group of children; a voice being heard; an animal being connected with the discovery of the special tree (either by the animal's illness prompting the discovery, or by the animal behaving strangely or even kneeling at the tree); miraculous acts of healing; unsuccessful attempts to move the Lady into church, during which she makes it clear that she prefers to stay in the tree; an eventual compromise with some kind of premises constructed as close to the tree as possible; the establishment of a pilgrimage to the site; and the proximity of special water, often a spring. These common themes may reflect the main elements of an early tradition which survived in various forms in various places. As to how early the tradition was, we as yet had little idea.

We were able to investigate some of Frei Agostinho's sites at first hand, to see what remained of the holy trees and their resident deity. At Cortes de Leiria in central Portugal the Lady had appeared in an olive trunk. On the ceiling of the village's 17th-century church, we found – still clearly visible – a lively illustration of the story including cows, sheep, herdsmen and angels, with the Lady wedged right inside the trunk (Fig. 25). The mixture of biblical-looking robes and the wide-brimmed hats of the painter's time gives the picture a quaint flavour. A verger in a red cardigan, who was busy running a choir practice and organising the church's rewiring, found time to give us some information.

The Virgin Mary is here called 'Our Lady of the Birdcage', apparently because she was originally worshipped in a cage-like structure made of willow and other branches, which was built around to stop her running away. As in so many of the other stories, her image was originally found by herdsmen; Frei Agostinho reports the find in an olive tree but notes that is not certain whether she spoke to them or whether they had a supernatural experience. In the early days she performed many miracles, but few in his day. The verger lent us a historical leaflet researched by a local journalist Carlos Fernandez, from which we could establish that the tradition is a lot older than the church. There is a record of the 'Birdcage' mentioned as early as 1344, and of a rural chapel or *ermida* being raised to Our Lady of that name in the 16th century. There is no modern holy tree, but there is a surviving festival: in 1542 the King of Portugal gave an authorisation for a local religious brotherhood to collect money on the first Sunday of May, the date of a big annual festival recorded in 1721 and still celebrated on a grand scale today. I noticed that – consistent with Merceana – there was a solid 14th century date for the earliest written text mentioning the phenomenon.

Further north in central Portugal, a visit to Oliveira do Conde was very different. There the story tells that the Lady (*Nossa Senhora dos*

Carvalhais) appeared in the trunk of an oak. Local people directed us to an area of woodland and pointed out a very old oak, hollow and reclining on its side but still putting out tall branches and a thick canopy of green leaves. The church beside it – at least 18th-century by a date on one of its bells – was abandoned and wrecked. The cult image bears on its base the date of 1001, and Frei Agostinho would like to trace it back to the time of Caesar. We learned that it had been removed to the house of a nearby priest, who was reluctant to let us into his house to see it. The Lady of the Oak Tree was thus no longer worshipped at the site of the tree where she was said to have been found. However, on a wide clearing adjacent to the church a fair still takes place regularly, and sometimes a mass is held beneath a tree on the other side of the clearing, perhaps reflecting some kind of memory of the earlier tradition. In his passage on Oliveira do Conde, Frei Agostinho writes about the oak tree's leafy branches and cool shade, and describes the oak as a symbol attributed with many qualities including courage, protection, heroic virtue, beneficence, providence, humility and constancy. Surprising words from an 18th-century cleric. I went back to look at the original oak. Lying down to rest on the horizontal sun-dappled trunk, I shut my eyes to see what qualities might spring to mind. Perhaps the centuries of fairs and merrymaking had left their mark, because the only mood I felt was one of celebration.

Pala, near Mortagua, gave an idea of how these country sites may have functioned in their prime. Here the Lady who appeared in the heart of an old chestnut tree deep in the forest is still honoured there in an autumn festival at chestnut harvest time. We were lucky to be in the area. A slow line of cars made the pilgrimage into the woods, where a crowd of several hundred stood beneath the trees outside the tiny chapel to hear mass. Some of the children were dressed as angels. The congregation included many mothers in smart clothes and high heels who stood patiently to hear a long sermon about the Virgin Mary and women's work. Then there was a procession through the forest carrying an image of the Lady perched on a wooden frame surrounded by flowers. A long stream of people followed her in silence between the trees, some of the children carrying balloons. At the same time, back near the church a big fair was opening up, selling everything from carpets and cassettes to crucifixes, china dogs, shoes, T-shirts, sides of pork and heaps of shining chestnuts. Barbecues sizzled under marquees, neatly packed picnic baskets were opened, wine was drunk from plastic cups, music played. People returning from the procession joined in the festivities. Overall it seemed to be an occasion for physical, economic and spiritual expansion.

I was beginning to get the impression that the whole of central Portugal was teeming with traditions of holy trees in which the Virgin Mary had appeared.

In addition to Frei Agostinho, we were now armed with a 1967 book by P Jacinto dos Reis surveying all the cults of the Virgin Mary in Portugal, and we scoured through it for references to tree apparitions. Searching for the hamlet of Gondolim near Penacova we finally found a small cluster of houses in a rain-drenched forest. Here the Virgin is said to have appeared in a tree trunk after bells were heard ringing in a thicket. Twice they took her to the church, but both times she fled back to the trunk of her tree. Gondolim's church had an even bigger key which was even harder to track down than usual. As a small crowd gathered to help us in the muddy main street, surrounded by buildings from another century, the encircling forest and the insistent dripping of the rain added to a sense of having stepped beyond the reach of modern Europe into a fairytale world where anything was possible.

Inside the church, a large mural above the altar showed the scene of the apparition of the Virgin, with a large Lady seated full square on a tree stump and a substantial bell beside her. Little paintings hanging on the church wall showed sickbed scenes of healing by the Lady. We were told that she has a spring fiesta, when her image is carried round the village. The elderly gentleman who showed us round the church remembered travelling some 20 km by boat – using sail and oars – to take this very same image down the river to Coimbra to be repainted 50 years before, when he was 12 years old. As often, an explanation was offered to rationalise the miracle: that the image of the saint had been hidden in time of war and had been lost until the shepherd and his animals found it.

In Dardavaz, Our Lady of Guadalupe was said to have appeared in a mimosa tree, though stories varied. On arrival at Dardavaz we found that her small chapel was empty apart from her image, but the priest up at the village's main church had a surprise for us. He told us excitedly that about two years earlier they had moved the altar of the main church back a little, and had found beneath it a plaque dated 1786. The priest brought it out of a cupboard. It carried a picture of someone ill in bed and a text of thanks for recovery to Our Lady of

Gaudalupe. It thus provided primary evidence for a healing cult in the parish at that time. He had found, and showed us, supporting evidence in the form of a parish record from 1700 mentioning a sisterhood of Our Lady of Guadalupe, made up of local parishioners and based in the little chapel. A careful hand with large cursive letters had penned into the register a list of names of the women attending the prayer sessions week by week. The healing Lady was active here under another name.

Dardavaz led off in a direction I could not pursue, offering a fascinating peek into a wealth of similar material outside Portugal. Guadalupe is in Spain, and a cult of Our Lady of Guadalupe also enjoyed great popularity in Latin America. Jacinto dos Reis states that her cult came to Portugal from Spain after the battle of Salado in 1340, so she evidently has a long history. Even without taking the path into Spain to investigate this Lady's origins, I learned from a small amount of reading that a few centuries ago in Spain stories and beliefs were current which were very similar to those in Portugal. William A Christian in *Local Religion in Sixteenth Century Spain* gives a list of apparitions, or images which had strangely appeared; he notes the frequent role of animals and the statues' persistent habit of returning to the sacred location where they were found. Our Lady of Salceda had appeared in a willow tree. Our Lady of the Madroñal appeared in Auñón on a tree stump and – like the Portuguese Lady – returned to the site later. After a fresh water spring appeared at Fuensanta, Our Lady of the Remedy was visited for healing, and I was interested to learn that it was especially for healing of the eyes and stomach just as at the first Cretan holy tree. In Morata a certain cow separated from the herd and knelt at the chapel of Our Lady of the Vega.

William Christian comments on 'the sense of divine participation in the landscape' which was a feature of local religion in that period. He describes how the Church tried to bring local religion under clerical control, for example by limiting the length of pilgrimages and clamping down on overnighting in the countryside, where it was suspected that people enjoyed themselves too much. The early 16th century saw the persecution of visionaries by the Inquisition. The ambivalence of the Lady's image about being in the church rather than the countryside was perhaps a metaphor for a similar ambivalence in people who lived in villages but worked in the countryside, or a conflict between the congregation and the Church establishment. He suggests that 'Mary offered alternative sacred places to the village center, taking the villagers out from the society to nature ... The legend motif of the return of the image to the country site, rejecting the parish church, may be an echo or a metaphor for what was in some sense a liberation of devotion from parish control – or, put another way, the resistance of local religion to the growing claims of the Church.'

Although we were not ourselves able to investigate modern survivals in Spain, the issue there is clearly not dead. While working on this part of the research, I was shown an article in *Time Out* magazine about a series of modern 'miracles' in El Escorial, a monastery town near Madrid, where the Virgin Mary had appeared in an ash tree, and was transmitting messages through the medium of an older peasant woman. The reporter Rob Stone had visited the site: 'A breeze pushes through the heat and sunbeams flicker through an ash tree. Twenty thousand people fall to their knees and cry in ecstasy: "La Virgen!" For a split second, exhilarated by their faith, I think I see the sacred apparition in the play of light and leaves. A miracle?' The sacred ash had been attacked by arsonists, and fenced off by a secular local council, but Stone saw it being 'kissed and fondled by a ring of ecstatic women'. What seemed a miracle to me was that despite the centuries of repressive measures by the Church establishment to control religious activities around the natural world, the same battle for the tree was still going on.

Two years later, I read in a Portuguese newspaper about another tree apparition in Spain. Trinidad Eugénio, a woman in her fifties living in the county of Huelva, was seeing the Virgin on the thirteenth of every month above a holm oak, 'wrapped in a circle of light, as brilliant as the sun'. The journalist Idálio Revez interviewed the parish priest who dismissed the visions as 'the fruit of the imagination of a person with little religious knowledge', but Trinidad Eugénio reported a number of miraculous cures, and had a large local following.

In general, Marian apparitions continue to be fairly frequent events in Catholic societies. On a trip to Guatemala we visited a site where an apparition of Our Lady of Guadalupe in a tree had been reported as recently as the early 1990s, and there are celebrated cases such as the Marian visions of the six children of Medjugorje in Bosnia-Herzegovina which started in 1981. However, what interested me particularly about the El Escorial and Huelva accounts was the role of the tree in the apparition and the particular involvement of women; it had also been four young girls who famously had a series of visions of the Virgin at Garabandal in Spain between 1961 and 1965. The religious historian Karen Armstrong on a TV programme *Do You Believe in Visions of the Virgin Mary?* suggested that visions bring in aspects of experience which are denied in the cerebral orientation of the Church establishment, and give a voice to women who are often not allowed one. She pointed to periods of history which have seen a growth of Marian devotion simultaneous with a resurgence of women's involvement. I noticed that, if not women, other relatively powerless groups such as landless peasants and children were often involved in the holy tree phenomena of Portugal.

By now what we had named 'Our Lady of the Tree Trunk' at Merceana was looking less like an unusual phenomenon and more like an Iberian epidemic. But despite learning about these other cases, I was slow to recognise the relevance of the most famous incident ever to have linked the Virgin Mary to a tree: the miracle at a place called Fatima.

The Disappearing Tree of Fatima

Fatima is one of the biggest centres of pilgrimage in the Catholic world as a result of events which started on 13 May 1917, in a small and remote valley in central Portugal. Here Mary appeared above the branches of a holm oak to three shepherd children named Lucia, Francisco and Jacinta, aged ten, nine and seven. She promised to reveal herself again on the thirteenth day of every month until October. By the date of her final apparition over 50,000 people gathered to witness it. Newspapers reported that those present were dazzled – and many apparently healed of ailments – by witnessing the strange phenomenon of the sun turning into a fireball and shooting coloured light to earth.

However, the children remained the only ones who could see the apparition of the Virgin, and the oldest child Lucia was the only person who could hear her message, which included a warning about the dangers of war and revolution in Portugal and Russia. The two other children died young, but Lucia became a Carmelite nun and lived in seclusion to a very ripe old age. While Portuguese and international pilgrims visit the site in a constant flow, it has remained a matter of urgency for Catholics and atheists alike to debate the truth of the children's account and to find a way of dismissing or accommodating an event which falls outside the norms of both the Catholic and the secular Western world view.

So what happened? How can one understand this strange story? Although at first the Church was reluctant to acknowledge the miracle, this experience of three children deep in the Portuguese countryside became an instrument for it to revive its fortunes under an anti-clerical government. The miracle also became an international *cause célèbre* in the propaganda war against communism. What particularly intrigued me was the way in which the sequence of events could be seen as encapsulating a process whereby the Church institutionalised and politicised local religious experience, particularly the honouring of trees.

My interest was not in proving or disproving the 'miracle', but in locating and understanding it. The whole picture of the event changes when it is seen to belong to the long tradition of similar appearances which we had traced back over the centuries in the Portuguese countryside, through Merceana and Brotas and beyond. So many of the familiar factors are present at Fatima: adults or children looking after animals in a remote place; a tree; an apparition; a voice. The children were, as Lucia herself described in her memoirs, desperately hungry as they used to mortify their flesh by passing their lunch to the sheep, and were given to long hours of prayer. Fasting, isolation and devotion breed visions. They were keen church goers in a locality where many similar apparitions had been experienced. They lived in the hamlet of Aljustrel, 20 kilometres from Cortes (of the Lady of the Birdcage), and had family contacts at Reixida near Cortes, whom they might have visited before the apparition. Also nearby was the church of Our Lady of the Fernery at Reguengo do Fetal. And at Ortiga two kilometres from Aljustrel, Our Lady had appeared in a nettle patch and had given a dumb shepherdess the power of speech. A Portuguese study book, *Aljustrel*, which investigates the children's day-to-day background, describes the poverty and harshness of peasant life in their village at that time. But it also mentions fairs and markets, religious festivals and visits to relations, all requiring a certain amount of travel between villages and therefore presumably contact, conversation and the spreading of news and ideas.

The children thus lived in terrain where 'Our Lady of the Tree Trunk' was a well-known figure, and their vision followed a time-honoured pattern of other visions experienced by people tending herds in the countryside of central Portugal. Although skilfully adapted by the Church to serve its political needs in the 20th century, the form of the vision of Our Lady at Fatima grew out of the vestiges of a centuries-old tradition. How old that tradition was, and what its origins were, were puzzles I had yet to pursue. The question arose whether it originally had more to do with a popular notion of a holy female tree than with the personified Christian figure of Mary herself. As suggested by the many attempts to relocate her within a church building, this female-identified tree linked to revelation and healing is an element which organised religion had a long struggle to master, whether through elimination or – failing that – appropriation.

At Fatima it seems to have succeeded. There is little at the site now except concrete, over a huge area which was once a hillside. Of the tree itself nothing has survived. It was very soon plucked apart by pilgrims seeking relics, and on its place stands a pillar at the centre of a glass and concrete chapel where mass is sung at regular intervals in different languages, summoned by an electronic bell and amplified through loud speakers. The English language service ended with the warning: 'Even here at Fatima the devil is at work. Hang on to your money and bags. Don't trust anyone.' At tourist shops pilgrims buy hologram pictures of the apparition, and wax images which are dedicated, melted down and sold again. From the top of the hill, on a marble path set into the concrete, an unending stream of suppliants approach the shrine on their knees, self-crippled, shuffling slowly and painfully on knee pads or laddered tights.

A chance purchase of a postcard in a small shop selling religious paraphernalia in Guimarães one rainy afternoon had reminded us of the Fatima connection. On re-examination, this same postcard seemed to embody the process of appropriation and changing priorities. Entitled 'Nossa Senhora de Fatima', it showed a romantically painted scene. Low in the foreground were three children with arms raised in awe or clasped in prayer. The boy was kneeling. Beside them were a goat and two sheep. Dominating the top two-thirds of the picture, surrounded by a turbulent blue-grey cloud, was the much larger and white-clad figure of the Virgin Mary towering above them. Beneath her feet, difficult to see and shrunk out of proportion to be smaller even than the children, was a tiny spindly tree. Every other postcard and picture we could find featured the tree in this same diminished form (see Fig. 27).

This dwindling of the tree can be seen as part of a wider picture in church history.

The Church and Tree Visions

The traditions of Judaism and Christianity are ambivalent about trees. God appears in a burning bush, and there are Old Testament passages which acknowledge the veneration of trees as a fact of life. Deuteronomy 33, 16 refers to 'the goodwill of him that dwelt in the bush'. However, there are also well-known passages that legislate against it, such as at Deuteronomy 16, 21: 'Thou shalt not plant thee a grove of any trees near unto the altar of the Lord thy God.' There are passages where Jehovah fulminates against such practices, as in Ezekiel 6, 13: 'Then shall ye know that I am the Lord, when their slain men shall be among their idols round their altars, upon every high hill, in all the tops of the mountains, and under every green tree, and under every thick oak, the place where they did offer sweet savour to all their idols.' There is a similar declaration at Deuteronomy 12, 2–3. Again at Deuteronomy 7, 5 instructions are given as to how to deal with those who do not follow correct practices: 'destroy their altars, and break their images, and cut down their groves, and burn their graven images with fire'. There are similar instructions at Exodus 34, 13, and the order to cut down groves is repeated at Judges 6, 25. And, again, at Deuteronomy 12, 2 we read: 'Ye shall utterly destroy all the places, wherein the nations which ye shall possess served their gods, upon the high mountains, and upon the hills, and under every green tree: and ye shall overthrow their altars, and break their pillars, and burn their groves with fire...'

Although sometimes specifically ascribed to other cultures, the vehemence of the denunciations suggests that these practices were not alien to the Israelite popular culture. Indeed, in some passages the children of Israel are specifically accused of making groves, serving Baal, choosing gardens, desiring oaks, and sacrificing in gardens (Isiah 1, 29 and 65, 3; Judges 3, 7; I Kings 14, 15; II Kings 17, 16). The planting of groves and the interest in hills and mountaintops for ritual activity are familiar from the Bronze Age and Early Iron Age Aegean, as discussed in Chapter One. Such elements, and rituals around trees, were evidently well known in the society which produced the Bible. Some of the passages move beyond banning the practices to give a picture of what they involved. Child sacrifice is sometimes mentioned, as at Isiah 57, 4–5: 'are ye not children of transgression, ... enflaming yourselves with idols under every green tree, slaying the children in the valleys under the clefts of the rocks?' This passage goes on to describe the veneration of stones. Idols and graven images are also often mentioned. Using incense, weeping for the near-Eastern vegetation deity Tammuz, and worshipping the sun, are three activities specifically described in a passage at Ezekiel 9, 7–18.

Without critical comment, however, the text at Judges 4, 4–5 records that '. . . Deborah, a prophetess, the wife of Lapidoth, judged Israel at that time. And she dwelt under the palm tree of Deborah between Ramah and Beth-el in mount Ephraim: and the children of Israel came up to her for judgement.' The role of a female figure here, sitting under a tree and being approached respectfully, resonates with material from the Aegean world discussed in Chapter One, including pictures such as Fig. 16. The community of Jews living in Pathros, Egypt, responded defiantly to the prophet Jeremiah's critical remarks and defended their practice of making offerings to 'the queen of heaven', at Jeremiah 44, 15–19. In a chapter in *Ancient Goddesses*, Karel van der Toorn discusses this 'queen of heaven', and more generally a whole body of overlooked evidence for the role of goddesses in early Israelite religion. In *Under Every Green Tree* Susan Ackerman has re-examined in detail some of the denunciation passages to draw out the evidence for popular – rather than official – religion in 6th century BC Judah.

The prevalent attitude towards trees in the Judaeo-Christian tradition is expressed not only in overt attacks like those quoted above, but also more subtly in the role allotted to trees in various biblical stories. It is eating the fruit of the tree in the Garden of Eden which corrupts Eve and Adam and leads to their expulsion from Paradise. It is also the tree which provides the wood of the cross on which Christ dies. In representations of the crucifixion in Christian iconography, the timbers of the cross are closely associated with the stretched, pain-wracked limbs of Jesus during his last hours on earth. So at the beginning and end of the Christian story there is a tree – one which is in both cases linked with the body. That story starts with the search for pleasure and ends in pain. The symbolism of the Garden of Eden and of the crucifixion are like two sides of the same coin, both subliminally identifying the tree with flesh, and with sex, mortality, sin and suffering. It occurred to me that perhaps attitudes to trees within a culture reflect that culture's attitudes to the body.

Mary sits under a tree in some versions of the Annunciation story, and as well as the apparition trees I have discussed there are marginal

Christian traditions based on biblical or apocryphal passages which associate her variously with cedar, palm, olive, rose, pomegranate and cherry tree. Within the dominant narratives of the Judaeo-Christian tradition, however, there is little to counter the generally negative attitude to trees. It therefore becomes tempting to suggest that the source of the vitality of the medieval Marian tree cults must lie in 'pre-Christian elements' or 'pagan traditions'. This is hard to prove. From surviving material of the early Middle Ages, it is hard to find substantial evidence for an alternative tradition of this kind, with a non-Christian ancestry, and even harder to trace a process whereby it became attached to the Virgin. As in biblical times, tree cults belonged to a popular culture which leaves fewer records than a centrally organised religion, and – again – sometimes all that survives is a collection of edicts by the organised religion banning its competitor. It is in fact these very edicts which most strongly give the impression of the existence and importance of nature rituals in the Iberian peninsula in the Middle Ages.

Thus a Madrid document dated 1603 preserves a text from the council of the north Portuguese town Braga declaiming against the heretical practice of burning torches and worshipping trees, springs and rocks ('*Si in alicuius Presbyteri parochia infidelis aut faculas incenderint, aut arbores, aut fontes, aut saxa veneratur. . .*') (*Fragmenta ex Conciliis Bracarensibus*, c.22, *Collectio conciliorum Hispaniae*). These were presumably trees which had not been drawn into the fold of the Church by an identification with the Virgin Mary. The banning of tree cult was only part of wider legislation in Portugal to keep the natural world at a safe distance from religious practice: another church edict, of 1563, from Lamego in north Portugal, specifically forbids processions to head for hills and rocks; they must go only to the church or chapel, where the holy service takes place ('*Defendemos e mandamos que com as procissões nam vam a outeiros, nem penedos, mas soomente aa igreja, ou hermida, onde se faz ho officio divino. . .*') (*Constituicões do bispado de Lamego*, 135). Sparse evidence as they are, these pronouncements do suggest a culture which encompassed tree rituals surviving into Christian times.

Such pronouncements start at an early date. The same Madrid collection quoted above includes an edict of the council of Braga dating from 598 AD which states that 'It is forbidden to observe iniquitous calendar customs. . . or to decorate homes with laurel and greenery. All such observances belong to paganism.' ('*Non liceat iniquas observationes agere Kalendarum . . . neque lauro, aut viriditate cingere domos. Omnis haec observatio paganismi est.*') The early date of some of the edicts is important if we are interested in evidence to bridge the gap between the tree rituals of the ancient and modern worlds.

If the Christian establishment gave the tree an ambivalent role in its ideology and banned tree rituals, it has also, historically, been unenthusiastic about visionary experiences. We saw that many of the Portuguese apparition stories told how attempts were made to move the Lady out of the tree and into a church building. In several cases there was also some ambiguity as to whether the appearance of Our Lady was as a vision or as a cult object. I began to wonder whether the Church had been instrumental in contributing to this confusion, replacing the vision in the narratives with an image or object which could be held in the hand and kept on the premises in clerical control. Marina Warner points out that 'A sacred image was not an illusion but the possessor of reality itself', especially if of superhuman origin, and comments on 'The progression from vision to sacred object. . . to cult site. . . to palladium of a people and a nation and a cause – a progression that occurs in many stories of Catholic attempts to contact the eternal'.

The official Vatican view is that since the word of God was revealed in the Gospels, no further direct communications are to be expected before the Last Judgement. In the case of Fatima, it is still possible to read a verbatim account of the rigorous cross-examination to which the visionary children were subjected, and attempts were made to silence them before the Church finally adopted their story and found it worked for them. A similar pattern of response has been followed by the Church with more recent apparitions. In the 1980s the children at Medjugorje were put under pressure by both the then communist regime and the regional Church hierarchy, although none of the visionaries have recanted and their experiences continued for 20 years. The vocabulary of faith includes the possibility of visions and miracles: there is a rich Christian tradition of visionaries, including venerated figures such as St Bernadette of Lourdes. At Medjugorje a dedicated local priest, Slavko Barbaric, did much to spread the messages of the Virgin around the world, latterly using the Internet; and the Bishop of Split claimed that his own blindness had been cured after visiting the hill site of the apparitions. However, in 1998 the Vatican itself finally ruled that there was no evidence of 'supernatural visions' at Medjugorje.

Visionary experiences may be acceptable to the Church establishment once they are recorded in texts and stories set safely in the past; contemporary visions, however, are clearly a different matter. By their nature such experiences are spontaneous and unofficial. Through attracting a huge popular following towards unordained individuals who claim direct access to the divine, they may undermine the authority of the Church's own personnel. Perhaps it is not surprising that they tend to attract the Church's disapproval. William Christian points out the political implications: 'The poor or the powerless have the visions, and the eventual imposition of their truth upon the town authorities is a sure way of showing that Mary or the saint has come to serve everybody; that the bond set up between the saint and the town is also a direct bond between the saint and each person of the town, beginning with the powerless.'

Members of the Church establishment are not the only ones to disapprove of visions: there is also a strong consensus voice against them from people who pride themselves on their common sense.

'Common Sense' and Tree Visions

Visions are a frequently attested aspect of human experience, and have an integrated and important place in the belief systems of many religions in non-Western cultures. However, the 'common-sense' view in Western culture has an investment in a picture of the world which does not include visions as a possibility, past or present. Certain forms of knowledge are privileged and others are dismissed as invalid on the basis of prevalent cultural assumptions. Thus accounts of visionary experiences have often been discredited as foolish or hysterical imaginings, or attacked as deliberate fabrications. I personally feel that this view is sustainable only from a fundamentalist position, which lacks curiosity and rejects anything challenging preconceived beliefs. It is easy to dismiss accounts of experiences from other cultures, or from within our own, simply because they do not fall within our cultural norms. I suggest that it would actually be more rational to set prejudice aside in order to explore ways of putting such experiences in context and understanding them.

After the death of Diana, Princess of Wales, large crowds gathered in central London to mourn her, piling up mountains of flowers, gifts and messages, with public displays of grief. On 4 September 1997 the

Independent ran an article headlined 'It's started: Diana's vision is seen'. Some of the crowd who had been queuing for 10 or 11 hours to sign the books of condolence in St James' Palace reported an 'appearance' of Diana in the top right-hand corner of an old painting of Charles I which was hanging at the end of the corridor. Everyone involved was very aware that this was a non-consensual experience. The journalist Clare Garner reports being approached by a 'hysterical' woman who told her, 'The light is shining on that painting in a particular way and Princess Diana's face is looking out of it. Everybody's seeing her face looking out.' The woman was then backed up by 'a sober-looking man in a suit' who commented 'This lady started and I thought: "Oh my God, she's mad..." ...but it's something very strange and it did shock me. I swear to God – and I'm not some nutter.' The image described by several people interviewed was a well-known image of Diana which had appeared on the cover of *Vogue* magazine, visible 'as clear as day' according to one woman. Another sobbing woman refused to give her name: 'You think I'm a crank.' All this is familiar in contemporary journalistic coverage of such themes: the 'tongue-in-cheek' style of writing; the reporter's need to emphasise the emotionality of those perceiving the vision; the percipients' need to re-affirm their own sanity.

An hour later, the journalist asked a second group of people to look at the painting of Charles I before they left, without giving any clues as to what they were looking for. The same vision was described. What conclusion can be drawn? Were these individuals lying? Or is it possible that when people are tired, stressed, acutely emotionally aware and focused on a particular idea they can enter a state where they have unusual experiences? How does the experience spread from one person to another? In our culture there is little curiosity about these questions. The word 'hallucination' is often brought in as a final and dismissive definition of such experiences, rather than as the starting point of a process of inquiry. Nor is the distinction sometimes made between ('internal') vision and ('external') apparition helpful, as it seems to reflect a rationalising construction after the event of experiences which are all felt at the time to be 'real'.

Similar tensions emerge in the way this topic is treated by academics. In 1993, Carol Burke published a study of *Vision Narratives of Women in Prison*, based on more than a year's fieldwork interviewing women prisoners and recording their stories of supernatural experiences. Burke interprets the women's stories exclusively along sociological and feminist lines, seeing them as coping strategies which help women to process their tragic life histories and recover self-esteem. Thus one prisoner's flash of concern about her family, which she herself experiences as 'a type of clairvoyance', is interpreted by Burke as separation anxiety. The women's accounts of being attacked by something supernatural in the night are explained as reflecting their experience of the dominant oppressive males in their lives. Everything has a 'rational' explanation. Reviewing the book in *Folklore* journal, Gillian Bennett comments on Burke's dismissal of supernatural belief systems, and regrets the 'tunnel vision' which leads Burke to marginalise 'all metaphysical and epistemological issues'. Bennett acknowledges the value of interpreting the women's confusing and frightening experiences as a 'cultural discourse' reflecting their circumstances, but points out that this is not always the only possible interpretation, nor is it the women's own interpretation. She goes on to say that for the women prisoners themselves, the whole significance of the stories rests on their being true. She argues for an 'experience-centred' approach which reasserts the dignity of the tellers and gives the stories back to them. This approach demands that folklorists 'believe their informants, or at least not disbelieve them on the basis of their own beliefs'. In her conclusion she doubts whether a feminist critique alone is adequate for dealing with such material and suggests that the women, 'like any others of us who have had any form of discrepant experience, . . . want to know whether it was "real" and, if so, what sort of reality it was'.

I find it interesting that several academics who have studied medieval visions similarly stress the importance of taking them seriously. William Christian offers 'a caveat against excessive skepticism in regard to the legends. That most of them were stereotyped or derivative by no means rules out the discovery of images or the historical phenomena of apparitions.' He suggests that real discoveries and visions became stereotyped after the event, as people organised these experiences into known patterns. In *The Medieval Vision: Essays in History and Perception*, Carolly Erickson sees the visionary imagination as 'an evocative symbol of the perceptual distance between our own times and the middle ages, and a touchstone for a tentative exploration of that distance'. She suggests that in the Middle Ages 'Their perceptual range was broader than ours. They were aware of more possibilities, because they were less inclined to dismiss any of them as unimaginable.' She points out that the capacity for visions was not incompatible with careful observation, and that in their 'watchful interrogation of the natural world', there was 'a quality of image-receptiveness, an openness to visual sensation that complemented the broader range of medieval sight'.

How might we think about that broader range of sight? We know that all body experience, including perception, is culturally constructed. We cannot retrieve the medieval experience, but it may be helpful to look at contemporary theoretical frameworks which – relying neither on mysticism nor on religious dogma – offer models for describing and understanding a broader perceptual range than that which we regard as normal. For example, one model which has interested me is that broadly known as 'subtle anatomy'. This is a system which is taught and practised in the West by a number of people in the health professions, including acupuncturists and some people working with massage, Alexander Technique, cranial osteopathy and meditation, amongst others. Although generally unacknowledged by conventional allopathic medicine, it is recognised and used by some nurses and doctors.

This body of thought suggests that there are subtle energy forces involved in the physical functioning of all living things, present in animal and plant life, and in the natural world as a whole, as well as in the human body.

The discipline has a long and coherent history in the East, while in the West its history has been more piecemeal and has only recently been drawn together into a coherent picture. For example, Wilhelm Reich, originally a pupil of Sigmund Freud, was working in a psychotherapeutic context in Germany and the USA before and after World War II when he developed his concept of 'body energy'. He came to see the free movement of this energy through the body as essential for the healthy functioning of the individual, while blockages and distortions were the result of trauma and tension often originating in childhood. His perspective was very different from that of Walter Kilner, a doctor at St Thomas' Hospital in London, who did a series of technical experiments on viewing the 'aura' through dicyanin-dyed screens, published early in the 20th century. Kilner reported that 'rays, or streams, or patches of brightness were noticed emanating from different parts of the body'. More recently Reich's follower John Pierrakos has integrated psychological understandings with a study of the 'aura' or 'energy field', and David Tansley in the school of Radionics has drawn various threads of anatomical study in East and West into a system of alternative medicine described in several books.

Bob Moore at the Psykisk Center in Denmark, who introduced me to this discipline as part of my massage training, emphasised in his courses that in his view there is nothing mystical about it. His understanding is that the movement of energy through and around the body follows laws like any other anatomical process. Those laws, he suggested – like the laws of many other anatomical processes – are as yet imperfectly understood. While teaching, he preferred to approach the subject in a dynamic way, using experiential workshops to help individuals develop their awareness of the movements of subtle energy within and around the human body. As in any discipline, theories vary in detail and overview, and differences are debated; his approach favoured experiment and inquiry.

The 'subtle anatomy' model suggests that permeating and surrounding the solid human body there is an 'energy body' which is crucial to our health – supplying, circulating, processing and eliminating subtle energy just as the solid body takes in air, circulates blood, processes and eliminates food. Visible to clairvoyants as showing colour, movement and blockages, palpable to some masseurs who sense it with their hands, the space around each individual is said to be filled with activity and changing energy structures. John Pierrakos has described it as a cloudy, pulsating envelope which extends for two to four feet around the visible body. And just as the solid body carries scars, stiffness, weakness and injuries as a result of tension, repression, stress and trauma during the past, so – it is suggested – the energy body bears a record of our life's experience and problems, past and present, imprinted in it.

From several thousand years of history of subtle anatomy studies in China and India, and from recent syntheses in the West, the broad basis of the current theory can be summarised as follows. The energy field around a person is said to be made up of a series of layers which react differently to experiences: the 'etheric' layer, a storehouse of energy, closest to the visible body; then the 'astral' or emotional level further out, linked with emotional activity; the 'mental' layer around the head and shoulders, which expands when an individual is thinking or meditating; and finally the outermost layer which encircles the visible body at a distance of several feet, said to carry the 'qualities' which are ours to express in life if they can find a clear path in through the energy field to reach the physical body at the heart. These different layers of the 'aura' are believed to function with different kinds of energy, and also to reflect different aspects of human activity – whether physical, emotional, mental or spiritual.

In Christian pictures, holy figures are sometimes shown with a halo above their head, or with a large egg-shaped luminous glow – known as a 'glory' – surrounding their body, which could be taken as representing the aura. However, according to the theories of subtle anatomy, not only saints but all of us have an energy field which is more or less active and powerful. Far from being an amorphous glow, it has an anatomy as complex as the visible body, including not only these different layers but a number of streams circulating up and down and round the body, many specific points with their own functions and a series of energy centres. These last are usually referred to as 'chakras' after the Indian terminology; CW Leadbeater in his classic text on the subject points out that the seven forms of yoga recognised in India (Rāja, Karma, Jnāna, Hatha, Laya, Bhakti and Mantra) are all concerned in different ways with developing the chakras, and he correlates the five principal 'Vāyus' or 'pranas' referred to in Hindu books with the functioning of seven chakras ranged up the body. Others modify the Indian models in different ways.

Perceiving such energic activity around the body is not part of the consensual reality of contemporary Western culture. Writers and teachers in the field suggest that the ability to perceive it may derive from an individual gift/aptitude (the clairvoyant) or from hard work developing that faculty (eg through a yogic discipline) or from cultural conditioning which facilitates and encourages such perceptions. Even without any of those factors, unusual states induced by shock, fasting, stress, emotions, mind-altering substances or ritual processes may propel us into a particularly acute sensitivity triggering 'hallucinations' similar to experiences in the dream state. These may reflect a more or less confused perception of energy movements. If all the things we can normally see – and maybe some things we cannot normally see – have their own energy field, we may under such conditions apprehend their existence through our own energy field. Our consensual processes of perception through the five senses may at such times feed us unexpected experiences of temperature change, smell, 'seeing things' or 'hearing things'.

Perhaps these are the conditions of altered consciousness which generated the hovering fairy-like figures shown in the Aegean Bronze Age designs like Fig. 15, and the voice or glowing form of the Lady in the Portuguese accounts of Marian apparitions. Small, floating figures appearing in a kind of cloud are a standard feature of accounts and depictions of supernatural appearances (as on the early 19th century Portuguese 'ex-voto' which depicts Our Lady at a sickbed saving someone close to death, Fig. 28). While the faithful believe and the sceptical dismiss, there is here a physical vocabulary which can provide a context for such experiences, a vocabulary which allows us to start talking about the distance between our 'normal' experience and the different perceptual range of people in some other cultures.

But what is the process by which individuals come to 'see' or 'hear' things in a particular shape or form, such as a vision of the Virgin Mary who sits in a tree and gives specific warnings and instructions about human behaviour?

Envisioning Mary

Apparitions, though experienced as heavenly, have a strong connection to physical conditions. The historian David Blackbourn, in a study of an outbreak of Marian visions in 1876 in the German village of Marpingen, points to 'typical' criteria for such visions, which are of course by no means confined to trees. Both Marpingen and Medjugorje in former Yugoslavia, whose apparitions I mentioned earlier, were in borderland territory, both were mountainous (apparitions often happen on high ground), and both were involved in political and economic conflict, with local identity in crisis. In my own work I have noted other typical factors, such as the marginality and vulnerability of those who perceive the visions. Many are women, children or empoverished peasants, and may be suffering from trauma or loss; 15-year-old Ivanka Ivankovic, for example, one of the Medjugorje visionaries, was grieving from the recent death of her mother, and the Fatima children were starving themselves. Discovering typical factors in the incidence of chickenpox does not make the disease imaginary, and these patterns do not explain away the visions; rather they give information which may help to understand the phenomena. More information can be gained by looking at the shape which the visions themselves take.

In 1999, Jürgen Beyer published a study of how apparition stories changed over a period from 1350 AD to 1700 AD in Scandinavia and those parts of Germany which became Lutheran during the Reformation. He traces a process of transformation whereby medieval apparitions of (often female) saints are replaced by apparitions exclusively of Jesus or of angels. Certain elements continued in the post-Reformation stories, such as the apparition wearing a white robe, bringing a message of instruction for the community, and in some cases inflicting a temporary paralysis so that the visionary could not get up from a seated position. But the message of the Catholic apparitions that the community must do penance is rephrased by the post-Reformation apparitions in a Lutheran terminology, so that the instruction is to do inner repentance. Moreover, in the Protestant period the site of the vision was never viewed as sacred, and the apparitions no longer ask for a shrine and cult to be established for them as they did in Catholic contexts.

Beyer identifies sources from which lay people could learn about which kind of divine revelations conformed to the new, Lutheran ideals: such sources included common knowledge, cheap print (pamphlets and broadsides) and oral communication (presumably he means on a more individual level). He also points to various types of intervention by the Church. Unacceptable elements in the stories could be censored, and their impact contained, at the pulpit. Or the authorities could intervene more directly. In 1538, a girl in Basel who died and came back to life again with stories of a vision of hell, and other 'olde wiues tales', was explicitly silenced: 'at the com-maundemente of the wise Magistrate shee was commaunded to sylence, leaste the vnconstaunte people myghte be wyth tryfles misseled'. Sometimes the response could be even fiercer. In 1573, Ingeborg Kjeldsdatter from Skiptvet near Oslo appeared in court because of some 'erroneous' teachings she had been spreading among the common people, namely 'that she had heard a voice and that the sky had opened and that she had seen a woman sitting on a chair and talking to her... The woman was alleged to be the *virgo* Mary...' Ingeborg Kjeldsdatter was sentenced to confess publicly in her local church and then to be executed.

Beyer notes that in general the message of the apparitions tends to be conservative, in that they call for a return to older patterns of worship. The timescale of the changes he identifies is, however, quite precise: visionaries' experiences were adjusted to Lutheran society in Germany from the 1550s, in Scandinavia a generation or so later: 'The preconditions for medieval apparitions of saints disappeared quickly.' He points out that changes in the actual patterns of experience of post-Reformation visionaries remain elusive since they took place inside people's heads, but concludes that 'Customs, beliefs, and memories of stories previously heard structured the experience of percipients and their listeners. The transformation of the available traditions took place in the decades following the Reformation, in interaction between the experience on the one hand and the interpretation in cheap print, sermons and everyday talk on the other.'

This case study showing how visions are influenced by the social climate suggests that 'other-worldly' apparitions have a lot to do with this world. Beyer's detailed account confirms observations which have often been made about the culturally specific content of dreams and visions. It has often been remarked in psychotherapeutic circles that Freudian patients have 'Freudian' dreams while Jungian patients have 'Jungian' dreams and visions, as if unconscious and 'extraordinary' experiences are influenced by a person's conscious and ordinary experiences. A Minoan involved in ecstatic religion, assisted perhaps by the repetition of ritual movements and dance, numinous awe, wine or opium (remember the poppies?), may have envisaged an aspect of the natural world – such as the energy of a tree – in a particular shape which reflected a thought-form familiar in the culture. We know from the floating figures on the rings that apparitions at tree rituals were visualised wearing flounced skirts in the current fashion just like the visionaries themselves. A Portuguese shepherd, as a result of prayer, loneliness and fasting, may have experienced a similar shift in consciousness to the Minoan, but in this case – in accordance with the repertoire of symbols available within his or her culture – the perception of an element of the natural world such as a tree may take a different form, such as the image of the Virgin Mary. In a Brazilian *candomblé* possession ritual, participants experience possession by a known and expected spirit; Tibetan yoga disciplines teach that the images and visions met in dreams or after death are shaped by the thought-forms of the person experiencing them. Beyer's work high-lights the commonplace realisation that visions of the Virgin Mary are only as widespread as the Catholic religion. In our attempts as human beings to make sense of our perceptions of what is regarded as non-consensual or supernatural, we apparently clothe the unknown in the shape of the known. There may be more things in heaven and earth than our philosophy, but it seems we can usually perceive them only in forms which our cultural conditioning allows.

There are various ways of understanding this process. One is to say that the visions must be an external projection of deeply unconscious material, as witness the conservative message of most of the apparitions. Beyer's description of the transformation of visionary experiences in response to social pressures highlights what is already known and is the basis of psychotherapeutic practice: that the unconscious can be retrained and its contents restructured.

Alternatively – although these may all be different ways of saying the same thing – one can apply the terminology of body energy. The theories of subtle anatomy suggest that visions of saints and devils have been mediated through the astral level of the energy field, which carries the individual's emotional debris from past experiences and unresolved hopes, fears, angers and so forth. So whatever the individual is perceiving, by the time the experience has reached the level of sensory awareness, it has been filtered through, and shaped by, the individual's fantasies, beliefs, limitations, expectations and emotional preoccupations. I am reminded here of George Bernard Shaw's description of a process whereby in childhood legendary and religious personages are impressed upon the mind's eye, so that 'all the thinking of the hallucinated adult about the fountain of inspiration which is continually flowing in the universe, or about the promptings of virtue and the revulsions of shame: in short, about aspiration and conscience, . . . is thinking in terms of the celestial vision'.

Yet another account of the process is given by Carlos Castaneda, who wrote a series of well-known and controversial books (published 1968–1998) describing a long apprenticeship with a Yaqui Indian – 'Don Juan' – in a native American tradition of esoteric knowledge. Castaneda, initially involved as a graduate anthropology student doing fieldwork for a doctorate at the University of California, described how he was taught an alternative view of the universe as an agglomeration of energy fields. Perhaps unsurprisingly, he was criticised variously in his lifetime for being a fool or a liar. Many of the descriptions in his books tally with those of practitioners of subtle anatomy. As regards visions of God, angels, saints and demons, the tradition Castaneda describes is sceptical; this scepticism is based on a precise anatomy which suggests how such visions happen.

Like subtle anatomy practitioners from other cultures, Don Juan's tradition of knowledge sees the energy field of a human being as a shiny egg-like shape, which is here called a 'luminous cocoon'; inside, it is full of luminous fibres which show the person's wishes and problems, everything they are and everything they feel. When he learns to 'see' energy, Castaneda describes perceiving people as white iridescent elongated footballs. He also gives an account of a day in Mexico City when he 'saw' energy in the world at large, perceived as filaments of brilliant colours superimposed on the buildings and on the traffic, lines of light which were bursting with energy.

This model of the human body suggests that of the many lines of energy or 'emanations' in the world at large, we as humans admit very few into our luminous cocoon. We admit only those which are aligned with a spot high on the energy field, termed the 'assemblage point'; Castaneda 'sees' it as an intensely shiny spot near the crest of the oblong energy field. Variations in perception are accounted for by the explanation that the emanations we admit determine the view of reality we perceive. I suppose a parallel might be sitting in front of a bank of telephone points: which one you plug your phone into determines which outside line you get connected to, and which voice you hear. In children this 'assemblage point' is mobile, but gradually they learn to keep it fixed steady so that they perceive the same consensual reality as others in their culture. If the point moves, it aligns with different emanations in the world at large (like connecting with a different telephone line) and therefore a different version of reality is assembled. The assemblage point moves involuntarily in sleep, leading to dream experiences, and as part of his training Castaneda learns to move it voluntarily which leads to a series of waking visions.

Which way on the surface of the cocoon the point moves determines the nature of the visions. If it moves *laterally* to either side of the band of emanations normally perceived by humans, the individual taps into what Don Juan describes as a morbid storehouse of human junk. A slight shift will give fantasies, a more extensive shift hallucinations. It sounds to me as if these small sideways moves give a different type of experience from normal, but that the accompanying fantasies and hallucinations reflect only unprocessed emotional material couched in symbols which are culturally available. I imagine it might be a bit like plugging in to one of the telephone points and finding it is only someone calling from a different room in your own house, in a mood.

Which side of the normal band of perception the assemblage point moves is said to determine the kind of visions which are experienced. Castaneda is taught that on the right-hand side of the normal band are visions of violence, killing and sensuality, while on the left-hand side there is spirituality, religion, God. On this left hand side, Castaneda (brought up a Catholic) experiences a vision of a church's altar glittering with candles and a giant crucifix combined with a sense of elation and profound love. He might as easily have had a vision of the Virgin Mary. The school of knowledge in which he is training finds little interest in these sideways shifts, and Castaneda is taught rather to make a shift *in depth*. If this is shallow, it leads to heightened awareness with a slight emotional vulnerability; but a deeper shift leads to a change in perception which is conducive to understanding and examination, the basis of the training which he is following.

Don Juan stresses to Castaneda that none of these shifts are purely 'mental', as common opinion might have it: in other words, they are not imaginary but are physical processes. However, he does distinguish between the value of different visions, suggesting that some reflect only the debris of human experience. He explains to Castaneda that the 'assemblage point' tends to adjust itself to fit others around us, and that the consensual position changes from one era to another. In our time and in Western culture, for example, the 'assemblage point' is generally fixed at a position which favours emanations which enable us to see the solid body, but disregard the energy field. Since the exact position of the point is an arbitrary one determined by our cultural heritage, it can move, and once it does so it forces new alignments of emanations and therefore new perceptions not usually accessible to people in our society. Described as going into another layer of the onion, we might also imagine it as turning a radio dial or as a TV switch changing to a new channel or a computer mouse accessing a different file. Don Juan explains that the assemblage point can be moved by 'power plants' (drugs), hunger, tiredness, rituals, fever and other events. This could apply to our visionaries of the Bronze Age and of the Middle Ages.

Don Juan tells Castaneda that the sole value of the bizarre devices and procedures associated with 'magical' traditions is to break the fixation of the assemblage point. His own tradition decided to bypass all rituals and incantations, and to move it in a different way. One-off mystical experiences and visions induced through unusual procedures are seen as having little significance. In the terms of his discipline, the important work is to learn to move the assemblage point deliberately and to reinforce its stability at new positions offering prolonged experiences of different versions of reality. Learning to move it in this way is a very slow process and involves life changes. Stilling internal chatter and clearing emotional clutter allow an inner silence to develop in which the point becomes more fluid; but this is not easy. So, while there may be valuable alternative possibilities of perception, this tradition asserts that getting to know them takes hard work and disciplined living.

With this material, the Castaneda books describe a theory and a practice which could provide a context for the varied visionary experiences described in this book. The hungry shepherd children seeing the Virgin Mary at Fatima, and the many other people who also reported seeing the Lady in trees in lonely places, could – from such a perspective – be seen not as liars or as lunatics but rather as people who have perceived an alternative reality due to a temporary shift in their subtle anatomy. In some cases the (to us) divergent experiences could in any case have been more consensual: due to a different cultural context, the Minoans, for example, might have had a differently disposed energy field – with the assemblage point positioned differently from ours – allowing a different range of perception to be accepted as normal. These alternative approaches suggest that the form of the visions which our culture finds so puzzling might be determined by changes in the energy field mediated through the symbolic repertoire available to the individual. The ability to envision, like the ability to visualise, is perhaps, as George Bernard Shaw suggested, 'part of the normal permanent equipment of all human beings'. It is just that contemporary Western culture prefers not to use that equipment. We do not have to be either dismissive or impressed into a conversion by the reports of the visionaries. Their experiences have a place.

Our Lady of the Tree Trunk in France

The visionary tree aspect of the cult of the Virgin Mary has not received much attention. In her classic book on the Virgin, *Alone of All her Sex*, Marina Warner makes almost no mention of it. After the work tracing these little-known accounts and cults in Portugal, I began to wonder how widespread the phenomenon was. Did such apparitions happen only in the Iberian peninsula? Curiosity prompted a search for signs of similar stories further north, starting with France.

Apparitions can be elusive, and this proved especially true in France. Stories about healing trees are rarely found in general guide books, history books, or even books on folklore. I was looking into a side-alley of the past without street lights. A series of phone calls to tourist offices in different parts of the country also drew a blank until I rang the town hall of Cerizay in the area of Deux-Sèvres in north-west France. There they told me a local legend about the *Beauchêne* (Fineoak). It concerns a herdsman who found one of his oxen out at pasture licking a particular oak tree and refusing to pasture anywhere else. The ox became the most vigorous of the whole herd. His curiosity aroused, the herdsman discovered in the tree a statue of the Virgin Mary. There is still a tree on the spot, but nowadays more interest seems to focus on the nearby church and monastery. The earliest evidence of a chapel at the place is from the 12th century, a time of Benedictine influence, and the site continues to be much visited, with a special pilgrimage in September. In 1955, as many as 15,000 pilgrims attended the ceremony of the crowning of the statue.

With its herdsman, the animal behaving strangely, the discovery of an image of Our Lady, and subsequent setting up of worship at the place, this was clearly the same story as we had found in Portugal. It led Constant Vaillant, writing in a local history book, to the conclusion that 'The Church, which could not stop the backward practices of paganism, replaced them with Christian practices' ('*L'Église, qui ne pouvait pas empêcher les pratiques attardées du paganisme, leur a substitué des pratiques chrétiennes*'). A similar process seems to have taken place at Bar-sur-Seine in the region of Aube (north-east France) where, the town hall told me, there is a pilgrimage (also in September) to a chapel dedicated to *Notre Dame du Chêne* (Our Lady of the Oak) in the middle of a wood. I was told, however, that there is now no particular tree associated with the chapel. We heard of another tree apparition tradition in the region of Vendée.

So there were examples in France of the same story we had found in Portugal, but so far no existing 'holy' tree to match the one in Crete. The only significant tree I could locate over the telephone was one which had its own phone number, a tourist attraction in the Normandy village of Allouville. It was a curious experience dialling an oak tree; I was answered, not by the rustling of leaves which visitors to Dodona may have expected, but by a helpful French voice keen to encourage tourists. I was told that the tree is believed to be 1000 years old, and that since 1696 it has had a chapel inside it. Its 15-metre circumference gives it a claim to be the oldest oak in Europe. This mighty specimen, though now dedicated to the Virgin and for a long time the site of outdoor services (Fig. 29), had no story of apparitions or healing like those in Portugal. Still, it was a start, and on a camping trip to Normandy we found out how far you can get in a neglected area of research when you are out in the field with luck on your side.

Some of the ancient trees we have visited look as if they have suffered for their fame, and Allouville's oak is one of them. Nowadays it has not only a chapel built inside at ground level and a staircase built around it to a room and balcony at first-floor level, but also cladding like patchwork applied over the top of its main trunk, and huge wooden props and crutches all around to stop it from falling over. The greenery was relatively meagre, and what was left of the actual tree seemed to be kept alive against the odds, like a comatose patient on a life support machine. Still, the tiny chapel inside the hollow trunk, with its shiny wood panelling, was a curiosity. And even if the tree wanted to give up the ghost, Allouville's tourist industry was thriving. It had an information centre and we found a local magazine – *Patrimoine Normand* – with an article about the tree and a list of other old oaks in Normandy. The publican gave us directions, and we set off to search.

At Vatteville-La-Rue we were disappointed because the sacred oak tree had been replaced in the early 20th century with a lime tree. A woman living next to it left her dressmaking class in the village hall to go home for an old photograph of the oak tree in former times, showing an icon of Our Lady in a small box attached to its trunk. In La-Haye-de-Routot it was not an oak but two yew trees in the churchyard, each about 1000 years old, which had become sanctified. One of them held an altar of Our Lady of Lourdes inside its trunk, dedicated late in the 19th century, with a small statue of the Lady on top of the altar looking out of the cavernous opening in the tree trunk. Again there was no story, but in the tiny village museum, at the bottom of a pile, we found a book by a local scholar, Jean Fournée, about the iconography of the Virgin in Normandy. This showed that ideas about her appearing in a tree had occurred in the recent past: one 19th-century illustration from the Benedictine monastery of Notre Dame de Bon-Secours in Caen showed her seated in the branches surrounded by a series of miniature scenes of healing (Fig. 30). The captions on these cameos identified scenes where the Lady, surrounded by a golden glow, was curing someone who was paralysed, a blind person, a sick person and a child, as well as one where she was chasing out a demon, and one where she was healing a girl who was dumb.

We drove to Caen to find the original of that picture, a colour print by a local firm, Picard-Guérin, which was held in the library. The librarian, interested in our quest, recommended to us the work of Henri Gadeau de Kerville on old trees of Normandy. We tracked this down in the public library of Rouen, and found a mine of information about a series of holy trees in the nearby area. We visited magnificent examples at Elbeuf and Bosguerard de Marcouville. In most cases, local people knew of them as special trees and could direct us to find them, often on the edge of the settlement or in a wooded area. Some had a little box holding an image of the Lady attached high up on the trunk. But the most striking find was at a village which was itself called Le Troncq (The Trunk).

It was near noon on a shimmering day at the end of June when we arrived at this scattered village looking for a yew tree mentioned briefly in Jean Fournée's book. He said it contained a statue of the Virgin. We drove past fields of ripe wheat and delicate blue-mauve flax flowers, wondering where to start looking for a holy tree. Stopping at the open door of a large square building by the roadside, we walked into a big room decorated with children's pictures where a lanky young man was sweeping up. 'Are you the teacher?' 'Today I'm the cleaner.' It was the first day of the summer holidays and he was able to direct us to the yew, which was right next to the church. Even the way he said, 'You can't miss it' didn't prepare us for the strange and beautiful sight awaiting us.

In front of the doorway of the church towered an immaculate yew whose sinews parted to create a pointed doorway in the trunk like the entrance to a fairytale castle. Inside, looking out, was the statue (see front and back cover). She was leaning slightly towards the church. On her light grey stone, tiny traces of paint showed where she had once had fair hair, blue eyes and pink skin. The baby she used to carry was long gone, leaving a bowl-like shape which she nursed with an expression of mildness and patience. Her base was coated in green mould, and ivy was climbing up the stone, gradually reclaiming it as part of the natural world. On either side the trunk had grown around the statue, giving the impression that she was a living part of the tree and was growing inside it. She was almost warm to the touch.

Later enquiries revealed that the statue can be dated to the end of the 14th century, but no one knows when she was placed in the tree. The yew, whose trunk is over 5 metres around, has been variously dated as up to 1000 years old. The oldest wall of the church dates to the 11th century, and most of the existing fabric is 14th–15th century. There is no record of what role the tree played in the life of the church, although statues inside graveyard yews are particularly common in Normandy. The teacher had told us that there is no longer a priest in the village, and mass is heard in the church only once or twice a year. The church and the tree with its statue now stand facing each other beside the flax fields as monuments of ceremonies celebrated on this site in past centuries, and both have been listed for their historic interest. Here the struggle between church and tree seemed to have been resolved in a truce. Leaning on the tree, I felt a mood of calm without coldness.

In his survey of Normandy trees, Fournée lists trees of many varieties sacred to other male and female saints including St Anne, St George, St John, St Christopher, St Laurent and St Germain. Some are preserved in place names, like Saint-Martin-du-Tilleul (St Martin-of-the-Lime), an association of saint with tree found in seven Normandy parishes. Among the trees sacred to Our Lady, Fournée lists not only oak and yew trees but many other varieties such as lime, ash, beech, elm, osier (willow), bramble and hawthorn. The statuette in an oak tree at Pressagny-l'Orgueilleux was allegedly placed there after it was dug up at a place where a team of oxen stopped and refused to move. At Lignou near Couterne, a chapel of Mary has a story about her appearing in a hawthorn. These apparitions, miraculously discovered images, and strangely behaving animals were all familiar elements of the story, and some sites had early dates too: at Houlbec a church was founded in the 15th century to replace a pine tree where a statue of the Virgin was worshipped. In terms of dates and legends, there was enough evidence from Normandy alone for a healing tree of Our Lady in France consistent with that in Portugal.

Renaud de la Baume adds a few more examples further afield: a giant oak still standing with an image of Mary at Saint-Martin-de-Connée in Mayenne, west of Paris; Our Lady of the Osier (Wicker or Willow) at Vinay, much further south, near Grenoble; where her apparition stopped an axe-wielding anti-Catholic, and Our Lady of Epinal in the Vosges, east of Paris, where legend says that other-worldly singing coming from the tree stopped the woodcutter's axe. From another source, a 19th-century woodcut gives an impression of how some holy trees looked on French-speaking soil when in full use, hung with offerings from the ailing (Fig. 31).

The final and most poignant evidence – which also gave the fullest hints about early beliefs and practices at these French holy trees – was from a textual source. As often with textual evidence about trees, it is negative evidence. It comes from the trial of Joan of Arc and is the list of things which, during her cross-examination, she denied doing at trees.

Joan of Arc was born about 1411 or 1412 in the village of Domrémy in northern central France. She was burnt for heresy, witchcraft and sorcery at Rouen on 30 May 1431. Her trial proceedings describe in the third person what was said in court in two versions, Latin and the French of the time; I used both in making my translation. Each section gives a series of insights into popular beliefs and rituals of the period.

The topic of trees is raised at the third session of the trial, on 24 February. 'She was cross-examined about a certain tree which stands close to her village. To which she replied that, fairly near to Domrémy, there is a certain tree called l'Arbre des Dames [the Tree of the Ladies or the Tree of the Queens], and others call it l'Arbre des Fées [the Tree of the Fairies]; nearby there is a fountain. She has heard tell that people ill with a fever drink at this fountain and seek to recover their health from its water. That, she has seen; but does not know whether they get better or not. Also she says that she has heard tell that sick people, when they can get up, go to the tree to take the air. And it is a big tree, a beech, from which the fine "May" comes, and it belonged, according to reports, to Monsieur Pierre de Bourlemont, gentleman.' It is impressive to see how adroitly Joan of Arc manages to avoid the traps her interrogators set for her as they try to implicate her in these non-Christian practices. Yes, she knows what people say and do; no, she does not know if it works. The presence of a spring by the tree is a familiar element. The connection with May also cropped up in Portugal, although Renaud de la Baume in his guide to the festivals of France sees it as a national speciality: 'It is certainly one of our ideas, indigenously and essentially French, to represent the Virgin at the time of the awakening of birds and greenery, among the hedges . . . bursting with spring.'

The proceedings continue: 'Also she was saying that sometimes she used to go to take the air with the other girls, and made at the tree headpieces of flowers for the image of Our Lady of Domrémy; and several times she heard old people – not from her family – saying that the fairy ladies used to go there... She heard tell from ... her godmother that she had seen these fairy ladies. But she herself does not know if it was true or not. She also says that she never saw the aforementioned fairies at the tree, to her knowledge. Asked if she has seen any elsewhere, she does not know if she has seen any or not. Also she says that she has seen young people put headpieces of flowers in the branches of the tree, and she herself has done the same occasionally with the other girls; . . . She does not know at all whether she had danced by the tree since she had understanding; but sometimes she might well have danced there with the children; but rather singing than dancing.' It was certainly not the interrogators' intention that their questions would leave a unique record of specific activities at special trees in 15th-century France; but they have done. From this passage we learn that there was dancing and singing, and dancing seems to be the activity Joan is most reluctant to own up to. She seems intent on protecting her family, and so she stresses that she was one of many young people who decorated the tree with coronets of flowers.

There follows a line of questioning about a certain wood near her father's house associated with the fairies, about people saying that the fairies at the tree had influenced her, and about a popularly known prophecy that a girl who could work miracles would come from near that wood. Joan of Arc gives no credence to any of this, but acknowledges that such things are said. The text as a whole provides references to prophecies, miracles, water with special qualities, healing, dancing, singing, tree-dressing and the May; these were evidently part of a popular culture which existed like a subtext to the main narrative of Catholicism. They had a place in village life, and an uneasy relationship with the Church. And they were all associated with a female-identified holy tree like the ones in Crete and Portugal.

Joan of Arc's trial tells us about the early 15th century, but what happened before? Fournée notes that in Cerisy-la-Forêt, in the district of Saint-Clair, the chapel of *Notre-Dame de l'Épine* (Our Lady of the Thorn) existed before the 13th century. How far did the phenomenon of the holy female tree go back in France? The apochryphal Gospel of Pseudo-Matthew tells a story linking Mary with a palm tree which bent down to offer her fruit; composed 550–700 AD, it rapidly became popular and was read in Rheims in the 9th century AD. Wilhelm Mannhardt cites a ruling of the Council at Nantes in north-west France in 895 AD which made it the bishop's duty to exterminate 'trees consecrated to demons which common people tend and hold in such veneration that they do not dare to cut off either branch or shoot' (*'arbores daemonibus consecratae quas vulgus colit et in tanta veneratione habet, ut nec ramum vel surculum audeat amputare'*). He also mentions a tree which the 7th-century Saint Amandus found being worshipped in northern France, dedicated to a demon (*'daemoni dedicata'* could also mean 'dedicated to a spirit', depending on the attitude of the writer). Mrs JH Philpot in her wide-ranging *The Sacred Tree* mentions that in the 4th century AD at Auxerre (south-east of Paris) there was a pear tree hung with trophies and venerated like a god. Before that we have the Roman writers' disparaging descriptions of the religious customs of the Gauls they conquered; Lucan, for example, wrote in the 1st century AD in his *Pharsalia* (iii. 405) about human sacrifice to trees at Marseilles.

Could such shreds of evidence ever provide a coherent history of holy trees in France across the wide gap between the ancient and medieval worlds? Is it significant that the above examples are mostly from northern France? Where would the female holy tree find a place in the story? At what point did the Virgin Mary become part of it?

While I was writing this book, a friend commented that the project itself was like a tree. Certainly new branches of inquiry kept leading off in different directions. If so, there were some branches I could follow and others I could not. Every area I approached, like France, raised new questions. There was also the question of how far the phenomenon of Our Lady of the Tree Trunk went within the continent of Europe. An intriguing illustration of a festival beneath a tree (Fig. 32) pointed us towards Holland, where the miraculous image in an oak tree at Scherpenheuvel, Limburg, was honoured in a pilgrimage to 'Our Lady of Scherpenheuvel' a few weeks after Easter. In nearby Belgium, the

Virgin appeared in a hawthorn tree to children at Beauraing in the 1930s. Again, there were glimpses of a wealth of material in Italy: there were classical references, for example, to the sacred fig tree of Romulus and Remus at the heart of ancient Rome, the identification of the oak as 'Jove's tree', the beech Jupiter Fagutalis and the prophetic ilex grove sacred to Faunus and Picus on the Aventine Hill; there were also recent Italian visions of the Virgin associated with trees. But I had reached a point where I wanted to go back and gain a better understanding of the origins and history of Our Lady of the Tree Trunk. What were the links – if any – between the material from western Europe and the first holy tree which we had found in Greece?

Returning to Crete, I found that tracing the path of transmission of a parallel legend – that of the magical staff – gave a clue about the possible passage across Europe of the Lady tree story. It also brought the holy tree suddenly very close to our home, in the UK.

Book References

Ackerman, Susan, *Under Every Green Tree: Popular Religion in Sixth-Century Judah*, Scholars Press, Atlanta, GA, 1992

Agostinho, Frei, *Santuário Mariano e História das Imagens Milagrosas e das Milagrosas Aparecidas, em Graças dos Pregadores e dos Devotos da Mesma Senhora ano de 1707*, Vols. I – X, Oficina de Antonio Pedrozo Galram, Lisbon, 1707–1723. Livro I: Titulo VIII (Guimarães), XXXV (Brotas). Livro II: Titulo XVIII (Oliveira do Conde), XXVI (Merceana) 326ff, XXVI [sic] (Dardavaz) 228ff, XLIX (Bucellas) 394ff, LXXVIII (Pala near Mortagua), XCII (Gondolim). Livro III: Titulo II (Lady of Guadalupe), VI (Cortes de Leiria), XXIII (Ortiga)

Aljustrel, see JR Abrantes, MS Pinto and MP Carvalho, *Aljustrel: Uma Aldeia de Fátima*, Santuário de Fátima, Fátima, 1993

Armstrong, Karen, speaking on *Do You Believe in Visions of the Virgin Mary?*, A Roger Bolton Production for UK TV Channel 5, transmitted 10 August 1997

Baume, Renaud de la, *Le Guide Familier des Fêtes de France*, Les Éditions La Boétie, Éditions des Deux Coqs d'Or, Paris, 1981, 112

Bennett, Gillian, 'Vision Narratives of Women in Prison. By Carol Burke' [review], in *Folklore* 105 (1994), 110–112

Beyer, Jürgen, 'On the Transformation of Apparition Stories in Scandinavia and Germany, c. 1350–1700', *Folklore* 110 (1999), 39–47

Blackbourn, David, *Marpingen: Apparitions of the Virgin Mary in Bismarckian Germany*, Oxford University Press, 1993

Brotas, see P Henrique da Silva Louro, *Brotas Através dos Tempos*, Fábrica da Igreja Paroquial de Brotas, Brotas, 1985

Burke, Carol, *Vision Narratives of Women in Prison*, The University of Tennessee Press, Knoxville, 1993

Carvalho da Costa, P Antonio, *Corografia Portugueza e Descripçam Topografica*, Vol. 3, Typographia de Domingos Goncçalves Gouvea, Braga, 1869, Capitulo XL

Castaneda, Carlos, *Journey to Ixtlan: The Lessons of Don Juan*, Penguin Books, Harmondsworth, Middlesex, 1974, 267 (energy lines in the world)

—, *The Fire From Within*, Black Swan, Transworld, London, Australia and New Zealand, 1985, 124–185 (assemblage point)

Christian, William A, Jr, *Local Religion in Sixteenth Century Spain*, Princeton University Press, NJ, 1981, 75ff, here 82, 89, 91, 208

Erickson, Carolly, *The Medieval Vision: Essays in History and Perception*, Oxford University Press, New York, 1976, v, 32–3

Espírito Santo, Moisés, *Origens Orientais da Religião Popular Portuguesa*, Assírio & Alvim, Lisbon, 1988, 9–10

Fatima, see *Documentação Crítica de Fátima Vol. I Interrogatorios aos Videntes–1917*, Santuário de Fátima, Fátima, 1992. Also Louis Kondor, ed, *Fatima in Lucia's Own Words*, Postulation Centre, Fatima, 1989 (first publ. 1976) 30–32 and *passim*

Fontaine, Abbé, *Allouville Bellefosse*, La Maison Delamare, Yvetot, 1914

Fournée, Jean, *Le Culte Populaire et L'Iconographie des Saints en Normandie. La Sainte Vierge*, Vol. 1, Société Parisienne d'Histoire et d'Archéologie Normande, 1976, 209–218, 227

—, *L'Arbre et la Forêt en Normandie*, Vol II, Le Pays Bas-Normand Société d'Art et d'Histoire, 1985, 140–48, 225–9

Gallop, Rodney, *Portugal: A Book of Folk-Ways*, Cambridge University Press, 1961, 128–130 (Mercena)

Garabandal, see F Sanchez-Ventura y Pascual, *The Apparitions of Garabandal*, San Miguel Publishing Company, Detroit, 1966

Garner, Clare, 'It's started: Diana's vision is seen', *Independent*, 4 September 1997, 1

Gressman, Hugo, *Die Orientalischen Religionen im Hellenistisch-Römischen Zeitalter*, Gruyter, Berlin and Leipzig, 1930, 99

Jacinto dos Reis, P, *Invocacões de Nossa Senhora em Portugal*, Cinquentenário das Aparições de Fátima, Olisipone, 1967, 115–118 (Brotas), 144–5 (Oliveira do Conde), 145 (Bucelas), 156 (Pala), 256–268 (Our Lady of the Fern), 281–2 (Our Lady of the Birdcage), 294–5 (Our Lady of Guadalupe), 570 (Varatojo), 604–607 (Ortiga) and *passim*, with references to Frei Agostinho

Joan of Arc, see *Procès de Condamnation de Jeanne d' Arc*, Bibliothèque du XVe Siècle, Pierre Champion, Paris, 1920. See Tome XXII Vol. I Texte Latin, 49–50 and Tome XXIII Vol. II Introduction, Traduction et Notes, 43–4

Kerville, Henri Gadeau de, *Les Vieux Arbres de la Normandie*, Libraire J-B Baillière et Fils, Paris, 1930

Kilner, Walter J, *The Aura*, Samuel Weiser, York Beach, ME, 1981 (first publ. as *The Human Atmosphere*, 1911)

Leadbetter, CW, *The Chakras*, The Theosophical Publishing House, Wheaton, IL, 1985 (first publ. 1927)

Lucan, *Pharsalia*, ed DR Shackleton Bailey, Teubner, Stuttgart, 1997

Mannhardt, Wilhelm, *Wald- und Feldkulte*, Vol. I, Verlag von Gebrüder Borntraeger, Berlin, 1904, 71

Marques, João, *Santuário de Nossa Senhora da Piedade da Merceana*, Confraria de Nossa Senhora da Piedade da Merceana, Merceana, 1988

Medjugorje, examples of press coverage, see Anne McElvoy, 'Visions on the Mount', *The Times Magazine*, 24 February 1996, 30–34; Alberic Stacpoole, 'Fr Slavko Barbaric' (Obituary), *Weekend Review, Independent*, 2 December 2000, 7

Patrimoine Normande 2 (1995), Éditions Heimdal, Bayeux, 30–39, here 39

Philpot, Mrs JH, *The Sacred Tree or The Tree in Religion and Myth*, Macmillan, London, 1897, 20

Pierrakos, John C, 'The Case of the Broken Heart', in David Boadella, ed, *In The Wake of Reich*, Coventure, London, 1976, 400–422

—, at the head of The Core Group of the Institute for the New Age of Man, 'Life Functions of the Energy Centres of Man Part 1' *Energy and Character* VII 1 (January 1976), 54–67, here 54–5

Reich, Wilhelm, *Character Analysis*, trans. VR Carfagno, Touchstone/Simon and Schuster, New York, 1972 (first publ. 1933). See also David Boadella, *Wilhelm Reich: The Evolution of his Work*, Arkana, London, Boston and Henley, 1985 (first publ. 1973)

Revez, Idálio, '"Diálogos" com a Virgem', *Publico*, 12 March 1997, 5

Scherpenheuvel, see Jules Frere, *Volkskunde in Limburg*, Stichting Mens en Kultuur, Gent, 1992, 168–9

Shaw, George Bernard, *Saint Joan*, Penguin Books, Harmondsworth, Middlesex, 1946 (first publ. 1924), Preface 21, 25

Stone, Rob, 'Dispatches Madrid', *Time Out*, 1298, 5–12 July 1995, 6

Tansley, David V, *Radionics and the Subtle Anatomy of Man*, Health Science Press, 1972 (republ. CW Daniel, Saffron Walden, Essex)

—, *The Raiment of Light: A Study of the Human Aura*, Arkana/Routledge and Kegan Paul, London and New York, 1984

Vaillant, Constant, *Cerizay, Ville Historique et Martyre*, Vol. I, Les Éditions Hérault, Maulévrier, 1980, 25

Van der Toorn, Karel, 'Goddesses in Early Israelite Religion' in Lucy Goodison and Christine Morris, eds, *Ancient Goddesses: The Myths and the Evidence*, British Museum Press, London, 1998 and University of Wisconsin Press, Madison, 1999, 83–97

Warner, Marina, *Alone of All her Sex: The Myth and the Cult of the Virgin Mary*, Vintage Press/Random House, London, 2000 (first publ. 1976), 292, 303

3

THE MAGICAL STAFF
AND THE HEALING BOUGH

It was again from the small town of Ayii Deka – close by the archaeological site of Gortyn in south Crete – that we were led to another story connected with trees. A story which refers back to early Christianity and could even be a survival from that time. It offers insights about how elements of popular culture can survive and be transmitted by word of mouth. It also suggests paths along which the Lady tree stories might have travelled.

We had arrived in Ayii Deka late one summer afternoon. After dinner we went for a stroll up the main street, which was full of lights and life in the warm evening air. Groups sat and chatted at tables outside the cafés, while the occasional lorry thundered through along the main road. In a large hardware shop full of sacks and boxes, an elderly couple sold us a shaving mirror. They wrapped it meticulously in newspaper and string, enquired where we came from, and told us about their granddaughter at university in Heraklion. Trade was quiet and they seemed pleased to chat. Eventually we sat down and became involved in a discussion about local history. They were keen to tell us about the original 'Ayii Deka' which translates as the 'Holy Ten' or 'Ten Saints' who gave the town its name. These were, they told us, victims of persecution who were killed during the Turkish occupation (which lasted in Crete from 1669–1898 AD). In the local church, they told us, was a slab of marble which bore the imprint of the saints' knees where it went soft as they were beheaded. One of the martyrs, they said, was ploughing when they came to get him. He had a stick to drive the animals, and before they took him away he stuck it into the ground. It took root and grew into an olive tree.

The legend, then, concerns ten Christian martyrs, and was preserved with the help of the Church. However, the changing versions we were to learn gave an insight into the way local memory had preserved this story, showing the tenacity and waywardness of oral tradition even amidst the technology of late industrial capitalism.

The following morning, from Manolis Apostolakis the owner of our pension, we heard a rather different story about the taking root of the magic olive tree. In his version, the 'Holy Ten' were the victims of persecution not by the Turks but by the Romans, far earlier as Christians under the Roman Empire. 'Myths are wonderful,' he concluded. 'Although they are lies, they have truth in them. The Romans *did* kill ten people – and many more.'

A nun at a monastery further north in central Crete knew a more actively pro-Christian version: nine people were going to be martyred when they met an old man working the fields with a stick (*vergili* in Greek) which he was using to drive the animals. They explained that they were going to be martyred because they wanted to believe in the one true God rather than many false gods. The old man then stuck his staff in the ground saying 'You were nine, now you are ten,' and joined them. His stick grew into an olive tree.

The fourth version we heard locally came from an older woman whom we found sitting doing fine crochet work by a sun-filled window at the back of an Ayii Deka café during the morning hours when business is slow. To the basic elements of the story she added a date of 450 or 250 AD, and she told us that the tree was in the town down the back of the houses somewhere; she had always heard about it but had never seen it herself.

While we were in town we went to the local church and saw in a glass case the marble stone with hollows in it said to be the imprint of the saints' knees. (The archaeologist Antonis Vasilakis in his guidebook on Crete comments that it is actually a '*kernos*', a ceremonial vessel used for making offerings in ancient Greek and early Christian worship.) At the church there was no image or symbol referring to the sprouting staff, nor outside the church could we find any special olive tree linked to the story.

We could view this example as a cameo revealing in miniature the way stories may be transmitted and distorted. The Greek Orthodox church discarded the motif of the staff and the tree; this fits a common pattern whereby institutions are selective in their preservation of legends, dropping certain elements which they cannot fruitfully use. As for our informants, for them the chronology – like elastic – seemed to stretch or shrink depending on who told the story. The story of the ten martyrs, historically placed in the great persecution of Christians by the Emperor Decius in 250 BC, was brought forward by our friends at the hardware store into the time of the Turkish occupation. Again, this was typical of a pattern we have noticed, whereby people living on the spot or involved in a popular ritual or custom often have only a vague sense of its history. Some attribute great antiquity to the custom: 'We have always done it'; 'It goes back to ancient/primitive times.' Or the opposite may happen: the source of the custom or belief is pulled closer in time, and sometimes attached to a relatively recent political or historical landmark.

In the event, the story of the magical staff which sprouted turned out to be a lot older than Christianity in Greek culture. Pausanias was a travel writer who produced a kind of 'Blue Guide' to Greece in the late 2nd century AD, describing the monuments, customs and lore of the places he visited. In his Book X, he tells the story of Orestheus, king of the Ozolian Lokri in central mainland Greece, whose dog gave birth to a stick instead of a puppy. Orestheus buried the stick; in the spring a vine grew from it, and the local people got their name from the branches (*ozoi* in Greek). In another story also told in the 2nd century AD, the appearance of sprouting boughs is linked with a female deity: the grammarian Athenaeus in his collection of after-dinner discussions and anecdotes *The Deipnosophists* tells how one Herostratus was sailing from Paphos to Naukratis carrying in his ship a small idol of the goddess Aphrodite. As he approached Egypt a storm broke, and the whole crew ran with prayers to the sacred image. The goddess then suddenly made everything around her to be full of fresh myrtle boughs, and filled the ship with a delicious fragrance amidst the crew's despair and 'much vomiting'. The sun shone out, and they arrived safely at Naukratis.

Considerably earlier, the story of dead vegetation miraculously sprouting also appears in Book VIII of Herodotus' histories. Writing in the 5th century BC, Herodotus was giving an account of the Persian

Wars earlier that century. His text (Book VIII, 55) tells that when the soldiers of the Persian king Xerxes took Athens, they burnt the temple of Erechtheus on the acropolis. Along with the temple, the Persians burnt the special olive tree placed there, according to legend, by the goddess Athena as a symbol of her patronage of the city. On the next day when the Athenians went up to the temple to sacrifice, they saw a fresh shoot about a cubit long growing out of the old trunk. (Pausanias in his Book I, 27.2 makes the shoot two cubits in length, on the same day as the burning.) This portent is seen by modern commentators as symbolising the city's regeneration.

So the motif of dead wood sprouting is met in the Aegean in the 5th century BC and the 2nd century AD before appearing in modern times connected to events of the 3rd century AD. It also has an independent life in recent times, as shown by a song collected by Lucy Garnett in the Turkish provinces of Greece in the late 19th century:

> He leant him there upon his staff, to say his Alpha, Beta,
> And though the staff was dry and dead, it put forth buds and branches;
> And from the branches forth there gushed and flowed out freshest fountains,
> And all the birds came flying down to wash and preen their plumage;

The person whose staff renews itself so extraordinarily is St Basil, the saint linked with the New Year.

The motif, then, has an impressive antiquity and longevity in Greek culture. We were to learn that it also travelled widely. The tenacity of the story suggests the possibility that the healing tree motif had a similarly long life.

Ancient and recurring motifs like this one have in the past prompted some folklorists to write about 'universal' themes. This particular word – 'universal' – has often seemed to pre-empt any further inquiry into the role of human beings in using, transmitting and adapting such themes and stories. I found myself attracted to the possibility of looking at widespread and longstanding traditions in another way.

The Life and Death of Traditions

Setting out to discover whether traditions such as the magical staff, and the sacred Lady trees in Portugal, France and Greece, can be traced back to antiquity leads into a major debate in the folklore world.

On one side of the debate is the James Frazer camp. Published between 1890 and 1915, the volumes of Frazer's massive compilation of popular religious customs in different parts of the world, *The Golden Bough*, has had a huge influence. His thesis was that these customs were recurrently underpinned by the theme of the death and resurrection of a divine king representing fertility and vegetation.

Thus he suggests that 'At a certain stage of early society the king or priest is often thought to be endowed with supernatural powers or to be an incarnation of a deity, and consistently with this belief the course of nature is supposed to be more or less under his control, and he is held responsible for bad weather, failure of the crops, and similar calamities.' To show a pattern whereby such god-kings had to be ritually killed and replaced before their strength failed, he gives examples ranging from the Shilluk of the White Nile to Cambodia, and from classical antiquity to his present day. In some cases the king is explicitly identified as a tree-spirit: 'the King of the Wood . . . , too, had to be killed in order that the divine spirit, incarnate in him, might be transferred in its integrity to his successor'. He states that such ceremonies 'bear the stamp of a dateless antiquity'.

Sometimes the practices involved the re-enactment of a 'sacred marriage' as a dramatic representation of the natural processes which were to be encouraged: 'They set forth the fruitful union of the powers of fertility, the sad death of one at least of the divine partners, and his joyful resurrection.' The theme of human sacrifice recurs: 'The tradition which associated the sacrifice of the king or his children with a great dearth points clearly to the belief, so common among primitive folk, that the king is responsible for the weather and the crops, and that he may justly pay with his life for the inclemency of the one or the failure of the other.' Frazer wrote mostly at second hand not only about European traditions, but about the Mediterranean and the near East: 'Under the names of Osiris, Tammuz, Adonis, and Attis, the peoples of Egypt and Western Asia represented the yearly decay and revival of life, especially of vegetable life, which they personified as a god who annually died and rose again from the dead.' Often the scenario included a 'Great Mother' who was paired with the youthful god as her son/lover, and who became very popular under the Roman Empire.

The bringing together of so much material from disparate sources into one basic template for magico-religious ideas at a certain stage of human development captured the imagination of a generation of scholarly and lay readers. Even archaeologists like Arthur Evans were influenced by Frazer in their interpretation of early religion, and it became common to write about a 'Great Mother Goddess' at the early stages of human development. The idea that *The King Must Die* was popularised in a series of novels by Mary Renault. The identification of universal themes and patterns in the human imagination received endorsement from the writings of Carl Jung, who suggested that people of all places and times share a 'collective unconscious' and so will always come up with the same formulations. He called these the 'archetypes, that is, universal and inherited patterns which, taken together, constitute the structure of the unconscious . . . the archetypes are the forms or riverbeds along which the current of psychic life has always flowed'.

Jung's theory had a huge impact not only in his own field of psychotherapy but also on writers like Erich Neumann, EO James and Robert Graves in their writing of religious history. It was taken up by some feminists, who have produced a number of books promoting the 'Goddess' theory, and it has also filtered through into general public awareness. When researching out in the field I often meet people who are disposed to see folklore customs and magical traditions as ancient or universal: 'People have always done this.' 'People did this everywhere.' 'We find the same archetypal symbol in all ancient societies.' Behind such ideas and comments there usually lies the direct or indirect influence of James Frazer and Carl Jung.

In the academic world ideas have moved on, and there has been a reaction against the Frazerian approach. For example, the use of the word 'primitive', and the generalisations about 'primitive' people, reflect a Victorian way of seeing history as an evolutionary development whereby human civilisation gradually got better the closer it got to their own time. Scholars nowadays would avoid that kind of assumption and would write more specifically and carefully about traditional cultures they are studying. Since Frazer's time scholars have also realised that context is very significant: what looks like a similar custom may mean something completely different for two different cultures. To bundle together a series of rituals from various times and places and suggest they are the same does not give sufficient respect to each particular circumstance and experience which is being studied. Even with material coming from different periods within the same culture, some scholars are resistant to acknowledging continuity, since the same ritual may mean something different at various points of history. There is also a far greater awareness in some current scholarship about the dangers of allowing recent psychological formulations to influence and shape the kinds of pictures historians build of the past. In the work of recent generations of folklorists, in particular, there has been something of a backlash against Frazer. 'Fertility' became a dirty word, and 'regeneration' can send shivers down the spine of some contemporary scholars in the field. Reacting to what they call 'the myth-ritual' theory (which suggests that myths are created to give an explanation for a culture's rituals), or 'the pre-Christian fertility rite theory', they prefer to work on the assumption that a custom or belief is a modern invention unless there is irrefutable evidence to the contrary. In 'It's an Ancient Custom – But How Ancient?', EC Cawte chose several 'traditional' British customs and questioned how old they actually are. Pointing to the upheavals caused in recent centuries by civil war, religious reformation and industrialisation, the article comments that 'It is surprising that any custom survived, much less that one can suggest continuity to a pre-Christian period.' Ronald Hutton has annoyed some neo-pagans by reiterating the point that the links between modern witchcraft ('Wicca') and any ancient pagan religion are very tenuous. This is not welcome hearing to those who have an investment in believing they are reviving an 'Old Religion' which had survived for a millennium underground. His writings support the very strong arguments for believing that Wicca was largely invented in the 20th century by a retired colonial civil servant, Gerald Gardner.

However, it is also possible to have an investment in iconoclasm, believing that you are heroically cutting swathes through the dead wood of past scholarship. On other aspects of paganism, I sometimes wonder whether Hutton overstates his case, and with his picture of 'a gap of almost a millennium with no surviving pagan religion discernible in western Europe' he resolutely sweeps aside some fascinating material. Although he admits the survival over the gap of some traditions, including ritual magic, cunning craft, an interest in classical art and literature, and 'some folk customs', I feel that this does not quite do justice to the surviving evidence of non-Christian traditions, and specifically the survival of tree traditions in popular life. He sometimes seems to be pressing the evidence to show as 'clean' a break in pagan tradition as he seeks to make between himself and the Frazerian school.

Another result of the reaction against Frazer is that, after what are seen as his excesses, some folklorists backed off from making any kind of symbolic interpretation of the material under study. Thus Georgina Boyes wrote a paper on the curious 'Castleton Garland' (a flower-covered man riding on a horse around the village of Castleton once a year) which did not touch at all on the possible meaning for the participants past or present, but looked only at the logistics of its staging. Folklorists of this school tended to shun the search to find meaning in ritual metaphor. Instead they preferred to look at a custom in purely localised social and economic terms. Who made the costumes? What is the breakdown of the shopping list to finance the event? What were the social dynamics of the casting? How did the class composition of the village affect the ritual? With such questions they bypass the more ambiguous issues of symbolism and belief.

Between these two extremes there is a middle path. Despite the huge contribution made by Frazer in gathering together such a staggering amount of material, his kind of voracious compilation can become reductionist if it is used to boil down many fascinating and diverse practices into a sort of historical mush where everything is vaguely 'ancient' and 'primitive' and the same. Sometimes his material does not really seem to fit the mould he puts it into; and without enough research into historical contacts between cultures, or into the routes whereby ideas and influences were transmitted, it is hard to find a reason for the supposed identity of customs. If people did not pass ideas from one to another, we are left with a mystical notion of a blueprint for the human mind, suggesting that it will come up with the same thing always, any time, anywhere.

In challenging this approach and deconstructing such notions, the recent sceptical school of folklorists made a huge contribution. They reminded us that all models of the past must be based on an interrogation of the historical evidence for each period, and that we cannot freely use analogies and parallels from other places and times to fill in gaps or as proof of an ancient date for any particular phenomenon. Each item has to stand on its own merits. I had the rather salutary experience some years ago of coming across a North

American pulp tabloid with the front page headline 'JACKIE KENNEDY'S GRAVE HEALS THE SICK'. 'It's a miracle! I touched her tombstone – and my pain vanished,' one visitor from North Carolina was quoted as saying. This reminded me that human culture is full of anomalies and surprises which pop up as if from nowhere. I wondered whether an archaeologist or anthropologist of a future century might be inclined to interpret this as a survival or revival of an 'ancient custom' rather than as an oddball on-the-spot invention of the late 20th century. In the same way, the attention paid to the graves of Karl Marx or Jim Morrison could be mistaken for a tradition of ancestor worship rather than two historically specific, and very different, phenomena.

Recent folklorist approaches have also contributed by highlighting the social dimension of religious activity. While Frazer's research work was based in libraries, all good recent anthropological study has involved rigorous fieldwork and the examination of first-hand sources. The material evidence and the social context are scrupulously considered. However, if the studies go no further, and exclude the religious element altogether from the discussion, this can in my view result in a different kind of distortion of the material under study: reducing rituals to shopping lists is like examining sheet music without ever listening to music. Religion, like music, is a reflection of the workings of human imagination and creativity. The communal shaping and sharing and passing of symbols and ideas between people is a fascinating process to follow. Diversity can be acknowledged. Where there are similarities in cultural expressions one can ask: Was this passed from one culture to another? If so, how? Why was it picked up? What need did it serve? Like tunes picked up by one person from another, symbols are elusive and hard to pin down. But they do travel, and the way they are sung the same or differently, the way they resonate in different settings, the feelings of singers and listeners, are all part of the story. Both the sheet music and the human experience of song are important. It seems to me a limitation on the part of the modern folklorists to imply that exploring symbols and beliefs is inevitably a suspect process. One can look beyond economic data and still be careful, thoughtful and self-reflective.

So when we learn from Moisés Espírito Santo, for example, about a recent tradition in the Beira and Tras-os-Montes areas of Portugal whereby white poplar trees are known as 'oracle trees' and are believed capable of speaking and pointing out the innocent and the guilty, we may remember the oracular oak at Dodona in early Greece mentioned in Chapter One. There the will of Zeus was learned from the sacred oak tree; and, as we saw, pre-classical traditions of the Early Iron Age suggested that holding a branch or staff would help a poet to sing true, or a king to judge fairly. However, the similarity of beliefs about oracular trees need not prompt the conclusion that this is a universal or timeless theme, embedded in the human brain or 'collective unconscious' of all people at all times in history. Nor do we have to assume an 'archetype' of a prophetic tree with an independent existence, available to enter the lives of human beings from time to time over the centuries, along the lines of Jung's theory. Rather we could ask: Is there a connection between these places, these people? How could this idea possibly have passed between them? Or did they think of it separately? If so, why? How does it appeal? What need does it fulfil in these peoples' way of life? Are there parallels between the environment and economies of these different peoples? What is it about trees which prompts such beliefs and practices? What is it about humans which responds to trees in this way? We can see perception and relationship as active processes, and follow their workings actively.

A case in point is the theme of the magically sprouting staff. As we have seen, this is an element in the Ayii Deka story of the ten martyrs, when the farmer's stick grows into an olive tree. Looking back in time, we found (above) that the theme was already in circulation in Greece in the 2nd century AD and that it was known there even earlier, in Athens in the 5th century BC. However, it is strange to learn that it also appears centuries later, and thousands of miles away, in Britain. How are we to understand this? The version which brings the story to the north-west corner of Europe, and which most keenly raises questions about its source and transmission, is the famous myth set at the legendary site of Glastonbury.

The Route to Glastonbury

The Glastonbury myth tells of St Joseph of Arimathea, a Phoenician tin trader in whose unused tomb the body of Jesus Christ was laid. He fled his native land to escape persecution and sought asylum in the island of Avalon with twelve of his followers. When they arrived, they climbed Wearyall Hill to survey the scene and Joseph planted his hawthorn staff in the ground to mark the end of their journey. It quickly took root and grew, blossoming in midwinter. The miracle was marked by the building of the first Christian church in England, which was dedicated to the Virgin Mary.

On a visit to Glastonbury, a cold stroll up Wearyall Hill took us to the modern windblown hawthorn tree still growing on the same site high on the slope; there are also several trees on religious sites in the town which are claimed to be descendants of the original thorn. They are of a type, *Crataegus Monogyna 'Biflora'*, which flowers twice a year – once in spring, once in the winter. A few weeks after Christmas I found the holy thorn at the Chalice Well site still sporting the decorations hung on it by modern tree-lovers at the winter solstice: ribbons, feathers, beads, stars, angels, an orange stuck with cloves, a North American Indian 'dream catcher'.

Meanwhile the story too has been through several transplantings by followers of the Frazerian/Jungian approach to myth, which has become very popular in 'new age' circles. Here the tendency is to believe implicitly in the great antiquity and mystic significance of the 'Holy Thorn'. There is also a tendency to draw into the web other beliefs. Thus in Frances Howard-Gordon's *Glastonbury: Maker of Myths*, the hawthorn tree is linked with 'the Goddess'. The author refers to the 'Greek Goddess Maia' who cast spells with the hawthorn. The same book comments that Joseph's staff 'suggests fertility and abundance', and describes the spirit of the three Glastonbury hills: the Tor representing dynamic power; Chalice Hill love; while Wearyall Hill stands for intellect, spiritual perception and creative illumination. In these passages the author leaves dates and sources vague; with this approach a second-hand source is readily taken as proof, and a suggestion that something is so is often taken as the truth. For example, the goddess Maia is often referred to on the basis of other modern writings, without any ancient reference or first-hand material being cited. As to the spirit of the hills, terms like 'spiritual perception' and 'creative illumination' are more in tune with contemporary 'new age' aspirations than with local textual material of the early Christian period.

These ideas thus seem to have more to do with reflecting modern needs and perceptions than with describing physical and historical realities. My difficulty with this approach is not just from the viewpoint of academic rigour, which demands clearly referenced evidence. It is also from the viewpoint of human respect, which requires that we do not make ungrounded assumptions about the lives and beliefs of other people, past or present. Last but not least, from a democratic viewpoint – which sees the acquiring of knowledge and understanding as a collective process – it seems to me important that writers always give their sources, whether textual, archaeological or visionary, so that others can revisit those sources in their own way and, if they wish, dialogue with the evidence for themselves. I do not feel that we can gain knowledge and understanding through a passive process of shutting our eyes and opening our mouths to be spoon-fed.

The approach of the modern 'deconstructing' folklorists to dating and interpreting the Glastonbury foundation story would be completely different from that of Frances Howard-Gordon. For them hard evidence, whether textual or archaeological, would be paramount. Since the earliest tight textual proof of the existence of a thorn tree at Glastonbury seems to be a 1535 reference to the thorn's Christmas flowering (in a letter from a Dr Leyton to Thomas Cromwell) and a 1645 quote from a clergyman, the Rev. John Eachard, stating that the thorn was of the kind used for Christ's crown, with the staff motif recorded in 1722 by the 18th-century historian R Rawlinson, these could be taken as the earliest dates for that aspect of the story, and any earlier history for the thorn ruled out. As Ken Dowden recently pointed out, 'self-consciously rigorous scholarship will tend to a negative view ("not proven" is a rare judgement)'.

Joseph of Arimathea appears in the gospels and the apocryphal gospel of Nicodemus linked with the death and resurrection of Jesus, as well as in a c1200 AD romance by a Burgundian poet Robert de Boron who is the first to link him with the Grail story. However, the first mention of Joseph coming to England is a c1250 AD rewritten version of William of Malmesbury's *History of Glastonbury*, which has Joseph building a church there for the Virgin Mary. An earlier 8th-century text mentioning the founding of the monastery does not mention Joseph; a 1000 AD text refers to a primitive wattle church dating from the time of Christ, but does not mention Joseph either. So he has no early credentials. The deconstructing folklorists might find much interest here in analysing the many later processes of deliberate interpolation and fabrication of texts and 'historical' objects intended to attract pilgrims and gain prestige for the abbey, retrospectively recreating and embellishing the story of its founding with Joseph and the thorn. Dismissing the dubious links with ancient goddesses, this deconstructing approach would also probably reject the association with fertility, would ignore the 'magical staff' motif, and would probably not attempt any interpretation of the Joseph story's symbolism. Thus it would, in my opinion, throw the baby out with the bathwater, and create a different kind of untruth by tackling only part of the phenomenon.

Deborah Crawford, in the journal *Folklore* for 1994, pointed out that the Joseph of Arimathea story might have existed or developed for some time in oral form before it was written down, and so is likely to be older than the first texts. She cites evidence for a 6th-century tradition that Christianity was first brought to Britain in the 1st century AD, and notes that Celtic Christianity had a particularly strong connection with Old Testament, rather than Roman Christian, practices: 'Was Joseph the personification of old memories of the "Jewish" character of Celtic Christianity?' Her attempt to shift the debate from examining historical evidence for Joseph's arrival to studying the content of the tradition, looking at the historical development of the medieval legend and the ideas it embodied, was met full on by the currently orthodox 'bricks-and-mortar' approach. 'If there was unusually early Christian activity at Glastonbury it has yet to be proved by the historian or located by the excavator,' John Clark concluded in his response in the next issue of the journal.

The story of Joseph of Arimathea is a fascinating one, which presents many striking and incongruous elements: the near-Eastern connections; the link with death (the tomb of Christ); the motif of the magically sprouting staff with its Greek forerunners; the followers, echoing the disciples; the binding together of a miraculous tree with the founding of Christianity in England; and the link – as in Portugal – between a special tree and the Virgin Mary. While 'new age' writers claim great antiquity for the story, and modern folklorists might stick to the safe earliest date for the thorn in the 16th century AD and dismiss Joseph of Arimathea as a fiction, we could look for different kinds of answers, wondering what the story meant to its tellers and listeners, and how and why, as well as when, it got here. We have seen that in Greece the theme of the sprouting staff is recorded in late antiquity by Pausanias and Athenaeus, and in the classical period by Herodotus. The fact that we have no proof to trace it back to the early period of Christianity in Britain, the period from which it claims to date but which has left relatively few records, does not mean it does not date back to then. The lack of material shifts the weight of likelihood, but we cannot be sure that elements of the story are not that old in Britain, any more than we can be sure that they are.

In such cases, archaeology can seem an important source of tangible evidence; but the archaeological excavations at Glastonbury have provided ambiguous material. Scholars debate whether the traces of early buildings point to a religious establishment in the first centuries after Christ, which could be the church associated in later tradition with Joseph of Arimathea. Even the sceptical view put forward by John Clark in *Folklore* journal for 1995 conceded that 'There seems little doubt that there was settlement on or near the abbey site in the Roman period' and that 'Something was obviously going on at Glastonbury in the sixth and seventh centuries'.

Background information about the spread of the cult of the Virgin Mary in Britain helps a little. It is known that there was a monastery dedicated to Mary in Glastonbury in the 8th century AD, and in her book *The Cult of the Virgin Mary in Anglo-Saxon England* Mary Clayton quotes writers of the 7th–8th centuries who discuss Mary's tomb and describe her as '*virgula radicis, gerula floris*' (a staff of the root, bearer of blossom). Clearly by that time, at least, the imagery linking the Church – specifically the Virgin – with a fertile staff was current. Mary Clayton also charts in some detail the Greek and near-Eastern influence on Marian cult, seen in religious language and in the introduction of a large number of Marian feast days between the 7th and 11th centuries. She suggests the influence may have come via Greek monks in southern Italy. She points out that Anglo-Saxons also reached the East, and at least one Greek monk reached Britain. She concludes that 'The cult seems to have reached England largely from Rome' especially under the Syrian and Greek popes of the 7th–8th centuries. She also notes the role played by the Benedictine monastic order.

An economic – rather than a religious – historian might bring forward other possible paths of transmission as additional factors for consideration. I find it interesting that Joseph of Arimathea is described in the later legend as a tin trader, and his landing place in Britain is in south-west England not far from the famous tin-mining area of Cornwall which was active, and widely known, in antiquity. Diodorus Siculus (V. 22. 1–4), writing 60–30 BC, described how Britons in the south-west worked tin into pieces the size of knucklebones and sold it to traders. Documentary sources apparently show that the tin was assembled at Ictis (perhaps St Michael's Mount off the coast of

Cornwall), and that Hengistbury Head, near Christchurch on the Dorset coast, was an important trading post. Excavations directed by Christopher Morris of Durham University revealed that the 5th and 6th century AD buildings at Tintagel in Cornwall held large quantites – perhaps 100,000 fragments – of Byzantine pottery, all manufactured in the eastern Mediterranean, including material from what is now Turkey, Tunisia and Greece. Archaeologists think the site may have been a base for the Byzantine shipping merchants; and small quantities of similar pottery have been found in Cardiff. Intermittent trade contacts such as these between Britain and the Mediterranean – both during and after the Roman Empire – may be a significant part of this picture.

Mary Clayton looks for possible carriers of new influences among individual religious personnel rather than in popular processes. I know that a lone cleric arriving in a distant country sometimes did have the determination and resources to have a surprisingly significant impact on that country's religious practices – witness the achievements of some of the Anglo-Saxon missionaries visiting Germany in the 8th century AD – but there are also influences transmitted on the ground by trade and movements of people which are more diffuse. I wonder whether such processes may also have played a role; if so, they would give a less tidy, less personalised, and less top-heavy picture of the forces working to create cultural change.

If the Marian festivals reached Britain from Greece and the East, by whatever means of transmission, it seemed to me that the story of the magically sprouting staff, which makes a sudden appearance linked to Joseph of Arimathea and the founding of Marian cult in England, might have followed a similar path at some point close in time. Then, to really set me thinking, its companion story – the apparition of the Virgin in a tree – suddenly turned up in England. First I tracked down one example, which was securely attested at an astonishingly early date. Then another example simply turned up, right in London itself.

The Lady Tree in England

At first there seemed to be no sign of the Lady of the Tree Trunk in England. There were a few special trees, like the Glastonbury Thorn and its offshoots, but none of them had any associated story about an apparition. There seemed to be no texts telling the familiar story. It was months before I tracked down the text of an 8th-century Latin manuscript held in the British Library which presented in detail a story parallel to those in Portugal and France. The manuscript, '*Vita Sancti Egwini*', dates from 731 AD and gives a contemporary account of the life of St Ecgwine, a bishop who allegedly founded the monastery at Evesham in Worcestershire. It tells how one of Ecgwine's swineherds found a sow with her newly born piglets hidden in a remote thorny place in the woods, and there saw an apparition of the Virgin flanked by two angels. Hearing about this, Ecgwine went himself to the same place and had the same vision. Although the Lady appeared in woodland rather than a specific tree, this story – with its apparition to a herdsman following an animal guide – clearly belongs to the same type as our other examples. As a member of the ecclesiastical establishment, Ecgwine responded true to form by promptly clearing the area of vegetation and building a church there.

It may be significant that this account is set in Evesham, in southwest central England and not too far from the Glastonbury area where Marian cult in Britain is said to have started. This version of the story – with an earlier secure date than can be verified for any of the Portuguese or French examples – seemed all the more surprising because of the dearth of later examples. Despite my searches I could find only one later story of the Virgin appearing in a tree (see below). The devastation of peasant life by land clearances, and the attacks on Catholic practices by Puritanism are, perhaps, the main reasons why such stories – which clearly had existed in at least one case – did not survive after the Middle Ages. In Europe, as we have seen, the Catholic Church made attempts to proscribe activities such as tree cults, but in practice sometimes followed the path of appropriation. The English Protestants, however, were less tolerant. Any stories and cults centred on Marian apparitions could have been eradicated by the same Puritan zeal which defaced the churches and allegedly hacked down one trunk of the Glastonbury Thorn.

Just such a hacking was the fate suffered by a tree which I found mentioned in Edmund Spenser's 16th-century poem 'The Shepheardes Calender'. Here he describes the felling of an oak formerly regarded as sacred and anointed by 'popish' priests:

> For it had bene an auncient tree,
> Sacred with many a mysteree,
> And often crost with the priestes crewe,

And often halowed with holy water dewe.
But sike [such] fancies weren foolerie,
And broughten this Oake to this miserye.

In punishing the tree for the beliefs and practices associated with
it, presumably the hope of the destroyers was that memories and
stories would die at the same time. They seemed to have achieved
some success in this, although the magic tree can be found as a motif
in medieval romances and interestingly there is evidence of the
survival of a very few traditions such as that associating the elder tree
with witches. To give just one modern example, Eleanor Hull in
Folklore of the British Isles quotes a Lincolnshire account about an old
man asked to chop a piece of elder wood, who responds that he will,
but that if it were alive 'I dussn't, not without axin' the Old Gal's
leave, not if it were ever so. . . You just says "Owd Gal, give me of thy
wood, and Oi will give some of moine, when I graws inter a tree."'
As an identification of a supernatural female figure with a tree, this
tradition has something in common with the Lady trees. By
remaining outside the arena of organised religion, such beliefs may
have escaped the organised attacks of Puritanism. However, by the
same token they have remained on the underbelly of popular culture,
never supported by buildings or public recognition. Whereas the Lady
trees in Portugal and Greece remain part of the religious landscape,
such beliefs as these about the elder tree in England have been
relegated to the ragbag of lost folk superstitions.

I had given up hope of finding another Lady tree story on the
British mainland when I read in a newspaper article a short piece
about the Anglican church of St Mary's of Willesden, stating that it
dated back to 938 AD when King Athelstan stumbled across some
men praying in the middle of a forest in Middlesex: 'A chapel was
built near a spring, deemed to have holy properties.' The mention of
the forest and the spring alerted me, and I discovered that the present
day church still has a spring which is used for holy water, with a
particular power to heal the eyes. On the telephone from the present-
day Roman Catholic church of Our Lady of Willesden, local
historian Nick Schofield took me through what is known about the
site's earlier history.

It is thought that pilgrims have visited the site since the Middle
Ages, and there is a record of a statue of the Virgin being made in the

13th century. And, yes, there is an apparition story: Our Lady appeared by an oak tree. The legend can be securely dated back only to the Victorian era, but there is strong evidence that something special happened at the site soon after 1474. Apparently at that date the priest of the church sent a petition to Rome asking to be removed because the living was so poor; but by the end of the 15th century the church had a sudden upturn in its fortunes. Our Lady of Willesden evidently achieved renown and was mentioned in a number of sources, including by Queen Elizabeth of York, wife of Henry VII. The suggestion is that it may have been the sighting of the Virgin which had caused this sharp upturn in the church's fortunes. In 1529 Thomas More defended Our Lady of Willesden against Protestant criticism in a fictional dialogue discussing heresy, so the church was evidently well known at that time.

The original image of Our Lady was destroyed by fire in the 16th century, and the present statue, a 'Black Madonna' made of dark oak in the 1890s, is still in use in the church of Our Lady of Willesden, and is visited by the faithful every day. Although the dating for the apparition is unsure, here is a surviving tradition located at a site which was attracting pilgrims before the Reformation, and there are enough familiar elements (the oak, the tradition of an apparition, the statue, the water, the healing of eyes, the link with Our Lady) for this story to be taken as belonging to the same series as those of Portugal and France. The fact that it is based in an area of north-west London where the crowded living conditions and heavy traffic would not now encourage you to think of trees, let alone rural visions of Our Lady, only added to the pleasure of the discovery. Although scattered and truncated, English examples do exist, and there may be more.

In his systematic review of the sources in *The Pagan Religions of the Ancient British Isles*, Ronald Hutton concludes that 'There exists now no place in the British Isles which can conclusively be identified as the exact site of a pagan sacred wood or single tree.' This does not mean they did not exist, but simply that the evidence which could guide us to specific sites has been lost. The lack of precise locations would not in itself prevent us from looking for a pre-Christian pagan ancestry for the Christian holy trees mentioned here; the problem is rather the fragmentary nature of the evidence and the fact that we are looking at not one but many paganisms.

Fig. 1 The holy tree of St Paraskevi in south-central Crete.

Fig. 2 Religious scene with tree and branches on bronze plaque from Cretan cave.

Fig. 3 Bird-headed(?) male figure with branch on Cretan bead seal.

Fig. 4 Bird-headed(?) female figures with vegetation on sealing from Phaistos, Crete.

Fig. 5 Ritual at tree shrine on gold ring found at Aidonia on the Greek mainland.

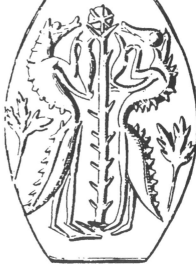

Fig. 6 Figure ecstatically touching or shaking tree at shrine on Cretan lentoid seal.

Fig. 7 'Genii' or 'daimones' in plant ritual on bead seal from central Crete.

Fig. 8 Moving with branches on seal found
at Midea on the Greek mainland.

Fig. 9 Saluting altar and palm tree on seal said to be
from Knossos.

Fig. 11 Sacred tree of Attis with offerings and
animals.

Fig. 10 Ritual scene at tree shrine on gold ring from Archanes Phourni in Crete.

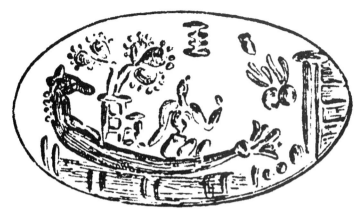

Fig. 12 Female figure in boat with tree and shrine on gold ring from Mochlos, Crete.

Fig. 13 Boat with hovering goddess and tree above, and couple on shore, on gold ring from Crete.

Fig. 14 'Ring of Minos' with tree rituals, boat, altar and hovering goddess, allegedly from near Knossos.

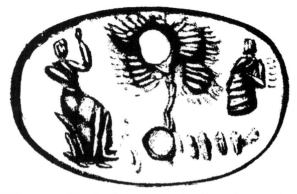

Fig. 15 Adorant, tree and hovering divinity on bronze ring said to be from Kavousi, east Crete.

Fig. 16 Scene of ritual at tree on gold ring from Mycenae on the Greek mainland.

Fig. 17 Hovering god at shrine with tree and column on gold ring from Knossos.

Fig. 18 Female figure (goddess?) with vegetation on Early Iron Age funerary urn of orientalising period from Arkades in central Crete.

Fig. 19 Women with branches approach seated priestess/goddess on Geometric bowl from Athens.

Fig. 20 Ritual with branches at funerary scene on urn fragment.

Fig. 21 'Hermes of the Tree' on bronze plaque
from sanctuary of Kato Symi, south central Crete.

Fig. 22 The Egyptian goddess Nut providing
sustenance to the dead from her sacred
sycamore tree.

N. S.ᴿᴬ DA PIEDADE DA MERCEANA

Fig. 23 Our Lady appearing to herdsman and ox from the oak tree at Merceana in central Portugal.

Fig. 24 Our Lady appearing to a herdsman and his dead cow from a pine tree at Brotas in the Alentejo area of Portugal.

Fig. 25 'Our Lady of the Birdcage' appearing in a tree at Cortes de Leiria in central Portugal.

Fig. 26 'Our Lady of the Holm Oak' at Varatojo in central Portugal.

Fig. 27 'Our Lady of Fatima' appearing above a holm oak.

Fig. 28 Portuguese oil painting of 1819 showing healing vision of 'Our Lady of the Conception'.

Fig. 29 19th-century engraving showing priest calling parishioners to worship at the oak at Allouville, Normandy.

Fig. 30 19th-century engraving from Normandy showing Our Lady in branches of tree with inset scenes of her healing miracles.

IMAGE DE NOSTRE DAME DE PITIÉ TROVVÉE A BANELLES, QVI FAIT PLVSIEVRS MIRACLES.

Fig. 31 19th-century woodcut of miracle-working image of 'Our Lady of Pity' in a tree with offerings on the branches and worshippers below.

Fig. 32 Miraculous image of Our Lady in oak tree at Scherpenheuvel, Holland.

Fig. 33 Child being passed through sapling tree in Campania, Italy, in 1979.

Fig. 34 Reconstructed drawing of precinct of Dodona's oracular oak in late 4th century BC.

Fig. 36b Detail of 'Ariadne'.

Fig. 35 Probable scene of tree cult on 2nd-century AD stone votive relief from Greece.

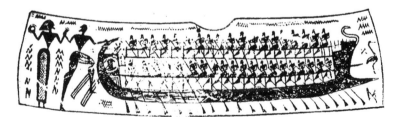

Fig. 36a Late Geometric vase decoration perhaps showing embarkation of Theseus and Ariadne.

Fig. 37 Visitors at the holy myrtle at Paliani Nunnery near Venerato in central Crete.

Fig. 38a

Fig. 38b

Fig. 38c

Fig. 38 (a), (b), (c), Lady in tree on coins from Gortyn in south-central Crete.

Fig. 39 Tree shrine on wall-painting in 1st-century AD Pompeii, Italy.

Fig. 40 16th-century German woodcut of peasants dancing around a lime tree.

'Celt', Roman, Saxon, Viking

What exactly do we mean by 'pre-Christian'? Taking the case of England – in the context of this chapter – there are at least four main areas of culture which could be looked to in the hope of finding an ancestry for the Christianised holy trees. For all of them, the evidence is at best inconclusive in terms of finding such ancestry. And they all overlap.

First, there are the pre-Roman inhabitants, traditionally termed Celts, although scholars in this field now question that term and often put it in quotation marks. Hutton describes how the poet Robert Graves contributed to the confusion about these elusive people with his book *The White Goddess*, a kind of 'sustained metaphor' or fantasy in which he invented from his own imagination a 'Triple Goddess', a 'Celtic Tree Calendar' and a whole personal religion which was never supposed to be literally true (he later described it as 'a crazy book and I didn't mean to write it').

The actual evidence is far more sparse. Described most clearly and accessibly by Simon James, Celtic civilisation occupied, in the 6th century BC, a huge area from the Iberian peninsula to the Upper Danube. Little is known of its early history, and the culture left no contemporary writings which could help those studying it. From our point of view particularly, holy trees without texts or buildings do not survive well in the archaeological record. There are the biased accounts of the conquering Romans, assessed and discussed by Ronald Hutton. They include the well-known account of Pliny (1st century AD) about Druids in Gaul cutting the mistletoe from sacred oak trees, accompanied by the sacrifice of bulls; he also refers to Britain as the home of Druidism. Substantial legal and religious power is attributed to the Druids. There are references to the practice of not only animal but also human sacrifice: three authors (Caesar, Strabo and Diodorus Siculus) refer to a great wicker figure of human shape which was filled with victims and then burnt in Celtic Gaul. The Roman authors write from a hostile, and therefore untrustworthy, viewpoint, but human sacrifice in England has been confirmed by the archaeological find of the ritually murdered body of 'Lindow Man', probably 1st-century AD, preserved in a bog and now in the British Museum. The texts' repeated mentions of trees and groves will have a basis: both Tacitus and Dio Cassius state that the British worshipped in groves of trees. Hutton draws attention to ash twigs in ritual shafts. From specialist work done on the subject, it seems safe to conclude that religion was concerned with trees, but the associations are male and there is no suggestion of the traditions of apparition, miracle or healing which are central to our story.

Then, after the process of conquest started in earnest in the 1st century AD, there is the Roman period, which brought outside elements into the local religion. At Bath, for example, an existing water cult of the goddess Sulis was dedicated to the Roman goddess Minerva, and in Lincolnshire Mars Rigonemetis was associated with a sacred wood. Names of deities of classical gods were thus introduced, but at the unofficial level popular cults could be imported from almost any part of the Roman Empire with the multiracial army, and there will have been additional influences through trade and other cultural contacts. Were different ideas about trees imported? Most of the early Lady trees in north-west Europe follow a seaboard pattern (south-west England and northern France – with the exception near Grenoble, up river from Marseilles); does this reflect seaborn influence at this or a later date?

Then, Angles and Saxons. David Wilson points out in *Anglo-Saxon Paganism* that he has almost no direct evidence for this topic: a picture has to be built up from a patchwork of other sources, such as evidence from the Germanic tribes on the continent before the Anglo-Saxon migration to England; evidence from England written soon after the Saxons' conversion to Christianity (such as the writings of the Venerable Bede); and evidence written after the conversion of England describing the heathenism of German peoples on the continent, whom some Saxons from England went back to convert. This last is fully discussed by Wilhelm Levison in *England and the Continent in the Eighth Century*.

These specialist works draw out certain themes as significant in the religion of the Germanic peoples (based in an area which in the 1st century BC was part of the great 'Celtic' civilisation spreading right across Europe). One is the importance of woods and groves; another is the recurring theme of animal and human sacrifice. The Roman historian Tacitus in his *Germania* (especially 7–12, 38–45) names gods and goddesses and mentions that some of the Suebi tribe sacrificed to Isis, and the Anglii (ancestors of the Angles) to Nerthus or Mother Earth; in her sacred grove stood a chariot covered with a cloth, from which the priest could feel her presence. Priests are again credited with wide secular powers, including capital punishment, imprison-ment and flogging. Among the Semnones, Tacitus says, no one may enter the hallowed wood unless bound with a cord to mark his inferiority. Divination by lot, which involved reading the runes on strips cut from a branch of a fruit tree, was conducted by a priest of the state or father of a family; there was also augury from the flight of birds and the neighing of horses.

These passages from Tacitus' Roman viewpoint dating to the 1st century AD may say little about the peoples who travelled to England in migrations starting from the 5th century AD. (There were also Saxon settlements along the north coast of France.) Wilson points out that Bede refers to Anglo-Saxons in England having religious buildings, rather than groves. The conversion of England to Christianity began about 600 AD, and Pope Gregory urged the missionaries to compromise, suggesting that the common people were to 'build themselves huts of the boughs of trees about those churches which had been turned to that use from temples . . . and no more offer beasts to the Devil'. The Anglo-Saxon 'Nine Herbs Charm' against snake bites refers to Woden striking an adder with 'nine glory twigs' inscribed with runes, recalling the divination strips of Germanic custom.

When Anglo-Saxons returned as missionaries to Germany in the late 7th and 8th centuries, what they found was closer in time to their own roots than Tacitus. Divination by lots and human sacrifice are again mentioned. Willibald's *Life of Boniface*, who preached in Germany in the 8th century AD, notes that some of the Hessians 'continued secretly, others openly, to offer sacrifices to trees and springs, to inspect the entrails of victims; some practiced divination, legerdemain [sleight of hand] and incantations . . .' Quoting him, Wilson notes that many of these practices are the same ones condemned in England by the penitentials and the synod of Clofeshoh, so they had evidently travelled in with the immigrants. The same passage of Willibald underlines the importance of trees, telling how Boniface tried to cut down 'at a place called Gaesmere, a certain oak of extraordinary size called by the pagans of olden times the Oak of Jupiter [Thor/Thunor]'. After he resolutely cut the first notch, a wind brought the tree to the ground, impressing the watching pagans to conversion; Boniface subsequently built an oratory from its timber to Christianise the site.

Levison cites a curious sermon, which has borrowings from Gregory, St Augustine and Caesarius of Arles, and gives further information about what the converting Christians perceived as pagan customs. In degenerated Latin, it claims that the Church can offer twice as much benefit as 'magicians, springs and trees', and it rails against debauched, sacrilegious singing, and dancing, at sacred festivals: 'For those people are miserable and wretched, who do not fear or blush to perform dances and miming movements right outside sacred places, even if Christians are coming to church... for that custom of dancing survives from the observations of the pagans' [my translation].

The success of the conversion of the Anglo-Saxons in England to the Roman Church, sealed at the Synod of Whitby in 664 AD, is stressed by Levison, who comments that: 'A new religious superstructure, rudimentary as it was, was built on the foundations of pagan England from materials brought over from the Mediterranean world.' Did those materials include the idea of associating special trees with a female saint? Renaud de la Baume imagines such a process to have happened in France: 'Veneration of the spring branch was well due to Her who purified the pagan mystery of the forests. Yews, ash trees and oaks, which the Celts adored with hope or fear, the Virgin freed them all from the cloven-footed gods, taking their place to save souls and the trees which they damned' [my translation].

The details of such a process remain elusive. When exactly did she do it? How was she chosen for the job of 'purifying the forests'? Who was backing her? Could she have done it if she arrived without any previously existing association with trees? Certainly, by the 8th century AD the Lady is appearing in a thicket in Evesham, as we have seen. How she made the journey is still unclear. Helen Waddell, who charmed a generation of readers in the mid-20th century with her breathless account of the early medieval *Wandering Scholars*, gives a highly coloured, impressionistic picture of the criss-crossing of people and poetry on the highways and byways of Europe – the characters, the songs, the friendships, the letters, the anecdotes, the careers made or wrecked, the enmities, the conversions, the romances, the happy and unhappy endings to various medieval lives. But scholars were not the only people on the move. She quotes a 5th-century dedication written by Sidonius Apollinaris: 'Go, little book, but take not the great roads whose arches are marked with Caesar's eternal name: take you the little familiar ways.' It is a metaphor for literary paths, but it is based on the fact that there were 'little familiar ways' around Europe. It is hard to tell whether the story of the Lady in the Tree Trunk was conveyed along official routes or made its own way along such unofficial, popular paths.

There was a fresh influx of paganism to England with the Viking invasions of the late first millennium BC, bringing in their own tree cults. So when Hutton cites the directives of Wulfstan, Archbishop of York, between 1000–1002 AD forbidding a number of pagan practices and condemning the existence of sanctuaries around wells, springs, rocks and trees, and when Wilhelm Mannhardt, in his huge work *Wald- und Feldkulte* (*Wood and Field Cult*), cites earlier bans, such as from King Canute (1014–1035 AD) forbidding 'the veneration of any kind of forest tree', and from King Edgar (959–975 AD) forbidding 'idle practices with elder and some other trees', this does not indicate an ancient tradition on English soil, but practices re-introduced relatively recently with the Vikings. Hutton points to evidence that they were rapidly converted to Christianity.

However, trees continued to be a contentious issue over the centuries. As elsewhere, some of the firmest evidence consists of the hostile pronouncements of the Church, and in the 13th century the Bishops of Worcester, Wells and Exeter all issued occasional orders against the veneration of trees. Although little evidence has survived beyond the Reformation, such edicts suggest a continuing tradition of interest in trees. Associated concerns about dancing continue: Wilfrid Bonser cites a range of material, including a ruling from a 1287 synod at Exeter against games and dances in graveyards, especially at festivals of the saints.

We are left with the question as to what was the source of the non-Christian, pagan element of that interest in trees. Even such a brief synoptic overview of what is known of the Celtic and Saxon religious traditions highlights the need for discrimination. Not all tree stories are the same. Those traditions are clearly different from the Lady tree tradition we have been investigating, associated as it was with apparitions, healing, flowering staffs and a female deity in its manifestations in later centuries in England, France and the Iberian peninsula. However, there are some resonances. One is the preoccupation with the oak. Another is the link with water in cult practices. Again, the 895 AD ruling from Nantes in north-west France against pagans who will not cut a branch or twig off a holy tree is echoed in the much later Christian stories from France, where strange voices from trees stop the woodcutter's axe. Our Lady tree tradition, being Christian, has no interest in animal sacrifices; but might not the Portuguese examples of the dead cow at Brotas (Fig. 24), and the herd of cattle dedicated to the Virgin at Merceana, reflect an adaptation of an earlier and different tradition in which the animals were sacrificed? Did the hostile Roman references to wicker figures represent a distorted picture of some activities with osier, whose memory was preserved in the later appearances of Our Lady of the Osier in France, and Our Lady of the Birdcage whose image was enclosed in a cage-like frame in Cortes de Leiria in Portugal? Were those wild Saxon graveyard dances taking place around sacred trees beside the church? Dancing is part of the Lady tree tradition; did those earlier traditions survive in the dances Joan of Arc denied doing?

Despite these shreds of possible connection, the Lady tree is clearly not a pagan tradition which has simply been suppressed, appropriated, or over-stamped with a Christian seal of approval. If it incorporates Celtic and Saxon material, that material has been substantially modified and effectively transformed.

The special case of Ireland – now famous for its Marian apparitions – does little to help to clarify the medieval processes at work. Converted before England, the Irish kept to their own version of Christianity in the face of the Roman initiative to convert England. By the 6th century AD, the Irish schools of learning had become the most famous in Europe, both developing Christian scholarship and preserving the traditions of pagan literature. They were a magnet for scholars: Helen Waddell describes how they travelled by the old trade routes, three days journey from the Loire to Cork, and quotes Bede's comment on how many went from England 'for the grace of sacred learning or a more austere life... All these the Irish willingly received, and saw to it to supply them with food day by day without cost, and books for their studies, and teaching, free of charge.' Subsequently she traces a centrifugal movement whereby the influence of Irish scholarship expanded towards England and the continent, where Columbanus (543–615 AD) and his disciples established over 100 monasteries. Was this influence a factor in our story?

In Ireland tree cults associated with healing are historically attested over a long period and are still in evidence at several sites today. Hutton notes that one holy tree was cut down by the King of Tara in 982 AD to humiliate the Dal Cais ruler in whose territory it stood. But the apparition motif associated with a tree is not prominent. As early as the 12th century AD, Geraldus Cambrensis noted the popularity of yews in Ireland as 'more frequently to be found in this country than in any other I have visited; but you will find them principally in old cemeteries and sacred places, where they were planted in ancient times by the hands of holy men...' Legend tells that St Brigid, who founded Ireland's first convent in Kildare in the 5th century AD, built her Church of the Oak next to a large oak tree on top of a hill. A cathedral was built on the site in the 13th century. A well dedicated to the saint still stands in the town, and pilgrims hang cloth on the bushes nearby. Hutton is inclined to think that she reflects the survival of a tradition of an earlier goddess. Here, on the very outer edge of Europe, a holy female tree was associated not with the Virgin Mary but with a local female saint, although the title 'Mary of the Gael' sought to identify her with the Virgin. St Patrick's Well Ash Tree in Ballyshannon, Co. Donegal – also still a local feature – shows that in Ireland too the association of holy trees could sometimes be with male figures.

The strength of the tradition here, and its diversity, so far from the point of origin of Christianity, raises many questions. Despite the lack of evidence, do we consider the Lady of the Tree Trunk as a pre-Christian phenomenon, who was later given the name of Mary? Or do we see her as the result of a synthesis of traditions, of a long-standing tree cult combining with a newly arrived Christian saint Mary? In other words, was this Lady an importation into Christianity, or a development of it? The Virgin Mary is given little emphasis in the Bible, so her persona in western Europe must have evolved as a result of some strong impetus in favour of a female holy figure. Was the source of that impetus Celtic Ireland? Or Greece? Or the near East, whence Marian cults spread across Christendom? Given the state of the evidence it is not always easy to disentangle the specific thread I am following in this book. There were many different paganisms, and it is not immediately clear which of them contributed to the creation of the remarkable synthesis of pagan and Christian, of plant and human shape, which was Our Lady of the Tree Trunk.

Thinking About Origins

Returning to the myths of the magically sprouting staff and the Marian tree apparitions, we can begin to see them in a historical perspective. Whether or not they carry any seeds of truth about actual events, for example at Glastonbury, is not important here. What seems important is to acknowledge that we are looking at stories which were originally articulated and preserved because they served a function, just as the modern 'goddess' and mystical additions to the Glastonbury myth serve a function for those who hold them in currency now. Each element would have been there for a reason.

Rather than suggesting mythical archetypes, the phenomena tell us about human interaction between the Mediterranean and northern Europe and the transmission of stories – or shared history – in the early centuries of Christianity in Europe, a period often pictured as 'dark'. The popularity of motifs such as the healing Lady tree and the flowering staff suggests people whose economic survival was dependent on the natural world, who needed to believe in its benevolence and miraculous powers of recovery – perhaps as a symbol of their own ability to survive a time of persecution and change – and who needed their concerns to be reflected in their religion's symbolism. It suggests people without access to medical care as we know it, who needed to develop their own system of treatment – again based on the natural world. The myths also speak of human imagination and creativity in developing and using symbols to forge a meaningful world view.

Other examples of the sprouting staff story fill out its history. It crops up linked with Mary in another context: a tradition from the Book of James, an apocryphal 'infancy' gospel about the early years of Christ's life. This tradition was commemorated in a feast observed in eastern Christendom from the 8th century onwards, becoming fully established in the 12th century. The tradition states that when Mary reached the age of 14, the high priest assembled the young men of the House of David and promised her to the one whose rod should blossom. This turned out to be Joseph. EO James traces the process of this story's introduction to the West by a French diplomat Philippe de Mézières (c1326–1405) who brought a transcript of the service back from eastern Christendom and established a festival, including a play of the story's events, in Italy and France in the late 14th century.

Because of its theme of unexpected blossoming, the sprouting staff might seem a particularly suitable symbol for the virgin birth, but I realised that this latter version of the story – with the element of a contest – has an even older history in the near East, which links it to another recurring motif: that of leadership. In the Bible's Book of Numbers 17, Moses, under instruction from God, asks the princes of each of the twelve houses of Israel to put a rod in the tabernacle. God says he will cause the rod of the man he chooses as leader to blossom. This turns out to be Aaron, chief of the Levites, whose rod puts forth buds, blossoms and almonds.

As we look to the other medieval versions of the story, outside Glastonbury, this link with leadership recurs. For example, in Portugal there is a curious story set in Guimarães. This is an ancient town in the north of the country – first capital of the early kingdom of Portucale until 1143 AD – which has some interesting tree connections. One of its main squares has an unusual Gothic canopy-shrine allegedly marking the spot where Wamba, reluctant king of the Visigoths, drove a pole into the ground and swore that he would not rule until it blossomed, whereupon it immediately sprouted. The square is actually named the 'Place of the Olive Tree', and it holds a 14th-century convent church dedicated to 'Our Lady of the Olive Tree'. In the legend, the original olive tree was the one which grew from Wamba's stick. As in the Biblical story, the sprouting staff is the means of pointing out someone who is to take on social/political power. As at Glastonbury, a male figure plants the stick which blossoms into a female holy tree – dedicated to Mary in both cases. Adolfo Coelho cites a tradition that nearby there was a Temple of Ceres, and notes that Mannhardt in *Wald- und Feldkulte* Vol. II finds traditions of similar trees near to temples in France, Switzerland and the area of Pomerania. Ceres is a Roman name for the Greek goddess of plant fertility, Demeter; one wonders whether such temples – if they ever existed – would originally have been pre-Roman, Romanised or Roman.

Stories about the lives of the saints show the motif of the magically sprouting staff recurring in a parallel role, as a symbol of hope and regeneration but also to mark or point out a special person and indicate their role as a powerful, authoritative or blessed figure. In her *Stories of the Saints*, Grace Hall ends her version of the St Christopher story with the child Christ – after revealing that it was he who has been carried across the water – declaring to the saint: ' "... If in thy heart thou canst not believe, I will leave a sign of My power and of My love for thee. Drive thy staff into the earth, so – and see, it shall bear leaves and fruit." While Oforo's eyes were fixed upon his staff, which, but now set into the ground, was already covered with verdure glistening in a radiant light, the Child disappeared.' In other versions the saint is known as Reprobus, 'the damned', before his conversion, and the planted staff blooms the next day. One of several artists who covered this story, Jheronimus Bosch in his version on a wooden panel (dated between 1490 and 1505) painted some leaves already sprouting from St Christopher's staff during the river crossing, following a German version of the story. The theme attached itself to the missionary exploits in Germany of St Boniface, bishop of the East Angles, who lived c680–755 AD; in this context it is used as a symbol of the triumph of Christian miracle-working over an existing heathen Saxon cult of real trees.

The theme is also popular in France where – as Paul Sébillot relates – folklore wove it into many saints' lives. St Martin's stick grew into an elm; St Gudwal woke on a journey to find that his staff had grown into a bushy tree sheltering him; the lances which had severed the head of St Volusien turned into undying ash trees. There are also traditions in France of trees miraculously flowering when they were old, dry or out of season.

The story of the sprouting staff does after all only exaggerate a little the miraculous processes whereby something dry and apparently lifeless (such as a seed) can – if planted in the ground – create life, leaves and fruit. Indeed, a willow or rose branch if stuck into the ground will regularly take root, and a thorn sometimes. Richard Gordon discusses such miracles in the context of the natural world: noting that 'Normality is of course neither fixed nor necessarily agreed', he comments that 'The natural world is that part of the empirical world which provides both the model and the matrix of the marvellous: the human effort invested since the Palaeolithic in the enrulement of the natural world is repaid many times over in that world's endless, obliging, productivity of marvels.' He points out the change that takes place when such marvels are invested with a social meaning, distinguishing between the strange and the marvellous: 'the strange is the unmarked product of a discrepancy between any norm and any claimed empirical event; the marvellous is the strange appropriated into a network of claims to power'. Certainly in these biblical and Christian stories the miracle of the sprouting staff is put to the service of claims to social power. To me it speaks rather of having trust in the natural forces at work in our world to create infinitely, out of nothing if necessary, as part of an abundant economy of the spirit. I think of Athenaeus' verdant ship, and of Kazantzakis' reverie, in *Zorba the Greek*, about sailing the Aegean: '. . . to cleave that sea in the gentle autumnal season, murmuring the name of each islet, is to my mind the joy most apt to transport the heart of man into paradise. Nowhere else can one pass so easily and serenely from reality to dream. The frontiers dwindle, and from the masts of the most ancient ships spring branches and fruits. It is as if here in Greece necessity is the mother of miracles.'

To return to Glastonbury, and to the staff of Joseph of Arimathea, perhaps the message was about the binding together of Christian and non-Christian elements, or the drawing into Christianity of a particular tradition about a holy tree with female associations. With its link between the tomb and the flowering staff, perhaps it is indeed based on the theme of fertility. Perhaps it was a pagan story about regeneration with a Judaeo-Christian overlay. With a long history elsewhere – in Greece and the Holy Land in the first millennium BC, as we have seen – it may have been adopted in Britain late, perhaps for political reasons in the Middle Ages by a clergy trying to incorporate a troublesome local tree cult. The eastern Mediterranean links suggest that area as a source for both staff and Lady tree. Perhaps the leadership motif was important in Glastonbury too. Perhaps the version of the story linked to Joseph of Arimathea was brought back from the East by crusaders, who carried so much Byzantine culture to the West in the 12th century, influenced by heathen themes which offered a touch of magic missing in current Christian doctrine. Or perhaps the story came to Britain earlier. Joseph's twelve companions recall not only the twelve tribes in the biblical version of the story but also Christ's disciples. Perhaps the story represents a creative imitation of the story of Christ, which followed some ramshackle path across Europe with the movement of peoples, like the 'relics' of the true cross. If so, it is notable for its link with tree and Lady, more reminiscent of religions outside the Judaeo-Christian tradition.

It seems to me that getting closer to the answer – whatever it is – would involve coming at it through a study of social history, migration, trade and economics, as well as in trying to reach some understanding of the hopes, fears, beliefs, visions and preoccupations of the people who transmitted it. Rather than looking into the past for a Grail to sip at eternal truths, we can try to trace the organic life of traditions which hitch-hiked across Europe, having various adventures and donning new clothes along the way.

The Healing Bough

As if to prove this point, new evidence suddenly emerged about the 'twig-splicing' ceremony which we had learned about at the holy tree in Crete, as described in Chapter One. At a photographic exhibition in London, with photos on a range of subjects, I came across a black-and-white picture from Campania in Italy which showed a young boy, held by adults, being passed naked through the split trunk of a young sapling tree. It was dated 1979, the record of the survival of a traditional custom of initiation or healing (Fig. 33). Tracing the photographer, Marialba Russo, I learned that the child was passed three times through the tree while the child's mother cried out three times as if in childbirth; at the end a picture of the Virgin Mary was attached to the bound-up tree trunk. All at once it became feasible that this practice too, rather than being simply a curious custom from rural south Crete, had an international life. I had not considered this possibility, but once I was looking, more examples emerged. The Portuguese 'Ordenacões philippinas' of 1595 condemn an 'abuse' carried out by rustic people whereby sick people are passed through trees such as dog rose and young cork tree, in order to be healed. It was extraordinary to recognise here another and very old variation of the Cretan healing ritual involving the splitting and rebinding of a branch or twig and the participation of a 'Mary' and a 'Manolis'.

In Portugal the work of J Leite de Vasconcellos gives a record of this ritual still being practised in the last 100 years. He lists a number of places, mostly in central or northern Portugal, where on the night of St John, very close to the summer solstice in June, an ailing child would be passed through a split branch. The type of tree varied – willow, oak, elder or elm – and the people conducting the ceremony, bearing the name 'Mary' and 'John', varied in number. In Fafe in northern Portugal, for example, a woman named Mary, who had to be a virgin, passed the child to a man named John with set words calling on the power of God and the Virgin Mary to make the child well. Sometimes there were three Marys and three Johns, or the ritual could be repeated three times. It is interesting that although the name of the male figure varies from Manolis (Jesus Emmanuel) to John, the figure of Mary remains constant from Greece to Portugal. The split branch was bound afterwards with the idea that if the plant healed, so would the child. Although we have not yet come across any evidence, it is

possible that somewhere among the woods and fields of modern
Portugal this extraordinary ceremony is still being practised. Even
more curious is the parallel with the twig-splitting tree ritual we had
come across in Greece.

Subsequently Gillian Spraggs drew my attention to evidence of the
very same practice in Britain. *A Dictionary of Superstitions*, under the
heading of 'Ash tree, child passed through', lists examples going back
to the 18th century, including one from J Cullum in Suffolk which
tells that 'A young ash tree was each time selected, and split
longitudinally about five feet: the fissure was kept wide open by my
gardener; whilst the friend of the child, having first stripped him
naked, passed him thrice through it, always head foremost. As soon as
the operation was performed, the wounded tree was bound up with
packthread; and as the bark healed, the child was to recover. The first
of the young patients was to be cured of the rickets, the second of a
rupture.' An 1804 account under the same heading brings in an added
dimension to the identification between child and tree: 'Thomas
Chillingworth..., now about 34, was, when an infant...passed
through...[an ash] tree, now perfectly sound, which he preserves with
so much care ... for it is believed the life of the patient depends on
the life of the tree...Instances of trees that have been employed in the
cure are very common.' I found that Frazer cites this example too, and
refers to a similar practice in Germany, France, Denmark and Sweden,
where however an oak is usually used rather than an ash.

At first I found it extraordinary to read in *A Dictionary of
Superstitions* that as late as 1913 F Wright records that 'An instance of
the old practice of passing a child suffering from rupture through the
split trunk of a growing ash tree was reported to me from Devonshire
last summer.' Then I found a reference from FW Mathews' book about
Somerset folklore: 'The "ground ash", that is an ash sapling grown
from seed, ...must be split for a length of two or three feet, then
prized open, and the child, naked, must be put through the rift from
East to West, handed in by a maiden and received by a boy. The split
tree is to be bound up again carefully...' The date was 1923. It seemed
very recent for such practices to be still happening until I read in a
Somerset county magazine of the late 1960s that a local farmer, who
had seen the ritual as a child of eight, and seen two of the three then
patients cured, decided to try it for himself 70 years later for an
unnamed long-running health problem: 'So, on May Day, the ash tree

in his garden was split, three feet from the ground, in readiness for the rite, which commenced at 4.30 a.m. Discarding all his clothes, and in the company of four other men, he was "passed through" the tree, so that he did not touch any of the sides...Two months later the old gent firmly declared that his trouble had disappeared...' It is interesting that in this secular version, although there were no religious names, certain procedures like the nakedness and the time of day were ritually adhered to even in the latter half of the 20th century. In *Somerset Folklore* (1965) Ruth Tongue records that the passing of the child must be done 'sunwise before sunrise', stresses the danger to the patient if the tree is subsequently damaged, and notes that two such trees are in the collection of the Taunton Museum. Curious what such trees look like, we set off to see one of them which is currently kept in store by the Glastonbury branch of the Museum.

The Keeper of the Somerset Rural Life Museum in Glastonbury, David Walker, a quietly spoken man in a grey sweater, came to greet us. He had checked the records and established that the tree was first listed in 1892 by the Somerset Archaeology and Natural History Society, the local learned body from whom, in the 1960s, the local Museum service grew. It was described in the records as 'Ash sapling used as a cure for hernia'. The person who made this donation of the tree to the society's collection over 100 years ago was recorded as a Mr Elworthy; this Victorian gentleman is known to have had a connection with the village of Quantock in Somerset, so David Walker thought the tree might be from there.

A short drive across Glastonbury got us from the Museum to the disused plastics factory which is used for storage. A nondescript door on a side street opened on to an Aladdin's cave of relics which the Museum has not enough space to display: ancient prams, tricycles, butter churns, mangles, saws, ploughs and fireplaces. Squeezing past an old bath chair, in a far corner we found the tree. It was a bare, slightly bent, trunk about three metres tall. It had no branches. It was sawn off at the top, and was mounted on a small wooden plinth. Down the middle of the trunk was a slit about two metres long, wide enough to put your hand through. Whether or not the hernia had healed for the invalid who had been passed through it, the tree had evidently not rejoined – although David Walker showed us faint bands of paler bark, as if it had once been bound.

He also pointed out that the tree had grown around the wound, so that it must have survived and been left in place for some years after it was slit. Then, when it was a sapling about 20 years old, somebody dug it up – evidently with the intention of keeping it, because an amount of root was included – and then mounted it, probably still in Victorian times by the look of the plinth. After its century of seasoning, the wood felt almost metallic hard to the touch, and its bent, truncated shape with the gaping wound made it look shocked and stricken. As we picked our way out past a 19th-century winnowing machine and a giant blacksmith's bellows, with a bird outside tapping insistently on the storehouse roof, it occurred to me that it was a strange fate for an ash tree planted about 1860 to end up as a dehydrated specimen on a side street in Glastonbury. While hostile accounts of tree cults in the past – whether Roman or biblical – sometimes mention the sacrifice of humans to trees, this seemed to be a case of a tree having been sacrificed for the health of a human.

It was only a couple of months after visiting this stricken ash that I stumbled on an extraordinary piece of history about the area it came from. Wilfrid Bonser in *The Medical Background of Anglo-Saxon England* cites a reference to 'an ash tree "which the ignorant call holy" [which] is mentioned among the boundaries of Taunton in a charter dated 854'. I struggled to decide which was more unlikely: that this should be a coincidence or that there might be a continuous tradition of ash trees with special powers surviving locally in the vicinity of Taunton. Even while I was wondering, I read on the same page an excerpt from a sermon of St Eligius which suggested an even longer history. Eligius was bishop of Noyon (north-east of Paris), and the sermon, dating from c640 AD, read: 'Let no Christian place lights at the temples, or the stones, or at fountains, or at trees... Let no one presume to make lustrations, or to enchant herbs, or to make flocks pass through a hollow tree or an aperture in the earth; for by doing so he seems to consecrate them to the devil.' This reference to passing an animal through the hollow of a tree gives the tree-splitting ritual a history of over 1300 years. I was at a loss to understand how a practice like this could travel so far and survive so long.

This particular inquiry was like a firework which you think has gone out but which keeps on spluttering back into life. Out of the blue I then received in the post from David Walker a cutting from the *Glastonbury Conservation Society Newsletter*. In a short article Ian Rands wrote that in the Taurus mountains east of the Rhine he spotted 30 years ago a young ash sapling slit not only from north to south but also from east to west. He had heard of local traditions about babies of families living in the forest being passed through a split tree as part of initiation rites, and wondered if this tree had been used to initiate twins. Returning in 2001, he took a camera and photographed the tree. The appearance of the custom so far outside the area in which I had recorded Lady trees was both thrilling and disconcerting, raising as it did yet more questions about the origins and travels of this cluster of belief and practices around special trees.

Another plant used for healing was the bramble. In *A Dictionary of Superstitions*, under the heading 'Bramble arch cures', another variation of this procedure came to light, with accounts from the 19th century commenting that 'There is an old superstition about these arches of brier hung out along the hedgerow: magical cures of whooping-cough and some other diseases of childhood can, it is believed, be effected by passing the child at sunrise under the brier facing the rising sun.' A similar treatment for ailing cows was also mentioned. *Practical Housewife* of c1860 scoffs: 'A mother will say, with great self-esteem in her look and tone, "I have taken out my child fasting for nine mornings, and put him through a bramble three times every morning; but his cough isn't no better".' However – still in the same entry – WG Black in 1883 clarifies the underlying philosophy: 'To crawl under a bramble which has formed a second root...is said to cure rheumatism, boils [etc]. The arch must be complete. If it is a child suffering from whooping-cough, who is thus symbolically to be re-born, he is passed seven times from one side to the other, while the operators repeat..."In bramble, out cough, Here I leave the whooping-cough".' The earliest bramble cure examples in the *Dictionary* are from the 17th century. It may also be much older, but this cannot be proved either way.

How can we understand that belief in the healing power of this ritual stood the test of the centuries? As appears from Black's 1883 account, the dynamic of the tree-splitting procedure seems to rest on the premise of 'sympathetic magic' whereby through the action of mending the tree the participants symbolically mended the sick child. The incantation quoted by Black also encapsulates the idea that an illness can pass from a human being into a plant which can apparently deal with it and 'hold' it safely as long as it is alive. The ash-tree examples show that if the plant dies, it can no longer keep the patient safe. Such ideas are generally regarded as 'primitive'; yet they recur in some modern 'new age' writings. For example, in *Tree Wisdom*, Jacqueline Memory Paterson gives instructions about how you can communicate with a tree and bring specific areas of healing to its attention by focusing your mind on the problem: after approaching the tree 'State your desires mentally, think them or even say them aloud, and remain in a calm state until you feel you have received an answer, or you feel healed or refreshed. If you have any negative states or emotions to clear, allow them to move from you, discard them and the tree will absorb them and transform them back into clear energy. This does not harm the tree in any way.' She stresses the importance of thanking the tree afterwards.

Here the same process is described: that of passing something negative to the tree – whether an illness or an emotion – for the tree to process. How we approach such an idea is affected by our whole understanding of how the process of healing happens. It was many centuries before humans understood how trees absorb carbon dioxide and transform it into oxygen. I am attracted to the idea that the healing practices described here reflect an inexplicit awareness of other parallel processes at work which are not magical so much as energetic. The holding of a strong hug, or of a compassionate listening ear, or of a calm presence, can – if we are sick or in trouble – relax tension and release resources inside our own organism which enable us to tackle the problem. Perhaps – if trees have energy fields – they may sometimes have a similar effect on someone with a health problem. I will come back to this idea in the last two chapters. Here I will mention only that one of the questions which has stayed with me throughout the work on this book was to understand what happened when I leant on the very first holy tree in Crete to see if it could help my bad leg. The day before visiting the tree I remember hobbling in anguish from the archaeological site at Mallia into town to catch the bus, each step a struggle. The afternoon immediately after the visit to the tree we spent two hours ranging over the hillsides above Kaloi Limenes looking for a tholos tomb; I clambered and climbed without any discomfort. After six months of walking only with stabbing sensations up my leg, alleviated but not cured by osteopathic treatment, I had rested my back against the tree trunk for several minutes and then walked away from the tree without pain.

Book References

Athenaeus, *The Deipnosophists*,Vol.VII, trans. CB Gulick,William Heinemann, London and Harvard University Press, Cambridge MA, 1957, 118–121 (15. 676 a–c).

Baume, Renaud de la, *Le Guide Familier des Fêtes de France*, Les Éditions La Boétie, Éditions des Deux Coqs d'Or, Paris, 1981, 114

Boniface, see M Tangl and Ph H Külb, eds, reworked by Reinhold Ran, *Briefe des Bonifatius. Willbalds Leben des Bonifatius*, Wissenschaftliche Buchgesellschaft, Darmstadt, 1968

Bonser, Wilfrid, *The Medical Background of Anglo-Saxon England*, Wellcome Historical Medical Library, London, 1963, 138, 144–5

Bosch, Jheronimus, 'St. Christopher carrying the Christ Child' in *Van Eyck to Bruegel: Dutch and Flemish Painting in the Collection of the Museum Boymans-van Beuningen*, KPMG and Museum Boymans-van Beuningen, Rotterdam, 1994, 84–89

Boyes, Georgina, 'Dressing the Part: The Role of Costume as an Indicator of Social Dynamics in the Castleton Garland Ceremony', in Theresa Buckland and Juliette Wood, eds, *Aspects of British Calendar Customs*, Sheffield Academic Press, 1993, 105–118

Cambrensis, Geraldus, *History and Topography of Ireland*, quoted by Thomas Pakenham, *Meetings with Remarkable Trees*, Phoenix Illustrated, an imprint of Weidenfeld and Nicolson/Orion, London, 1997, 100

Cawte, EC, 'It's an Ancient Custom – But How Ancient?', in Theresa Buckland and Juliette Wood, eds, *Aspects of British Calendar Customs*, Sheffield Academic Press, 1993, 37–56

Clark, John, 'Glastonbury Revisited', *Folklore* 106 (1995), 93–96, here 95, 94

Clayton, Mary, *The Cult of the Virgin Mary in Anglo-Saxon England*, Cambridge University Press, 1990, 13–15 (tomb and blossom), 25–51 (Marian feasts) and *passim*

Coelho, Adolfo, *Obra Etnografica*,Vol. I, Don Quixote, Lisbon, 1993, pp 215–6

Crawford, Deborah KE, 'St Joseph in Britain: Reconsidering the Legends. Part 1', in *Folklore* 104 (1993), 86–98

—, 'St Joseph in Britain: Reconsidering the Legends. Part 2', *Folklore* 105 (1994), 51–59, here 58

Dowden, Ken, 'West on the East: Martin West's *East Face of Helicon* and its Forerunners. Review Article', *Journal of Hellenic Studies* 121 (2001), 167–175, here 170

Dream of the Rood, see Michael Alexander, ed, *The Earliest English Poems*, Penguin Books, Harmondsworth, Middlesex, 1967, 103–109

St Ecgwine, see Rev. Dr Giles, ed, *Vita Quorundum Anglo-Saxonum: Original Lives of Anglo-Saxons and Others who Lived before the Conquest*, Caxton Society, London, 1854, 349ff

Espírito Santo, Moisés, *Origens Orientais da Religião Popular Portuguesa*, Assírio & Alvim, Lisbon, 1988, 19 note 56

Evans, Arthur, *The Palace of Minos at Knossos*, Vol. I, Macmillan, London, 1921, 3 (citing Frazer's *Lectures on the Early History of Kingship*, 128ff)

Frazer, James George, *The Golden Bough: A Study in Magic and Religion*, Abridged Edition, Macmillan, London, 1941 (first publ. 1922; the unabridged volumes first publ. 1890–1915), 168, 264–83, 292, 296, 315, 324, 325, 356 (dying king); 682–3 (hernia tree)

Garnett, Lucy MJ, *Greek Folk-songs from the Turkish Provinces of Greece*, Elliot Stock, London, 1885, 96

Glastonbury, see EMR Ditmas, *Traditions and Legends of Glastonbury*, Toucan Press, Guernsey, 1979; Willem P Gerritsen and Anthony G van Melle, *A Dictionary of Medieval Heroes*, trans. Tanis Guest, The Boydell Press, Woodbridge, England, 1998, 152–4 (Joseph of Arimathea); DJ Hall, *English Medieval Pilgrimage*, Routledge and Kegan Paul, London 1965, 45ff; AR Vickery, *Holy Thorn of Glastonbury*, Toucan Press, Guernsey 1987

Gordon, Richard, 'Imagining Greek and Roman Magic', in Valerie Flint, Richard Gordon, Georg Luck and Daniel Ogden, eds, *Witchcraft and Magic in Europe: Ancient Greece and Rome*, The Athlone Press, London, 1999, 159–276, here 168–9

Hall, Grace, *Stories of the Saints*, Harrap & Co., London, 1921, 25

Herodotus, see most accessibly *Herodotus*, Vol. IV Books 8–9, trans., AD Godley, Loeb Classical Library, Heinemann, London and GP Putnam's Sons, New York, 1930, 50–51

Howard-Gordon, Frances, *Glastonbury: Maker of Myths*, Gothic Image, Glastonbury, 1997 (first publ. 1982)

Hull, Eleanor M, *Folklore of the British Isles*, Methuen, London, 1928, 133

Hutton, Ronald, *The Pagan Religions of the Ancient British Isles*, Blackwell, Oxford, 1991, 145 (Robert Graves), 153–4 and 175 (Brighid), 166 (groves), 193–4 ('Celtic' human sacrifice), 199 (ash twigs), 211 (Mars), 280–83 (Vikings), 293 (no surviving tree site and King of Tara), 298–9 (tree bans)

—, *The Triumph of the Moon: A History of Modern Pagan Witchcraft*, Oxford University Press, 1999

—, 'Paganism and Polemic: The Debate over the Origins of Modern Pagan Witchcraft', *Folklore* 111 No. 1 (2000), 103–117, here 112 (gap of millennium), 109 (surviving traditions)

'Jackie Kennedy's Grave Heals the Sick', headline on *Weekly World News*, 13 September 1994, 1

James, EO, *The Drama of the Medieval Church*, Clarendon Press, Oxford, 1933, 263–265

James, Simon, *Exploring the World of the Celts*, Thames and Hudson, London, 1993, 47 (tin trade) and *passim*

Jung, Carl Gustav, *Symbols of Transformation*, trans. RFC Hull, Routledge and Kegan Paul, London and Princeton University Press, NJ, 1956 (Vol. V of *Collected Works*), 228

Kazantzakis, Nikos, *Zorba the Greek*, trans. Carl Wildman, Faber and Faber, London, 1961 (first publ. in English 1954), 18

Levison, Wilhelm, *England and the Continent in the Eighth Century*, Clarendon Press, Oxford, 1946, 1–5, 47, 75ff, 308–313

Mannhardt, Wilhelm, *Wald- und Feldkulte*, Vol. I, Verlag von Gebrüder Borntraeger, Berlin, 1904, 70

Mathews, FW, *Tales of the Blackdown Borderland*, Somerset Folk Press, 1923

More, Thomas, *A Dialogue Concerning Heresies*, Parts I and II, ed Thomas MC Lawler, Germain Marc'hadour and Richard C Marius, Yale University Press, Newhaven and London, 1981 (Vol. VI of *Complete Works*), 100–1, 486, 631–2

Opie, Iona and Moira Tatem, eds, *A Dictionary of Superstitions*, Oxford University Press, 1992, 6–7, 37

Paterson, Jacqueline Memory, *Tree Wisdom*, Thorsons/HarperCollins, London and San Francisco, 1996, 10

Pausanias, *Description of Greece*, Vol. IV (Books VIII–X), trans. WHS Jones, Heinemann, London and Harvard University Press, MA, 1935, Book X. 38.1, on 596–7

Rands, Ian, 'A Tale of Twins in the Forest', *Glastonbury Conservation Society Newsletter* 102 (January 2002), 3

Renault, Mary, *The King Must Die*, A Four Square Book/New English Library, London, 1965 (first publ. 1958)

Sébillot, Paul, *Le Folk-lore de France*, Vol. III, Éditions G.-P. Maisonneuve et Larose, Paris, 1968, 437–9, here 437

Spenser, Edmund, 'The Shepheardes Calender', Eclogue 2, February, ll. 102ff, here 207–212 (felled oak tree), in JC Smith and E de Selincourt, eds, *The Poetical Works of Edmund Spenser*, Oxford University Press, 1961 (first publ. 1912)

Tongue, Ruth L, *Somerset Folklore*, The Folk-Lore Society, London, 1965, 221

Vasconcellos, J Leite de, *Tradições Populares de Portugal*, Temas Portuguesas, Lisbon, 1986, 140, 147–9

Vassilakis (*sic*), Antonis Sp, *Crete*, I Mathioulakis & Co., Athens, 231–2

Waddell, Helen, *The Wandering Scholars*, Penguin Books, Harmondsworth, Middlesex, · 1927, 53, 55–62

Wilson, David, *Anglo-Saxon Paganism*, Routledge, London, 1992, 22–43

4

ORACLE TREES –
LINKING PAST AND FUTURE

So far the trail of the Lady tree had led back from the present to the Middle Ages, taking in along the way some extraordinary vegetation: branches which produced apparitions; trees attributed with healing powers; and sticks said to sprout magically to mark a special person.

I had also been wondering how such incongruous phenomena found their way into the Judaeo-Christian tradition, and asking where they came from and how far their history could be traced. The search for origins can lead infinitely back in time, and in multiple directions rather than to a single source. However, as the classical scholar Martin West has put it, 'one can often get back to the stage where what appeared arbitrary or illogical makes sense, and that is always a good place to pause'.

The religion of Minoan Crete is one such stage, where tree veneration and apparitions make sense as part of ritual practices focused on the natural world in many of its forms, including plants, animals and the sun, as well as the human body. But did the holy trees and branches of the Middle Ages have any connection to the Minoan sacred trees? On the soil of Greece itself, was there any historical connection over the gap of three millennia between tree cults of the Bronze Age and of modern times?

I decided to go back and look at evidence from the period of classical antiquity, to see if there were any hints that it might link back to the Bronze Age, or forward to the Middle Ages. Setting out to explore those gaps, I started with a closer look at the two most famous ancient Greek sites linked to trees: the oracles of Delphi and of Dodona.

The Search for Delphic Wisdom

It has struck me that the places which were secret, inaccessible or the object of pilgrimage in antiquity have also been hard for us to reach. So it was with Delphi. Over 2500 years ago seekers for help and truth beat out a path which we wanted to follow. As I tried to organise the trip, getting to Delphi did begin to feel like a pilgrimage. Not that it was as arduous for us as it would have been for a Greek in the 5th century BC travelling from Athens or some other part of Greece to consult the oracle. Many of them would have walked for days through mountainous terrain, sometimes in the burning sun, to reach the place where the *omphalos* or 'navel stone' marked out what the ancients called the navel of the earth. For us the obstacles to reaching Delphi were more mundane: first the site was going to be closed because it was Monday; then the hired car broke down; then there was no time left before we had to travel home. In the end it had to be a bus journey to the centre of the world and back in one day.

At 5 a.m. the Athens air was balmy. The taxi driver wove his way across the deserted city centre and down through darkened streets to come suddenly upon the edge-of-town bus station, an oasis of light which was tatty and crowded with people. Buses revving, a snack-bar selling breakfast *koulouria* (bread rings) and hot *spanakopittes* (spinach pies), a short-tempered ticket seller, passengers struggling with baggage, the last-minute rush to the toilet.

The midwinter sun rose slowly on our right as we drove north out of Athens. Its low angular light cut golden paths through the forest of grubby high-rise tenements and garish roadside hoardings, the pollution almost steaming like damp from a forest floor. Then gradually the air cleared. The messy sprawl of Athens' outskirts gave way to open road, hills, views and real forests. It was only then that I remembered the ominous phrase in the guidebook about taking warm clothing because Delphi is subject to 'violent changes of temperature'.

Memories of my previous brief visit to Delphi 30 years earlier came suddenly into focus. I remembered standing in midsummer heat that baked to the bone, gazing awestruck from Delphi's ridge down through a gap in the mountains to the tiny silver curve of water which was the Bay of Itea below. I remembered just how far below it was, just how high Delphi must be, and just how cold it might seem in January to us who – as recent arrivals from Crete – were travelling without coats. The snow-capped ridge of Parnassos appeared on our right; the bus slowed and started to wind ominously upwards round rocky curves towards it.

I am not sure how high we were when the bus pulled in to a rest-stop café hung all over with its merchandise of handicraft fabrics, and selling coffee. The tannoy was playing a familiar song: The Water Boys' 'The Whole of the Moon'. Curiously, it is about prophecy, or at least about someone who saw the wider plan of life. The singer tells that he wandered around the world for years, but saw only flashes of the truth. The other person stayed in his room and saw it all, not just the crescent but the whole of the moon. The refrain, like an incantation, coincided with a contemplation the journey had started in me, wondering what was the purpose of seeking knowledge if – as so often happens – it cannot be used fruitfully? In the ancient Greek myth, the Delphic prophecy about Oedipus's life prompted drastic reactions which sent him hurtling into the embrace of the very fate which he so feared. People I knew who saw 'the whole of the moon' often seemed to pay the price for their wisdom in terms of depression, despair and isolation from the futility of human projects and passions – rather like looking down on life from a great height. Cassandra was given the gift of prophecy with the catch that no one would ever believe her. If knowledge cannot change things, and gives no real security or protection from pain, why do humans – now as then, though in different ways – seek so avidly to know and control the future? The song was still ringing in my ears, and the coffee warming my insides, as we climbed back on to the bus, joined by a group of Greek students wearing skiing boots and heavy mountain jackets. The bus, now very full, revved up and then continued slowly to climb.

The ancient pilgrims went to Delphi with problems that were military, social, moral or emotional. Dedications of tripods and figurines, dating from about 800 BC, are taken as the earliest evidence of the oracle, and the first temple was built in the late 7th century. In the latter part of the Geometric period communities often sent for advice from Delphi about setting up colonies. Political and military figures from all over Greece and, later, from the East, would enquire whether it was a good idea to engage in a certain battle or invade a certain territory. Traditionally questions of blood-guilt would be referred to Delphi, and murderers would come to learn how to achieve purification. The oracle also gave guidance about cult, and individuals went there for cures. In Euripides' play *Ion*, written in the 5th century BC, a royal Athenian lady comes with her husband and servants to ask the solution for her childlessness. The play mentions sacrifice of a sheep or goat, and offering-cakes which could be purchased at the entrance (the minimum charge for the less wealthy) before seekers could enter the temple and consult the oracle. The appetite for answers may have been whetted by the journey; the hope for revelation fed by the harsh and beautiful other-worldly landscape through which they travelled. Perhaps it seemed a suitable habitation for the gods.

On arrival at the sanctuary of Apollo, we were greeted by a cold drizzle, and set off in quest of extra clothing through out-of-season tourist shops offering designer ski clothes and short-sleeved T-shirts reading 'Welcome to Delphi'. Then we stopped in a café where we lingered over tea, to use the toilet and add extra layers. The price of the tea – three times the usual – fitted with a time-honoured tradition of fleecing the pilgrims: the ancients were overcharged for the offering-cakes too. In some places arriving as an outsider can feel inauthentic, like an intruder whose presence spoils what they see. But Delphi was always about visitors. And the sanctuary always seems to have profited well; there has been a tourist industry here for nearly 3000 years.

In traditional accounts, the responses of the oracle, always in verse, are riddling. The most famous example is Croesus, king of Lydia, who was told that if he started a war he was planning on Persia he would destroy a great kingdom. Encouraged, he went ahead, but the kingdom destroyed was his own. In other cases success was apparently reached at a cost. As the historian HW Parke in his book *Greek Oracles* summarises the process: 'The leader of an expedition asks for success and is promised it in ambiguous phrases which, though ultimately fulfilled, lead first to misunderstanding and disappointment.'

Despite the ambiguous benefits, visitors paid highly for the service. Delphi was a powerful influence in Greek politics; perhaps it was important to keep on good terms. Spoils of war were often presented to the oracle, and the ancient city states of Greece seem to have competed in offering statues or constructing arches, colonnades, or whole buildings as gestures of thanks and civic pride. As we climbed up the steep hill from the sanctuary entrance towards the temple, followed by two large groups of tourists who had just arrived by coach, we passed one monument after another. In their state of ruin the grey stones looked tasteful and atmospheric; when new and painted in full colour, as they would have been, they may have looked garish and self-advertising like rival stalls at a trade fair. All around us visitors examined the remains intently, as if – like the ancients – searching for the answer to burning questions. I wondered if they were finding ancient wisdom or saw only the folly of vested interest.

We are reminded of the importance of the laurel at Delphi by numerous references from the whole period of antiquity. In Euripides' play, Ion sweeps the sanctuary with foliage from the 'sacred, immortal laurel groves', and the visitor Creusa decorates the altars with laurel branches. The eternal fire inside the temple was fed with pine and laurel. Vase paintings show Orestes being cleaned of blood-guilt with a wand of laurel. Parke mentions 5th-century BC references to prophets or poets chewing laurel leaves to achieve inspiration, and in the 2nd century AD texts tell that the Pythia, the Delphic prophetess, did so. Late texts have also recorded a tradition that the earliest temple of Apollo at Delphi was made of laurel. We read that the enquirer was purified with water from the nearby sacred spring, the Castalian Fountain, which also had its own special tree and the base of a statue of Ge, goddess of Earth, suggesting that it was the site of earlier religious activity. The Pythia, who is not mentioned in the *Homeric Hymn to Apollo* but is otherwise well attested, delivered her prophecies in a trancelike state, sitting on a tripod in the temple of Apollo, wearing a crown of laurel and shaking a laurel. (According to later, Hellenistic, writers the tripod stood over a chasm whose vapours rose to inspire her.) Male priests subsequently translated her cries into hexameter verse which they presented to the visitor, who was also required to be male. The texts mention not only the Pythia, always a woman of pure habits over 50 years old, who was the medium and mouthpiece of Apollo (at the height of the oracle's activity, this role was fulfilled by three women taking turns). There is also a more marginal figure, a Sibyl, linked in legend with a rock on which she stood to chant prophecies. HW Parke suggests that Sibylline oracles were first produced in the late 7th century BC; he traces their origin to Hellenic Asia Minor.

Although archaeologists have found no large chasm beneath the temple at Delphi, it recurs in tales about the oracle's early history. In one such story told by Diodorus Siculus (XVI, 26) near the start of the Christian era, the site was discovered by a goatherd who noticed that his animals made strange sounds and movements when they approached the chasm. This story reminds me of the accounts of the strange behaviour of the animals identifying the miraculous Mary trees in medieval times at the other end of Europe. In this case the goatherd, and other people who went near the chasm, were seized with prophetic frenzy and foretold the future. However, after some of them fell in and died, the story goes, a priestess was chosen to sit over the chasm on the safety of a tripod.

These traditions throw up certain themes. The natural world – including springs, rocks, chasms, goats, and especially the laurel or bay tree – played a key role in the process of prophecy; during the period for which there are textual records, a woman was central to the process; and there is a link with altered or ecstatic states, since the Pythia prophesied in trance. All of these seem to have more in common with the religious traditions of prehistoric Crete than with the institution which Delphi became. At this point another theme is perhaps crucial to explain the disparity: the recurring tradition that Apollo took over the oracle site from a previous occupant. This would be consistent with the archaeological picture: Nicolas Coldstream, in his book *Geometric Greece*, cites no fewer than five major sites, including Delphi, where a shrine seems to have changed hands from a goddess to a god during the 'dark age'. One tradition states that at Delphi the oracle originally belonged to Earth and Poseidon, who passed it to Apollo as gift or barter. In the story quoted above, shepherds were the first finders and founders of the site. The earliest story, of Apollo defeating a resident she-dragon to win the place (cited in Chapter One), is taken by some scholars as simply a myth symbolising Apollo's triumph over the disorderly aspect of the cosmos. Others think it may reflect a historical moment when a shrine like those of Crete was replaced forcibly by something new. Certainly there was an extensive Bronze Age settlement on the site, and nearby there seems to have been a Late Bronze Age shrine where nearly 200 small terracotta figurines were found; Coldstream concludes that 'It is conceivable that the earth-goddess had her original sanctuary here'.

Such a change of ownership could explain some of the contradictions at Delphi. It could also explain the sight that greeted us at the second turn of the Sacred Way winding up the hill to the Temple. There, next to a bay tree, stood the Rock of the Sibyl, part of a circle of rough boulders surrounding a cleft from which a small stream springs. This has been tentatively identified as the site (or one of them) of the sanctuary and primitive oracle of Earth or Ge-Themis, and it was treated very high-handedly by later builders. In the early 6th century BC the inhabitants of the island of Naxos disrespectfully erected on top of one of the stones an extremely tall column surmounted by a sphinx (now in the museum) as a monument of their civic pride and gratitude. Crowding the circle on the other side stands the Treasury of the Athenians, built in the early 5th century with spoils of war to house their offerings, and restored at the start of the 20th century. But the building which impinges most drastically on this circle of stones is the Temple of Apollo itself. When the *Blue Guide* states that part of the earlier sanctuary 'was destroyed to make way for the great retaining wall', it does little to suggest how the terrace wall supporting the temple was simply dropped, apparently with complete disregard, on top of half of the earlier circle of stones. Like Dorothy's house in *The Wizard of Oz*, the Temple of Apollo looks as if it has landed with a thump, bang on the sacred area of the wicked witch, and killed her stone dead.

Perhaps not completely dead. After the recriminations about the weather, the struggle to get warm, the overpriced teas, the heavily overcast sky blotting out attempts at photography, the rain-smudged notes, the steep climb and the arguments about which monument was which, the drizzle now thickened. Hooded in enveloping waterproofs, we continued our pilgrimage up to the front of the Temple of Apollo itself, and there – nestling beneath the corner of it – was another bay tree. At the centre of the huge ruin was the 'Adyton' (the inner or 'forbidden' shrine), a small space which housed the *omphalos* or 'navel-stone' (now in the museum) and the Pythia herself. She was screened in some way from both the priest and the pilgrim as she sat on the tripod, perhaps chewing the bitter bay leaves. Bitterness and ambivalence were for me the essence of that day at Delphi: the revelation it offered was of living life with difficulty and still carrying on with the journey. But, before we left, the sun came out for a few moments as it set in the west, and the huge cliff faces of the famous Shining Rocks overlooking the sanctuary suddenly shone with a magnificent pink. Despite the oracle's preoccupation with wealth, prestige and political power, did Delphi remain a place of inspiration in classical antiquity? Did the Pythia with her laurel-related trance have anything in common with those female figures on the Bronze Age rings? The earlier figures danced by tree shrines, and their exuberant gestures have been taken as part of trance-induced nature rituals; we have no way of knowing whether they may also have been prophesying. They seemed to dance free, but the Pythia sat cooped up on her tripod, just as Delphi's famous motto 'Nothing in excess' conflicts with the ecstatic elements of Minoan religion, which have always seemed to me more in tune with William Blake's dictum that 'The road of excess leads to the palace of wisdom'.

However, despite the differences, and despite the fact that the link with tree and prophetic tradition cannot be traced back in the prehistoric material from the site, the Delphic oracle does seem to represent some kind of parallel to the sacred trees of the Bronze Age. It was active over a terrific time span. Delphi was evidently functioning from about 800 BC right through to late antiquity. By the 3rd century AD only local people were still interested in the cult, and international interest was confined to tourism; after a period of declining prestige, the oracle was finally abolished by the Roman Emperor Theodosius in the late 4th century AD. So it lasted well over 1000 years.

I found an even more tenacious tradition when I started to research the oracle which was Delphi's main rival in the ancient world: the sacred prophetic oak at Dodona.

The Longevity of the Oracular Oak

Dodona lies in the area of Epirus in northern Greece. How early did the famous tree oracle actually start functioning? No Neolithic material has been found at the site, and it was cut off from southern Greece during the early stages of the Bronze Age, until about the 16th–15th century BC. The earliest datable finds from the site are pottery and bronze weapons which may be 15th-century. The cult of Zeus is thought by some to have come into Greece with invaders from the north in the course of the Bronze Age. The most recent excavator Sotirios Dakaris believes that an earlier stratum suggests the cult of an earth goddess who became a partner of the new male god, but he offers – and I have found – no evidence to back this up. Evidence for the role of the tree is not found till later, in the Early Iron Age texts of Homer, Hesiod and the Homeric Hymns, as described in Chapter One.

However, the insistence of the ancients' tradition which links Dodona with the Pelasgi, thought of by them as the earliest inhabitants of Greece, which stresses its great age, and which from Homer onwards refers explicitly to the holy tree, could be taken as giving the prophetic oak here a stronger early history than Delphi's laurel. Thus the Greek historian Herodotus in the 5th century states in Book 2. 52 his belief that the Pelasgian oracle at Dodona was 'the most ancient oracle in Greece'. He relates a legend about its founding by a sacred woman from Egypt: 'Two black doves flew away from Thebes in Egypt. One flew to Libya, while the other came to Dodona. She alighted on an oak tree, and – perched there – started to speak with human voice, and told them that at this place an oracle of Zeus should be founded.' Herodotus rationalises the story by suggesting that the Dodoneans called the prophetesses doves because their foreign speech sounded like bird chatter, and that after they learned Greek it sounded like human speech.

Evidence from excavation at the site has not confirmed the link between Dodona and Egyptian Thebes, but the presence of three priestesses linked in some way with doves and actually called *Peleiades* (Doves) is confirmed by Herodotus' first-hand evidence: in his own time three women with that title were giving prophecies at the site and he mentions meeting them and talking to them. Sotirios Dakaris in his booklet *Dodona* speculates that 'these had originally been connected with the cult of the fertility goddess, whose symbol was a dove, or three doves, and who manifested herself, as in historical times, in the form of a dove, which was also the symbol of Aphrodite'. What we can say for sure is that the elements of bird, tree, and priestesses were all very significant also in the religion of Minoan Crete in the second millennium BC. What connection there may have been – if any – to bridge the considerable chronological and geographical distance between Crete and northern Greece, between the Bronze Age and the Early Iron Age, remains an open question. In any case, Dodona's seems to be the sacred tree which, looking back from the historical period of

Greek antiquity, can claim the earliest and strongest tradition. It is also the tree oracle site which lasted longest.

At first worship centred on the tree itself, and this continued for many centuries. Reconstructed drawings show the later layout with a little temple next to the tree in a small enclosure (approx. 20 m x 20 m) from the 4th century BC onwards (see Fig. 34, which looks remarkably like the present-day church enclosure near the first holy tree we saw in Crete). During the period of antiquity, other structures were built clustering around the tree shrine, including a large Council Hall (*Bouleuterion*) in the late 4th or early 3rd centuries BC, a theatre which could seat 17,000 people in the 3rd century BC, and various temples. The cult building around the oracular tree itself became progressively more monumental and dominating. The site endured into the Roman period. In the 5th century AD a Christian Basilica was built over the top of two of the temples and in 431 AD Dodona sent a bishop to the Council of Ephesus. Despite various destructions, the site thus had a long architectural life. Oracular inscriptions incised on small lead sheets were important initially in helping archaeologists to identify the site. One lead inscription of the early 3rd century BC mentions Zeus, Dione and Themis as resident deities, showing that the king of the gods had two female colleagues. Apollo, Heracles and Aphrodite also feature at the site. Hellenistic authors knew of the sanctuary: Apollonius of Rhodes in his 3rd-century BC poem *Jason and the Argonauts* incorporates the tradition that their ship the *Argo* had built into it a sacred beam from the Dodonian oak, which spoke to them. And in late antiquity, several of Pausanias' stories include accounts of prophecies from Dodona; his reference to doves and the explicit statement that the prophecies were made *ek* (ie 'from' or 'out of') the oak, show that in the 2nd century AD the natural elements in the process were not forgotten. At the end of the 4th century AD the oracular tree was cut down and uprooted, leaving a huge hole to be found by the excavators.

The building of the Christian Basilica on the exact site of earlier temples at Dodona suggests a conscious intention to replace one with the other. Sotirios Dakaris concludes that the cult of the sacred oak was practised in the open from the prehistoric period up to the end of the 5th century AD, a period of 2000 years. While the precise start and end dates of the tree oracle's use are debatable, for me this sacred oak site is the one which gets the prize for longevity. And yet there is a problem. Parke comments that 'The oak of Dodona has its nearest analogies not in Greece so much as in Italy and still more in such distant parts of northern Europe as pagan Prussia' where a sky god is worshipped in an oak and the nearest analogies for the cult practices of the Selli (mentioned in Chapter One) can be found. As late as the 16th century, Erasmus Stella (*de Borussae antiquitatibus* II, 520) records the tradition that among the pagan Prussians tall oaks were consulted and gave replies. Overall it seems that although Dodona joined the Greek world, it may not have originally belonged to the same tradition as the other holy trees of Greece.

Greek Sacred Trees and Visionary Branches

For many other examples of holy trees linked with goddesses – and gods – surviving in Greece into the time of the Roman Empire, we can turn to the Greek travel writer Pausanias. On his journeys in the 2nd century AD he found trees associated with the cult of various divinities, especially Demeter and Persephone, and left detailed descriptions: 'Behind this temple there is a grove of trees – not large – surrounded by a wall. It is forbidden to enter inside the wall, and in front of it are statues of Demeter and her Daughter about a metre high. Within the enclosure of these Great Goddesses there is also a shrine of Aphrodite. And in front of the entrance are ancient wooden images of Hera, Apollo and the Muses...' This is how Pausanias described the sanctuary of Demeter and Persephone which he saw at Megalopolis during his travels in Arkadia. In this one area of Greece alone he recorded a number of such sanctuaries. A little way from Megalopolis he found another temple and grove of Demeter, here known as 'in-the-Marsh'; only women were allowed to enter it. A bit further away he found a sanctuary of Demeter 'Fury' at Onkeium.

Other deities also had groves dedicated to them. In the area of Phokis alone Pausanias visited a sacred grove of Athena, one dedicated to Artemis and one of the 'Gracious Gods'. Our sense of what was important in Greek religion is affected by what has survived: many temples still stand in some form but the trees are long gone, so we cannot see the relationship of grove and temple. At the sanctuary of Zeus in Nemea, excavators have found the 'planting pits' for the sacred grove of cypress trees beside the temple (mentioned by Pausanias). The cypresses recently replanted into the same pits give an idea of how the graceful trees may have competed with the temple for the glory of the place.

There is a pattern which emerges with many of the sanctuaries which Pausanias describes. He states that they open for their festivals only once or twice a year, and they are often far away from inhabited areas on a mountain or in some other site with special natural features. As with Delphi, visiting them often required a procession or journey. This adds up to a major difference in the organisation of religious experience in antiquity from what we know in the Western world today. Here, usually, a church is a building standing in the centre of a settlement and visited by the devout every week. It provides a social centre, serving to reinforce a community and its values. The ancient Greeks had shrines with a similar function to this, like those on the acropolis in Athens, but they also knew a different tradition: one where you leave the known to go and meet the divine. The word 'pilgrimage' sounds too specialised for what seems to have been a key element in religious experience: the worshipper travels, climbs, goes to another area, goes into nature to meet its magnificence in a wild and inspiring place. Instead of regular commitment to worship in an institution near where you live, you have a calendar of different festivals of various deities at shrines dotted around your locality and beyond. You set off into another world, both human and divine. The spiritual experience is not about consolidating certainties but about extending boundaries and making contact, both with nature and – at the same time – with other communities.

Remembering how people had travelled from all over the island to the saint's day at the Cretan holy tree, and recalling the experience of the forest festival at Pala in Portugal, I wondered whether the local Orthodox and Catholic saints of the Mediterranean world, with their once-a-year celebrations at special spots, were in essence continuing that tradition of the ancient world, so different from the ethos of regular Sunday church-going.

The classical scholar Richard Buxton, discussing the role of natural places like caves and mountains as they appear in ancient Greek myth, has commented on their symbolic role representing 'extra-civic otherness'. In the stories as perhaps to some extent in life in Greek antiquity – the relationship between the two is complex – a mountain was a place for reversals of normal social behaviour: 'Things normally separate are brought together, as the distinctions of the city are collapsed.' It was also a place for madness and for metamorphosis: a very different location for the spiritual experience.

Another huge difference between the ancient Greek experience and our own lies in the time frame. From our world of rapidly changing technology and cultural fashions which burn out and are supplanted even faster than the latest computer model, it is perhaps hard for us to grasp over what a span of years traditions could survive in the ancient world. Almost 1000 years after the Homeric epics were written down, Pausanias quotes the poems with familiarity, and makes it clear that a myth can be 'in circulation throughout the Greek world'. So it is perhaps not surprising to learn from him that his contemporaries at Chaeronia worshipped the 'sceptre of Agamemnon', keeping it in a priest's house for a year at a time and sacrificing to it daily. Evidently there was still belief in the power of plant life.

Sometimes the 2nd-century AD rituals and stories which Pausanias describes were downright magical in nature. On Mount Lycaeon the priest of Zeus used prayer and an oak branch, lowered into a spring, to break droughts. At Cithaeron a tree trunk – chosen carefully from an oak grove following a bird omen – was shaped into an image to be the 'bride' of Zeus. The story goes that in origin this was a trick to draw Hera out of a sulk. Placing the image on a wagon with a woman as a 'bridesmaid', the local people used to take it to the peak of Mount Cithaeron and light a huge bonfire. Pausanias also relates a story that along with the thunderbolt hurled at the bridal chamber of Semele there fell from heaven a log, which Polydorus decorated with bronze and called Dionysus. These stories may reflect some memory that the earliest statues of deities in the historical period were made of wood; art historians have noted how the first stone statues during the Archaic period show a certain stiffness and restriction, as if the artists had not yet adjusted to the fact that they were no longer working with a tree trunk.

Pausanias also knew the story about the brand given by the Fates to Althaea. This brand was linked to the life of her son Meleager, who was not to die until the brand was consumed by fire; but she burnt it in a fury and killed him when he could have lived forever. Themes from the Early Iron Age, such as the connection of trees with cycles of birth and death, are re-stated. The *Homeric Hymn to Apollo* told how on Delos Leto gave birth to Apollo by a palm tree. Centuries later the theme of divine birth by trees is still current, and Pausanias records in his Book VII a claim by the Samians that Hera was born on Samos under the withy (willow) tree which even in his time grew in the Heraeum. He also describes in his Book IX a sanctuary of Hermes in Boeotia containing the remains of a wild strawberry tree (*Arbutus Andrachne*) under which Hermes was nourished. Trees were also often located at tombs. At Thebes, for example, the tomb of Menoekeus had a pomegranate tree growing on it. Athena's sacred olive on the acropolis was beside the tomb of Kekrops. The hero Alkmaeon had around his grave cypresses which, according to Pausanias, the local people would not cut down because they believed them to be sacred, calling them 'maidens'. Pausanias knew the poets' story that in ancient times nymphs grew out of trees – especially oaks – and he recorded that the people of Tithorea claimed their city was named after one such nymph. Again, the material is diverse and not all the tree symbolism is female.

It is clear that in Greece in the 2nd century AD sacred trees, tree spirits and tree deities were still flourishing. In Arkadia Pausanias knew an oak sacred to Pan outside Tegea; and a plane tree by a spring at Kaphyae which was named after the Trojan War hero Menelaus and was claimed to have been planted by him. Comparing this with other sacred trees which were already ancient in his time, Pausanias mentions the withy (willow) growing in the Samian sanctuary of Hera as the oldest, followed by the oak in Dodona, the olive on the acropolis in Athens, and the olive tree on the sacred island of Delos. Here I have drawn only from a few of Pausanias' books, but even this small sample gives an impression of how significant trees were in local religious practices in Greece in late antiquity. And although history books are often silent about the importance of this strand of popular religion, there are pictures which tell the same story.

Fig. 35, for example, is a votive relief which probably stood in the villa of Herodes Atticus, in the area of the Loukou Monastery in Kynouria in the Peloponnese in the 2nd century AD. 'The interpretation of this symbolic scene is obscure' reads the label next to the plaque in the National Archaeological Museum in Athens. However, with its female figure seated beneath a tree, facing it with a bowl on her lap, a smaller-scale female statue standing beside the trunk on a base holding a basket with offerings, and another small figure actually in the tree and touching the branches, which are decorated with a ribbon or fillet, it does not seem rash to interpret it as some form of tree cult. The words carved around the scene give some more clues.

'EUTHENIA' carved on the base of the statue means 'prosperity'; 'EPIKTESIS' on the back of the seated woman's chair means 'additional acquisition'; and 'TELETE' ('rite' or 'ceremony') engraved in front of the woman's face, between her and the branches, confirms the impression that the scene shows a ritual focused on a tree, and designed to bring wealth and prosperity.

Other uses of trees and vegetation lived on. Pausanias in places records the use of plants and their unguents for healing, and his writings also make it clear that the traditional role of trees in accessing healing and inspiration had not been forgotten. In Arkadia (Book VIII) Pausanias records that among the Kynaetheans, not far from their city, there was a spring of cold water called Alyssus, which had healing properties and was known as a curer of madness, with a plane tree above it: a familiar combination of tree and spring. The special qualities of the plane tree feature in another story, from Achaia (Book VII) where a city is founded as a result of a man's vision experienced in a dream while sleeping under a plane tree. Hesiod's connection with plant life is remembered, as Pausanias mocks a statue at Argos showing Hesiod with a harp: 'not at all an appropriate thing for Hesiod to carry, for his own text makes it clear that he composed with a wand of laurel'. (He is familiar with, and referring to, the passage from *Theogony* about Hesiod's creative process, see Chapter One.) He also describes a famous painting at Delphi which includes a section showing Orpheus, the mystically inspired singer-poet, holding his harp in his left hand while with his right he touches a willow: 'It is the branches that he touches, and he is leaning against the tree.' Orpheus is holding his means of creativity, one in each hand: harp in the left, branch in the right.

Pausanias' writings show that at the other end of the period of Greek antiquity, in the 2nd century AD, some special trees were known individually and tree cults were still flourishing.

Prophecies or Fantasies?

This material raises a question: how can we explain the fact that tree rituals in the past were so tenacious and so durable? Do we imagine that the ancient Greeks – so admired for their contributions to the beginnings of philosophy, drama and literature – were foolish and deluded in the way that they continued to show an interest in honouring trees? Do we separate off what our culture regards as inferior 'primitive' or 'magical' practices around trees from 'proper' Greek religion, despite the fact that for the ancient Greeks themselves these practices were an integrated part of their culture? Or do we accept that these religious practices on some level 'worked' for the ancient Greeks just as Christianity 'works' in contemporary Western culture? Rather than assuming that all non-Christian religions rest on projection and imagination, can we look at the texture of practices like tree cults with an openness to the idea that there may be a non-discursive reality – a physical experience which is not hallucinatory – involved in the relations with trees and underpinning these practices? Why are certain trees recurrently preferred? What state of consciousness was entered by those mediating between the natural phenomena and the spoken word, and how did they reach it? These are not questions which are usually asked or answered, but there are ethnographic parallels which put the evidence for such ancient tree rituals in an interesting perspective.

During his account of his apprenticeship in a native American tradition of esoteric knowledge, Carlos Castaneda retells a series of experiences with the peyote cactus, known in that context as *Mescalito*. The experiences resonate strongly with the ancient Greek tradition of looking to plants for wisdom and guidance. Castaneda was told that after eating the cactus buttons, Mescalito might appear to him as a figure like a man or as a light, and in the event his eating them did prompt an experience of both manifestations. What interests me is the explicit challenge to our culture's assumption that after ingesting a 'hallucinogenic' substance, in this case mescalin, the unusual experiences that follow are necessarily 'hallucinations'.

At the start of his apprenticeship, Castaneda saw himself as analysing a native tradition of belief from a superior vantage point of academic anthropology studies. However, after his experiences, he became convinced that whatever entity is contained in the cactus *Lophophora Williamsii* was not a figment of his imagination but had an independent existence out there in the world at large. On one occasion he attended a *mitote* (a peyote session lasting several days) during which he provided refreshments without eating any peyote buttons himself; on the last day he experienced unusual sights and sounds and a vision of his mother accompanied by a series of important insights, and afterwards was told that the others present saw Mescalito hovering over him. What some might term the 'spirit of the cactus' was experienced palpably without taking the drug. Palpable too were the consequences of such experiences: his teacher Don Juan stressed that meeting Mescalito sharpens everything and teaches a person how to live a better life. Mescalito was described as having a spirit which brings about change. In Castaneda's case this seemed to be confirmed, as he brought his academic training into service to tackle and describe the incredible world which Don Juan introduced him to, and committed his life to the apprenticeship.

Such accounts are easy to dismiss, and indeed there have been constant attempts to discredit Castaneda's writings. It seems to me revealing that his first book, written as an outsider to the esoteric discipline, earned him a PhD, but as soon as he entered the discipline and described his participation in experiences unfamiliar to the academic establishment, there were attempts to brand his writings as fraudulent. Like other researchers who have become fully participant observers in cultural traditions divergent from the dominant Western world view, he was seen as having 'gone native', and was disowned by the academic establishment. Don Juan's teachings suggested that the world of objects and solidity is a convenient fiction which makes our passage on earth easier. He offered Castaneda a different view of the world as an interaction of energy fields, where every person is in touch with everything else, through long fibres which come out at the abdomen. He suggested that if people could let go of the habit of always having the world conform to our assumptions, we could perceive things differently.

In his account of the apprenticeship, Castaneda relates much material about what I have described earlier in this book as subtle anatomy, although he uses different words and concepts. Thus, as I mentioned above, instead of using terms like 'aura' and 'energy field', Don Juan teaches him about the 'luminous cocoon' of all living things. He teaches that plants also have an energy field, telling Castaneda that the cocoon of a very large tree is not much bigger than the tree, while some small plants have a cocoon almost as high as a human being and three times wider. These are the 'power plants', some of which are known in the West as mood- or mind-changing drugs. The luminosity of plants is described as pinkish in general, but poisonous plants verge towards a pale yellow hue of pink, while medicinal plants are a bright violet pink and 'power plants' are different shades of white. Basing himself on a long tradition of clairvoyance or 'seeing', Don Juan tells Castaneda that the cocoon of a tree has more in common with humans than an ant's cocoon does, and because of their affinities it is possible for trees and humans to develop a strong relationship.

I remember during my massage training being taught by Bob Moore that if two people make contact between the outer 'quality' layer of their energy fields, this helps them to draw on their own 'qualities' to resolve problems and blockages in the body which may be causing tension or illness. The 'power of love' can be apprehended in physical terms by clairvoyants who can see energy from the 'quality' layer being drawn in to the body through the shoulder, expanding the heart chakra and coming out from it as rays of colour which turn into vapour less than half a metre from the body. The person giving out this beneficial energy to another may be no more aware of it than they are of other body processes like breathing. Sometimes the term 'spiritual' is perhaps used in an attempt to describe this experience of self and other in the 'quality' area. Meditation can be another way of accessing resources in the energy field which are not always available to us.

The teaching I received emphasised that the keynote of these experiences is that they are non-invasive. In a good relationship between two people there will be similar rates of energy flow and a mutual, gentle, exchange of energy which allows an expansion of the energy field to happen under its own momentum, in contrast to the more dramatic and sometimes draining sense of expansion which is often described as part of linking in to a powerful charismatic personality. Similarly, if a masseur or other type of physical therapist is able to enter the energy rhythm of the person they are working with, I was taught that the person's inner, 'etheric', energy layer may expand in an unforced way and become looser around the physical body, enabling healing work to be done below their areas of resistance. This facilitates deeper change without damage to the individual; it also allows insights to surface which they might not in their normal state be able to access. Similarly certain music can also gently loosen the energy field outwards, which makes it possible for an individual to draw on resources to strengthen the vibration of their own energy. Teachers of subtle anatomy suggest that contact with trees can work in a similarly non-invasive way, with a particularly beneficial effect on certain chakras.

Earlier I mentioned briefly the chakra system, which identifies a series of energy centres, ranging up the body from base to crown. Of these the first or root chakra is located at the base of the spine and regulates our relationship with the earth; it is linked to physical issues such as grounding, balance, mobility, daily work, sex, physical security, and the related emotional issues. The second chakra is at the belly, linked to instinct, creativity and 'gut reactions', and the third at the solar plexus, regulating the digestion and transmutation of experience and raw emotion as well as food. The fourth chakra, near the heart, circulates and releases disinterested emotion, joy and compassion, while the fifth, at the throat, is concerned with expression. The sixth chakra, between the eyebrows, absorbs and releases energy involved in processes of intellect and intuition, while the seventh chakra, on the crown, is associated with spiritual experiences and with the coordination of the whole system. It is said to be the root chakra and the heart chakra which are most attuned to the beneficial influence of trees.

Many people attest the relaxing effect of spending time in a forest. Some go further and seek out what they describe as a calming experience by holding, or leaning against, tree trunks. I was struck by the words of a young woman whom I met at a demonstration to save some ancient oaks from the chainsaw. She said: 'There's something wonderful about them, it gets to me here in the heart. I have so much admiration, especially for the old trees, they have seen so much. Sitting against them puts you in touch with their wisdom, and those roots going deep into the ground.' She had been living in a tree for several weeks, so I wrote down and considered her words carefully. I noticed how her mention of heart and roots tallied with what I had been taught as the areas of the body which were most helped by contact with trees: the heart and root chakras. I also noticed that she referred to being able to contact the tree's wisdom, and I wondered if the priestesses at Dodona, like her, were able to use the energy of the tree to reach a deeper understanding of human dilemmas, and to respond more wisely.

The Seasonal Mysteries of Persephone and Helen

Two of the Greek vegetation cults of antiquity had particular resonances with the Bronze Age material: that of Persephone at Eleusis and that of Helen at Sparta.

The myth of Demeter and her daughter Persephone tells how Persephone was in a meadow with some other young women picking flowers. She reached out to pick a narcissus and the earth yawned open. Her uncle Hades, god of the underworld, sprang out in his chariot and carried her back down below to be his bride.

Her mother Demeter eventually learned what had happened. She was distraught, searched, raged and went into mourning. She then buried herself in a temporary job working under an assumed name as nanny to the son of the king and queen of Eleusis, just outside Athens. Events led to that arrangement ending in tears and a row with the queen, after which Demeter told the Eleusinians to set up a temple to perform rites in her honour. Then she entered a period of pining for her daughter so intense that – as goddess of vegetation – she caused the earth to stop growing plants for food and the human race was in danger of dying out. Finally Zeus, who had originally given permission for the rape, sent word to Hades that Persephone must be returned. Before letting her leave, Hades tricked her into eating a pomegranate seed, with the result that she could return to the light only for two-thirds of each year, and would have to spend the remaining one-third with him below.

This is the version told in the earliest source, the *Homeric Hymn to Demeter*, which is usually dated to the late 7th or early 6th century BC. The picturesque details of the story are almost the only clue historians have about what actually went on in the mystery religion of Demeter and Persephone at Eleusis, where it is thought that elements of the story may have been re-enacted. The initiated kept the secrets of the mysteries' rituals so well that throughout the centuries of antiquity no word escaped to leave a record. Other things, however, are well known. It is no secret that Demeter was linked with vegetation, not only crops but fruit trees too, and this fact was central to her worship. Historians also know that two big festivals were celebrated in Eleusis each year, one in early spring and a bigger one in September. From the time of the *Homeric Hymn* onwards, there is much evidence that they were hugely popular, a religious landmark and household name in the ancient Greek world until the early centuries of our era.

We also know that the cult of Demeter was very different from that of Athena, although she too was linked with a tree. Athena's planting of an olive tree on the acropolis as a gift to the people of Athens is well known, and the myth tells how with it she won the role of being the city's patron deity – in competition with Poseidon who gave a well of salt water. The story hints at an early connection of Athena with vegetation cult. However, by the classical era Athena had become part of the civic establishment while Demeter remained on the margins. As patron of the city Athena had her temple at its heart, a symbol of community values, while Eleusis was out of town and was reached from Athens by a long procession. Demeter was not a fully integrated member of the community of gods on Olympus; perhaps her links with the natural world itself were too strong.

The Persephone story of a goddess linked with vegetation disappearing and reappearing may recall the Minoan female figures departing with trees in boats, as on Figs. 12 and 14. Both may have some connection with the well-known story of Theseus and Ariadne which first appears in texts of the Early Iron Age. This tells how Theseus kills the monstrous Minotaur in the Labyrinth at Knossos with the help of Ariadne, daughter of King Minos. Taking her with him in his ship as he leaves for Athens, he abandons her en route on the island of Naxos where she dies or is rescued by the god Dionysos (depending on the version). Again in this story we find the themes of departure, loss and death. Most of the tree-linked Cretan Bronze Age ladies in boats depart alone, as on Fig. 12 and 14, although in some cases a male figure is involved, as on Fig. 13. Many scholars have put forward the idea, mentioned in Chapter One, that the boat was associated with death in the Bronze Age. Stylianos Alexiou has suggested that it symbolised the transport of the dead to the other world. Martin Nilsson suggested that a sea journey to Elysium was a Minoan idea originating from Egyptian beliefs. AW Persson suggested that the boats represent the boat of the setting sun.

Male deities became more prominent during the Late Bronze Age (as on Fig. 17) and chariots started to replace boats in funerary symbolism during the Late Bronze Age. The later written variations in which the female figures leave with a man, like Ariadne, or with a man by force in a chariot, like Persephone, may reflect the changes in technological and social conditions of the Early Iron Age when they were written down. They are developments of the same theme of female departure.

Ariadne herself is first mentioned in literature in a famous passage of Homer's (*The Iliad* Book 18, 590ff) which describes a festal dance at her dancing-place at Knossos, and later sources suggest that her cult combined joy and sorrow; so far this is consistent with Bronze Age Minoan themes. Nilsson comments that Ariadne is one of the best-known figures of Greek mythology, and that common opinion in his time had reached the conclusion that in origin 'she was an old goddess of Nature venerated on the islands of the Aegean'. He too points to a similarity with the story of Persephone. He points out that although some of the tales about Ariadne in classical texts may reflect tensions between different cults (eg between her cult and that of Dionysos), the salient point of them all is her death: 'She hanged herself when she was abandoned by Theseus; she died on Naxos ...; she was buried in the temple of the Cretan Dionysos at Argos; she was killed at Dia at the instigation of Dionysos; and she died in childbed at Amathus and her tomb was shown there. No other heroine suffered death in so many ways as Ariadne, and these different versions can only be explained as originating in a cult in which her death was celebrated.' He acknowledges that the combination of mourning and celebration was typical of near-Eastern vegetation rituals, and points out the originality and uniqueness of this cult in being centred on a female figure. Despite parallels in the journey of Ishtar to the underworld, he points out that the idea does not occur in Asia in this form: he therefore regards it as 'an original product of Minoan religious genius'.

There is thus a recurrent pattern associating a female departure variously with Crete, the sun, the seasons and vegetation. Fig. 36, the decoration on a Geometric vase in the British Museum, is often taken as showing the departure of Ariadne with Theseus. The radiant circular object which she holds in her hand was interpreted by the archae-ologist Nicolas Coldstream as the 'crown of light' with which, according to Pausanias (V.19.1), she had illuminated the Labyrinth. Perhaps it also represents the sun travelling into the darkness to illuminate the underworld.

Persephone, with her seasonal disappearance, thus seems to have something in common with the ladies on the Bronze Age rings, but sadly there are no story texts surviving from the Bronze Age to compare. Nor is there archaeological evidence from Eleusis itself which could confirm or deny such connections. Remains of a Late Bronze Age shrine were found on the site at Eleusis, but there is no material to associate them with Demeter and Persephone, and continuity of worship from the Bronze Age to the Geometric era is far from certain. What historians know for sure is that the mysteries of Eleusis were established well before the classical period: the site underwent successive enlargements, first in the Geometric period and again about 700 BC. It thrived throughout the period of classical antiquity and survived well into the Christian era: the Roman Emperor Marcus

Aurelius was initiated into the mysteries in the 2nd century AD, and the site was still being refurbished in the 3rd century AD.

It is also the goddess Demeter who is linked with one of the earliest stories of environmental barbarism. If myths reflect the consciousness of a people, the story of Erysichthon shows that as early as the classical period the Greeks had a sense of the dangers of desecrating trees and over-consuming natural resources. The *Oxford Classical Dictionary* states that the earliest source of the story is Hellanicus in the 5th century BC, although a fuller version is given by the Hellenistic writer Callimachus in later classical antiquity (3rd century BC). The story is set in Thessaly and tells how Erysichthon , wanting timber, tried to cut down a sacred grove of Demeter, although she made a personal apparition to warn him against it. After committing this act, he was taken over by an insatiable hunger which drove him to sell everything he owned to buy food, and eventually ruined him. The story seems to me to offer an allegory applicable to the corporate greed of late capitalism which destroys irreplaceable resources, and the associated patterns of voracious consumption into which individuals are indoctrinated. Denying your connection with the world through an act of abuse creates an emptiness inside which no food can fill. There could hardly be a more explicit fable about the price of human greed and disrespect for the natural world.

As I surveyed the poems and myths produced in Greece in the classical and post-classical periods, I found there was to be another episode in the life and death of the departing female figure. In the 3rd century BC, the poet Theocritus wrote a poem which describes the consecration of the plane tree of Helen at Sparta. The choir of local young women hang fragrant garlands on it, anoint it with oil and write for all passers-by to read: 'Honour me, for I am Helen's tree' (XVIII, 43–8). This is the same Helen, Queen of Sparta, who left her husband and was carried off to Troy by Paris in his ship, causing the Greeks to come after her and thus start the Trojan War, as related in Homer's epic poem *The Iliad*. There is textual evidence that she was worshipped as a goddess at Sparta, and Pausanias (III.19.10) refers to worship of 'Helen Dendrites' ('Helen of the Tree') on the island of Rhodes. This celebration of 'Helen's tree' suggests that at Sparta too she was a goddess linked with the natural world, a tree spirit or deity, as well as an unfaithful wife in a warrior saga. Although her role in that story dominates in the Homeric epics, the Theocritus poem shows that centuries later her incarnation as a tree goddess was a live issue. The plane tree was a well-known feature of Sparta and some scholars have argued that this poem was written to explain the origin of a Spartan cult of Helen of the Plane Tree.

There were several aspects of the poem which I found interesting. One was that the mention of the choir hanging flowers on the tree and anointing it recalled the same rituals to honour trees taking place in medieval France and England, as described in Chapters Two and Three. Also, as I looked at the poem, some lines in it particularly aroused my curiosity: 'Lovely, O Lady Night, shines the face of the rising dawn, and the clear spring at winter's end; just so golden Helen shines amongst us.' It was something about the way the metaphors for Helen's beauty compared her to the sun and the spring which reminded me of the sun rituals and seasonal festivals I had worked to identify in my study of Minoan religion. Then I remembered an article by Otto Skutsch, in a classical journal, which drew attention to a recurring variation of the Helen story – namely that it was only an image of her which went to Troy, while she herself went to Egypt. Drawing on the work of another scholar, Martin West, he presents a case that in the story Helen went to Egypt because 'she went to the south like the sun' during the winter months, and that her return was celebrated in Sparta at a spring festival, as described in Theocritus' idyll. This resonated with the spring festivals of the Lady trees in other parts of Europe.

As for Homer's poem, Skutsch concludes that 'It seems to me, in fact, as good as certain that Helen originally had nothing to do with Troy' and comments on the poetic genius which 'made Helen, who disappeared, go to Troy with Paris because he wanted a reason for the great war which he was going to describe', mirroring a story of an earlier abduction of Helen by the Greek hero Theseus. He draws attention to other indications connecting Helen with the sun, including a derivation of her name as 'the shining one'.

This notion of a goddess who disappears in winter reminded me of the apparent importance of the sun in Minoan religion, and of those ring engravings showing a female figure travelling by boat with a tree on board, accompanied in some versions by a male figure, discussed above. Was 'Helen of the Tree' another manifestation of the pattern of the female figure representing sun/summer/vegetation who travelled away for the winter? Of a seasonal loss and return where the return was greeted with the celebration of spring? Was there any link with the loss and return of Persephone, also abducted by a male figure and greeted with a return of vegetation – as well as her mother's joy – when she re-emerged from the underworld in the spring?

The Virgin Mary re-entered the picture dramatically when we visited another holy tree dedicated to her, this time a myrtle with healing powers in a nunnery in central Crete.

The Magic Myrtle of Mary, Aphrodite and Artemis

After many fruitless enquiries about holy trees in contemporary Crete, it was an archaeologist, the curator of the archaeologists' hostel at Knossos, who suggested to us the holy myrtle at Venerato. Clearly signposted off one of the main roads south from Heraklion, the nunnery of Paliani encircles a large myrtle tree with a trunk of enormous girth. A maze of bare muscular-looking branches have lost their leaves in their lower reaches, apparently stripped by zealous pilgrims. Above, a mass of greenery rises like a shock of hair. Sitting huge, hemmed in by the small convent courtyard, the tree looks cramped, as if it would like to stretch and scatter the church and little dwellings around it. It looked about 10 metres high. We were told this is unusually large; apparently four to five metres is the normal height for myrtle trees. While nuns scurried around the courtyard, we watched a slow trickle of people coming in to kiss the tree on arrival and pay their respects (Fig. 37). As at many Greek shrines, tiny plaques of stamped metal had been hung on the tree by previous visitors as thanks for help. They referred to a wide range of ailments and life problems which had been brought there for a solution, with pictures of an ear, a heart, a leg, a house. I was told that the leaves boiled to make tea and drunk in the morning could help with headache, stomach ache and cancer. A woman visitor rebuked me for smelling a leaf: like an icon, it should only be kissed. Beside the tree was a spring which is also regarded as sacred: 'Drink some, put it on your head!' a small wiry nun exclaimed, before leading us away to her cell to buy some needlework. The age of the tree tradition is guessed at over 1000 years and there is a festival on 24 September when people gather around the tree and in the church from the early morning onwards. On Good Friday crowns are brought and hung on the tree.

It was the tree's story which took us completely by surprise. While some sources say that the tree became acknowledged as sacred after an icon of the Virgin Mary was found at its foot, the nun pressed into our hands an A4 flier dated 1940 and typed in Greek rhyming verse which told a far more curious version. In former times the area was covered by a forest. One day this caught fire, and from an old briar bush a voice was suddenly heard crying out 'No! No!' After fearfully putting out the fire, local people found an icon which showed the Virgin in the branches of a myrtle tree. The girls of the local school burned incense and tended the icon, seeking help from the Virgin, until:

> One day it made a miracle
> For the sinless children,
> And the painted branches
> Became real.

The girls planted them and they grew heartily. The villagers built a church and put the icon in it, but three times it fled back to the branches of the myrtle tree and so it was left there. Other accounts tell how the tree then grew around the icon (a phenomenon we had seen at the first holy tree). At the present day the tree is touched and prayed under as an embodiment of the Virgin Mary herself.

This story told on the A4 flier is remarkable in the way it combines the sprouting staff and various of the tree motifs. The wooden icon suddenly taking root recalls the magically sprouting staff story. The fire story – involving children and telling of the discovery in a woody place of a miraculous icon of the Virgin which preferred her tree to the church – is clearly another version of the one we had heard in Portugal and France. The fact that in the story the icon itself shows the Virgin in the branches of a myrtle tree incorporates the theme of the Lady's apparition in the tree. Our informants on the site assigned the events in the story, and the founding of the church, to the 4th century AD. Although this cannot be verified, it is not entirely impossible given the dating of the nunnery, which was mentioned as an antiquity in a document as early as 668 AD.

Did this suggest a significant shift in the time frame? In western and northern Europe the earliest evidence of this phenomenon – and this story with its particular cluster of elements – had been from the 8th century in Britain, as described in Chapter Three. Here the suggested date pulled it back substantially earlier in the first millennium AD. I already knew that some elements in the 'Lady tree' story were very old: Diodorus Siculus' account of the foundation of Delphi – written around the start of the Christian era – included other aspects of the same story: as described earlier in this chapter, he tells how the site was identified by a goatherd who noticed that his animals were behaving strangely at a certain spot. At Venerato there was no evidence for such an early date beyond hearsay, but I felt inspired to scour the sources again.

This was when I discovered that we were not alone on the trail of this particular inquiry. Someone else had noticed the parallels between modern Cretan tree cults and the Minoan evidence. Professor Peter Warren of Bristol University wrote asking about our visit to the very first Cretan tree, to include it in an academic paper on contemporary Cretan tree cults. Being a Minoan specialist, he too was interested in possible evidence of continuity between the second millennium BC and the modern examples. He pointed out that late 5th and 4th BC coins of Phaistos show a young god, Velchanos, sitting in a leafless tree. These offered further interesting evidence of tree cults' durability, but without a female connection did not advance our search for the history of the Lady trees. More relevant were Cretan coins which Warren mentioned from late 5th to 3rd century BC Priansos, showing a goddess on a throne under a palm tree stroking the head of a snake, clearly recalling aspects of Minoan cult practice; also some coins from Gortyn showing Europa in a tree. I made a note to look up these coins in the library when I next had the chance. He also mentioned some further examples of modern Cretan holy trees, and referred to a Cretan author Nikos Psilakis as having identified over 50 such sacred trees.

Over 50 sacred trees? With the help of Peter Warren, we made contact with Nikos Psilakis and arranged to meet him.

There is a place in the centre of Heraklion, by the lion fountain, where tables spill out from restaurants and cafés all over the courtyard and the alleyways around it. In midwinter, on warm evenings, the tables are full of fashionable Cretans sitting with their families and friends, eating, drinking and talking. A tuneful murmur rises from the tables as the cadences of conversation interweave like birdsong. On a midsummer day the murmur is subdued by heavy heat as the sun beats down on Greeks and tourists sweltering under the awnings over ice creams and coffees. It was on such a baking June midday that we met Nikos Psilakis, a celebrity in Crete for his local radio show, and his wife Maria, an author in her own right and collaborator in his books which range from Byzantine monasteries to local cookery specialities. While visitors in sunclothes perspired around us, they managed, like many Cretans, to look both smartly dressed and cool despite the temperature. We exchanged notes about the progress of our researches: they were interested to see photographs of sacred trees in France and Portugal, we were interested to hear about Crete. Yes, he knew of many holy trees in the area. In fact, they were visiting one that very evening and we could meet them there. It was at a monastery called Moni Angarathou, where they would be attending the baptism of the child of some friends. Following the unbending rules of Cretan hospitality, Psilakis insisted on paying for the ice creams as we parted.

The road to Angarathos Monastery led through a picture-book landscape of small round hills covered with olive trees, picked out sharply by the late afternoon sun. The name 'Angarathos' reflects the story that the first church was built at the place where an icon of the Virgin Mary had been found under a bush of the herb *angarathia* (Jerusalem sage). A monk told us that legend placed this in 12th–13th century AD. The earliest records of the establishment go back to the early 16th century, and in following centuries it became known as a seat of learning. Psilakis' book tells how in the early 17th century it was one of the wealthiest monasteries in Crete. Its fort-like layout, with buildings backing on to an encircling wall, reflects a troubled past with many ransackings during fighting against the Turks. When we arrived it was peaceful in the evening light. The present church, dedicated to the Virgin, is late 19th-century; from inside it we could hear the rich tones of the priest's incantations from the baptism already in progress. Psilakis had told us how to find the holy tree, against the outside wall of the church at its east end. The present tree – after a graft – is a pomegranate. We found it rather squashed behind an orange tree, a fence protecting its delicate scarlet flowers. In front of it a 'saint-box' held a little dish of oil and a faded picture of the Virgin and Child. The famous icon itself was, we were told, inside the church. The story of its discovery was familiar, although what we heard lacked other elements such as the flight of the icon from the church, and the apparition of the Lady.

We missed too the appearance of the Psilakises. After paying our respects to the tree, we waited outside the church door, but the crowd leaving at the end of the baptism did not include them. We later learned that we had made the unusual mistake of arriving too early: their friends' baptism was a later one, at which we also failed to appear for them.

Nonetheless, this day marked a turning point. It had become clear that we were not looking at a few oddities, but at a tradition which was endemic in Cretan culture. After the Venerato myrtle with its fantastic collection of motifs, at the Angarathos monastery we had found the plant, the icon, the discovery, and the Lady. Warren had provided more examples – some linking trees with male saints – and Psilakis had dozens more. The frequent epithet '*Phaneromeni*' meaning 'she who appears' refers to the miraculous discovery of an icon, and its ubiquitousness in the Cretan countryside was another confirmation of the prevalence of that element of the story in Crete.

Back in the library, some of the themes turned out not to be exclusive to Crete; they could also be found in other parts of Greece in modern times. In Messenia, according to popular legend, monks from the monastery of St Basil one night saw a flaming tree on Mount Ithome opposite. They crossed the valley and found an icon of the Panayia ('All-Holy', the Greek term for the Virgin) on a tree with a lighted candle beside it. They carried it across to their monastery, but it miraculously transferred itself back to where it was found. The monks eventually abandoned their monastery building and moved across to join it. In the early 20th century, Mary Hamilton recorded examples as far afield as Mytilene, Macedonia and Karpathos of traditions involving tying rags or threads on a special tree growing at a sacred site, to symbolise the sick leaving their illnesses behind and expressing their thanks to the tree. Arthur Evans himself records seeing such a thorn tree hung with different coloured rags at a 'Mohammedan saint's' tomb in Macedonia.

If this was such a common phenomenon in recent times, were there no antecedents from Greek antiquity relating not just to generalised tree cults but to the specifics of the Lady tree story? As I returned to the library the myrtle proved important, leading to the goddess Aphrodite and a whole new set of links. In a passage in his Book V on Elis, Pausanias describes how after crossing the River Hermus the traveller sees an image of Aphrodite 'made of a living myrtle tree', said to have been dedicated by the legendary figure Pelops to propitiate the goddess. So here we had another divine female literally embodied in a myrtle tree. Primarily seen as the goddess of love, Aphrodite also has epithets in the Greek texts associating her variously with the sky ('Ourania' or 'Heavenly') and with the hill, and she has strong links with the sea. In Chapter Three, I cited Athenaeus' 2nd-century AD story about her preventing a shipwreck, and he has several other relevant tales: about shrines of Aphrodite on board ships, and about her planting a pomegranate tree in Cyprus. Most interesting of all, in his Book IX he has a description of an annual 'Festival of Embarkation' in Sicily, which marks the embarkation of the goddess Aphrodite for Libya followed by her return. So we have yet another goddess linked with vegetation and seasonal sea travel.

LR Farnell, in his classic study of Greek cults, refers to one story where the Delphic oracle advises Theseus to take Aphrodite as his fellow-voyager; he notes Aphrodite's close connection with Crete and suggests that 'As we follow the voyage of Theseus back to Athens it becomes clear that his beloved whom he leads away and deserts is Aphrodite herself or her Cretan representative; the divinity of Ariadne and her real personality are betrayed in the Cypriote worship and legend.' According to a Cypriot version of the story, when Ariadne was deserted by her lover, she hanged herself on a tree. Farnell derives the cult of Helen Dendritis and this story of Ariadne hanging herself on a tree from the same source: the custom of hanging images or masks of divinities in trees. He points out that in another version she died in Cyprus in a grove named after a composite figure 'Ariadne-Aphrodite'. He points to the island of Delos as another place where there are traces of the Theseus–Ariadne legend and of Aphrodite-worship. Ariadne and Aphrodite were perhaps different names given to the same divine female figure associated with a particular scenario of events.

Aphrodite has a number of other intriguing associations. In a reversal of the gender roles of the Theseus story, an early mention in Hesiod's *Theogony* (lines 900–901) tells of her carrying off Phaethon, a sun-related male figure whose name means 'Shining'. She herself sometimes goes under the name of 'Pasiphae' ('All-shining'), and Farnell quotes a description written by Macrobius c400 AD of Aphrodite mourning Adonis in which she sits with head bowed grieving as the image of winter, and is happy when the sun comes up from the underworld. A number of cults centred on her tomb, and in Cyprus evidence suggests a ritual of bringing her back to life. Farnell cites a number of other references from classical and post-classical sources about cult practices which tie in with our themes of seasonal loss and return.

Again we have tree-associated goddesses involved in these recurrent themes. Farnell argues for an oriental origin of these aspects of Aphrodite; from my own viewpoint what are most interesting are the Bronze Age Cretan resonances around the theme of tree/sun/sea/loss/death/return.

Artemis is another goddess who was identified with specific trees in the ancient texts. Pausanias tells how at Hypsoi she was worshipped as *Daphnaea* (of the Laurel), and at Kariae ('Walnut Trees') she had a sanctuary with an outdoor image of her as *Karyatis* (of the Walnut Tree): 'Here every year the Lakedaimonian girls hold chorus dances; they also have a well-established special local dance.' Dancing at the tree was a feature of tree cults in northern Europe, and other Artemis passages offer other specific parallels with the Lady tree stories. For example, in his Book III on Lakonia Pausanias describes at Limnaion another image of Artemis called both 'Orthia' ('Upright') and 'Lygodesma' ('Willow-bound') because it was found in a thicket of willows, and the willows around it made the image stand up straight. This has an uncanny similarity to the story of 'Our Lady of the Bird Cage', the Virgin Mary mentioned in Chapter Two whose image was worshipped in a cage-like structure made of willow and other branches built around to stop her running away. Only that was in Cortes de Leiria in Portugal, first attested in the 14th century AD.

Another Artemis story has an element involving prophecy, still in Pausanias' Book III; it is about a displaced community told by an oracle that Artemis would show them where they should settle. So when they landed on shore they followed a hare (one of Artemis' animals) which had appeared to them. It dived into a myrtle tree so they built a city at that place, 'and they still worship that myrtle tree and call Artemis "Saviour"'. An animal pointing out a holy tree, a goddess who miraculously helps; these too are familiar themes from north-western European Lady tree stories. Of Kaphyae in Arkadia (Book VIII) Pausanias tells another curious story. Once some children in play put a noose round the neck of the idol of Artemis and said they were hanging her. Adults stoned them, but the goddess was angry at the death of innocents and ordered them to set up a cult of 'hanging Artemis'. Farnell again derives this from the custom of hanging an image of the deity of vegetation in a tree to secure fertility. This may be so, although I am uncomfortable with the use of 'fertility' as a catch-all explanation; I also wonder whether there might originally have been more unpleasant associations which Farnell did not consider.

Most intriguingly, Pausanias describes also in Arkadia a statue of Artemis which stood actually *inside* a great cedar tree, because of which they called her 'Kedreatis' or 'Lady of the Cedar'. There is no picture, only Pausanias' description; while commentators like Frazer debate whether the image stood in the hollow tree trunk or among the branches, I am reminded of the examples of images of the Lady in both places in the trees recorded in France and Portugal, and wonder whether the effect of the Artemis statue was more like that at Merceana, Brotas and Caen (Figs. 23, 24, 30) or – if inside the trunk – like Cortes de Leiria (Fig. 25) or like the graceful statue inside the growing tree at Le Troncq (on the front and back cover).

It is noticeable that Artemis appears in cults linked with trees only in particular areas of Greece. Aphrodite's tree cults are again thematically and geographically specific. I have long thought that the names of Olympian deities are a superficial layer overlaid on a range of local cults; the name chosen seems to depend partly on which deity seemed most suitable, and partly on historical accident. The same schema of ideas seems to be connected with Aphrodite in one place and Artemis in another. A variety of deities are associated with different kinds of trees in antiquity. In the Bronze Age there may have been even more diversity, as names of divinities preserved in the Linear B script suggest that some of them may have been specific to different localities. What interests me is to enquire whether the variety of local cults reflect any shared ideas or underlying themes. I am not looking for an 'archetypal' pattern, but for recurring motifs which have a geographical context and which travel over time.

Gortyn and a Last Piece of the Jigsaw

Only a few weeks before I had to complete my research, I was in the library and remembered that I wanted to check the Gortyn coins mentioned by Peter Warren. Going to a first-hand source always has something of the thrill of entering the unknown. What you find may not be what you expect: it may be much more, or less, than secondary sources implied; the material you unearth may fell your theories at a blow or it may make them burst into blossom. It might seem strange that a heavy tome about ancient Cretan coins could make anyone feel excited, but Georges Le Rider's volume on *Monnaies Crétoises* turned out to be worth it. Opening the illustrations pages I found myself faced with literally dozens of photographs of small coins impressed with designs of a lady sitting in a tree (Fig. 38). On the reverse was a bull. The text referred to the lady as Europa, on the basis of the legend in which Zeus as a bull carried her to Gortyn and had his way with her beneath a plane tree. Europa may well have been the name given to her when these coins were in use (c360 BC on, according to Le Rider's estimate). But she is not shown on the bull or mating with Zeus; she is sitting in a tree, in a position directly comparable to that in the illustration from Merceana (Fig. 23). The bull associated with this Europa, on the other side of the coin, also has parallels at Portuguese sites, such as the herd of bulls at Merceana.

Suddenly I had what I had been missing – a specific link between the tree ladies of Greek civilisation and the Lady of the Tree Trunk in western Europe. The fact that it was such a good iconographic match was all the more incredible given that it was still unclear how this lady in the tree had made the journey.

Gortyn itself still has a plane tree, which turned out to provide independent evidence for continuity of tradition at the site. The town has a long history, starting with a hill settlement around 1000 BC and continuing through classical Greek, Roman and Byzantine times until it fell to Arab raiders around the late 7th century AD. It was from nearby Ayii Deka – again – that we were sent to look at the special tree which stands on the north of the archaeological site. It is a plane tree of an unusual – evergreen – species. Local people told us that it is miraculous because it never sheds its leaves and because it can heal people. We heard that it possesses special powers to help women who want to have children. Surrounded by a fence, it bears a plaque giving its Latin name – *Platanus Orientalis* – and explaining that it does not shed its leaves. The plaque also points out the tree's mythological interest: that after the god Zeus pursued Europa in the shape of a bull it was here that they conceived Minos, the legendary king of Knossos.

This story does not prove anything about the antiquity of a tradition of trees on this site; such connections can be written in after the event, just as trees can be replanted. For this reason I had not thought much about it; however, a search through geographical sources in the library turned up mentions in classical texts of a sacred plane tree at Gortyn in antiquity. Varro wrote that near Gortyn there was a special plane tree that retained its leaves in winter; Theophrastus and Pliny also mentioned the Europa myth.

Such texts from different periods give evidence which, when combined with the 4th-century BC coins, gives a very solid history to the tradition of Gortyn's plane tree. I mentioned above some of the material reflecting the strong tradition in the ancient Greek world linking trees to deities, often goddesses – including Helen, Artemis and Aphrodite. Here at Gortyn we had the presence of a venerated modern tree and ancient reference to an ancient sacred tree on the same site – and therefore the possibility of continuity from that time. It cannot be proved or disproved, but it is possible that folk memory preserved a tradition of a sacred plane tree at this place from late antiquity until the present day. Here was one tree whose roots did seem to reach back to the classical world.

The survival of this tree site, combined with the coins of the lady in the tree, made me think seriously about the problems of survival and transmission from the ancient to the modern world.

Survival Against the Odds

To suggest that a cultural motif has survived is to raise the question: how?

To survive through the 'dark age' from the Bronze Age to the Early Iron Age, an idea had to survive movements of people, economic setback, technological decline, and a contraction in cultural contacts. In a community which did not move, a local tree cult might be thought to have a good chance of continuing, especially since the first literature of the Iron Age reveals the existence of a rich cultural tradition of ideas about plants, including tree-nymphs, inspiring boughs, prophetic trees, healing leaves and so on, as we saw in Chapter One.

However, to survive from late antiquity in the Greco-Roman world into the early Middle Ages, would be a different matter. An idea of this sort would have had to survive serious persecution from the newly established Christian church, economic setback at the end of the Roman Empire, movements of people and a decline in cultural contacts. If we are considering the western European examples, and if we really think the two traditions are connected, the idea would also have had to negotiate a transplanting to new soil: the notion of a healing lady in a tree would have had to travel from the eastern Mediterranean to Portugal, France and England.

To take the last point first, we have to face here an asymmetry in our sources. Because of the nature and the abundance of the material evidence left by the Minoans, and particularly their tradition of engraving complex religious scenes on seals and rings, we know far more about Crete in the second millennium BC than we do about Portugal, Spain, France or Britain in the same period. We know more about Greece in the first millennium BC too; there is so much literature that even little local tree cults get mentioned, while we have no comparable body of evidence from western Europe. This does not mean that there were not any tree cults there: as we have seen, the sparse evidence clearly suggests that there were.

When we get to the early first millennium AD, we can – as I noted in Chapter Three – point to the massive circulation of cultural ideas at the height of the Roman Empire, which could theoretically have disseminated some tree cults. However, this would not explain the vitality of tree traditions in unconquered Ireland in the most distant westerly part of Europe. Nor is it consistent with the distaste of the conquering Romans in their descriptions of some different kinds of tree cult, those of the Celtic and Germanic tribes, which they found as they moved north and west. In the first centuries of the Christian era, ideas from Greco-Roman paganism did influence local cults in a number of places, as the work of historians like Miranda Green suggests for Britain, but there was no proselytising zeal to start new cults from scratch on a wide scale. I suspect that the spread in the late first millennium of the cult of the Virgin Mary, herself tree friendly, was useful in appropriating tree cults of different sorts which already existed in various parts of northern and western Europe, giving them a form in which they could be brought into the fold of the Church.

But how and why did she become tree friendly? This remains the question: how, after centuries of Christianity, could the Virgin Mary travel to distant parts as an ambassador who was amenable to manifesting herself in trees in an area extending from Portugal to England? At the same time, how did female holy trees survive in Greece itself, as they apparently did, close to the heart of the Christian world? Certainly, many Christian writers wrote vociferously against tree cults, like Athanasius in the 4th century AD: 'Formerly everywhere was filled with the deceit of oracles . . . demons cheated men with their illusions, taking possession of springs or rivers or woods or stones, and thus by their tricks stupefying the simple. But now that the divine manifestation of the word has taken place, their illusion has ceased . . .'

However, on a closer look, the picture is complex. Richard Gordon, writing in *Witchcraft and Magic in Europe: Ancient Greece and Rome*, points out that in late antiquity the final decision about what was acceptable in civic religion lay in political hands, while members of the Church were often less severe. Pagans who had suddenly been denied their traditional spiritual frame of reference were like people shipwrecked and adrift, and many Christian thinkers were happy to hold out a hand to them. Valerie Flint, in the same volume, writes about Christian redefinitions of pagan religions, especially of those elements of pagan magic which were seen as being the most important and the most assimilable. Once the victory of Christianity was established, such elements could be allowed to be 'drawn into Christian territory, complete with their lesser "daimones". These energies were then retranslated and absorbed.'

Several writers make it clear that such acceptable elements included the healing of the human body and the protection of agriculture. Thus Iamblichus (4th century AD) insists that '. . . we often have occasion to perform rituals, for the sake of genuine bodily needs, to the body's tutelary gods and to good daimones'. St Augustine (4th–5th century AD) allows certain medical remedies, 'where there are no enchantments, invocations, or characters' if the object, herb or potion used heals through its own properties rather than through a magical bond, adding that 'when we do not know the reason for the efficacy of a thing, the intention for which it is used is important in so far as concerns the cure or alleviation of bodies, whether in medicine or in agriculture'. Constantine the Great (as recorded in the 5th-century Theodosian Code) distinguishes between good and bad daimones, and protects similar areas of activity: '. . . remedies sought for human bodies shall not be involved in criminal accusation, nor the assistance that is innocently employed in rural districts in order that rains may not be feared for the ripe grape harvests or that the harvests may not be shattered by . . . ruinous hail'. Flint points out that many Christian leaders performed rituals to protect the harvests.

She also notes that 'One very large loophole and means of

concession lay in the idea of divination.' Though many writers railed against charlatan diviners, even the Old Testament had prophets, whom Origen defended in the 3rd century AD: '...there is nothing inappropriate about the fact that the prophets among them uttered predictions even about everyday matters for the consolation of those who wanted that sort of thing'. Flint comments that the recognition of the human need for consolation and encouragement in the face of irreducible anxiety was an important aspect of Christian compromise. Again, in the face of a medical profession which was variously expensive, incompetent or non-existent, the use of renamed pagan statues for the cure of disease was in places allowed by the Church.

Our contemporary culture's distinction between divination and healing was in any case not so clear-cut in antiquity, where the processes of diagnosing, working out the best solution, giving advice and offering a prognosis – whether on a medical or other problem – could all fall within the realm of divination or 'iatromantic' ('doctor-prophet') activity.

It is notable that the very aspects of pagan 'magical' activity which received specially lenient treatment in this process of re-interpretation and re-incorporation were those which survived in the cults of the Lady trees, particularly those associated with healing. It is possible that the tree spirits were seen as good 'daimones' and, in areas like Crete, were allowed to continue to function once they had been renamed as saints. Warren, struck by the parallels between prehistoric and modern tree practices, concludes that 'There is, then, an abiding response to natural features, without direct, causative continuity but with a subconscious sense of the antiquity of practices which adds strength to current belief and practice...' We do not have the evidence to say more. For such cults to reappear autonomously in Crete since antiquity would in itself be very striking; hardly less striking than the real possibility that there may have been a lived and consciously remembered continuity of practice – changing in significance but retaining salient features – over several millennia on the island. The possibility that such a tradition could in turn have contributed to mothering kindred tree cults in north-west Europe may seem even more unlikely, but sometimes the unlikely happens.

Did the Lady Travel?

Amidst a great variety of male and female deities, and a great variety of tree cults, I was impressed by a recurrent theme. It appears in the Bronze Age in the female supernatural figures who are linked with vegetation, travel by boat, are associated with rituals of mourning, and appear floating in the air near trees, associated with dance and joyous movement. We do not have adequate textual evidence to give these ladies names. I suggest that in the hard times of the 'dark age' these ladies took to the woods and were remembered as tree-nymphs. During the Early Iron Age they learned to sit in trees, taught by near-Eastern, or – as I have suggested – Egyptian models. Such influences are never far away, as in Herodotus' story (Book VII, 31) about the Persian king Xerxes who stopped to honour a lovely plane tree in Sardis on his way to Greece.

In the classical and post-classical period I suspect that the distant descendants of those Minoan tree-spirits – too similar to be unrelated – may be found in some of the goddesses of the Greek world, goddesses who are linked with vegetation, who travel by boat or chariot (sometimes with a man, willingly or unwillingly), are left or lost, and appear again seasonally – either in person or in the form of their cult image – at trees, associated with dance, joy and helping people. We have the names of goddesses, like Helen, Ariadne, Aphrodite and Artemis, who are described in surviving texts as participating variously in aspects of this cycle. The loss of vegetation is tied to the seasons, and there are hints that their departure is linked to the movement of the sun, travelling south in the winter.

Finally, in medieval times in the Iberian peninsula, France and Britain, we have stories of a supernatural female figure who appears – either as a vision or in the form of her cult image – at trees, often in spring, associated with dance and healing and a determination to stay in the tree at all costs rather than move to a church. She seems to have ensconced herself in non-Christian tree cults of different complexions which already existed in those areas. We have the names of various saints, but it is usually one saint: the Virgin Mary. She too, as Marina Warner describes, is linked with the heavens, death and the sea. Her mysteries too are both sorrowful and joyful; her appearance is linked to spring and is greeted with joy like the buds on the branches opening in May.

Did she have a connection with those earlier Greek goddesses?

After my researches I began to feel that I had started with the wrong question: that it was not a case of looking for the survival from the Bronze Age of a battered, attenuated tradition of female sacred trees, but more a question of identifying complex strands of interweaving traditions. Elements were lost and elements accrued in a dialogue between cultures.

The Cretan tradition shows a great adherence to place: why else would one find a male figure (Hermes) in a tree in the Archaic period and a female figure in a tree (Europa) in the classical period, both in the same area of south-central Crete where the healing tree of St Paraskevi is still functioning today? Central Crete is also the area where my studies of Bronze Age religion have thrown up most evidence about the significance of the sun, and where the orientation of the doorways of the Mesara-type circular tombs shows an interest in the reappearance of the sun at dawn. I suspect that the local traditions in Greece of disappearing and returning ladies were strong enough to respond vigorously to an incoming Christian tradition. In the early centuries after conversion, the Virgin Mary will have entered the scene and it seems that in some places she became assimilated to the seasonal tree scenario.

This Marian cult will have come, like the main narratives of Christianity, from the Middle East. One can only guess at the timescale. The official naming of Mary as Mother of God at Ephesus in 431 AD was a landmark in her growing importance. The 'identification' of her tomb in the valley of Josaphat, probably in the mid-5th century AD, sets a stamp on the nature of her cult, which was already reaching Greece. As Warner relates, in the 5th century AD a Basilica was built in Salonika to house a miraculous icon of her, and in the 6th century AD Athena's Parthenon was re-dedicated to her. Tree shrines were known in Italy (eg Fig. 39), and at Paestum in southern Italy the Madonna of the Pomegranate seems to have inherited over time a tree earlier associated with Hera at the site. Thus in parts of the Greco-Roman world she could perhaps slip into ready-made shoes.

There was also, however, a willingness to travel. Recalling Mary Clayton's accounts of the importance of Greek and near-Eastern influence in the conversion of England, I returned to her book and noticed that she quotes Aldhelm (died 709 AD) describing Mary not only as 'the rod of the root of Jesse' but also as 'a garden enclosed, a fountain sealed up, ...the dawn of the sun'. The symbols were familiar. From the evidence she considers, Clayton concludes that four Marian feasts were introduced to England during the 7th and 8th centuries, and two more (the Presentation and Conception) about 1030 AD. She notes that 'These two feasts were not celebrated anywhere else in Western Europe at this date and their adoption must be the result of Eastern influence on Anglo-Saxon devotion.' Evidently the cult of the Virgin Mary travelled on a well-used route from the eastern Mediterranean to Britain, apparently bringing with it some of the associations it had gathered in Greece and perhaps even earlier in the Middle East, including the affinity with trees. Clayton frequently mentions Greek influence, for example in the extravagant praise of Mary by Ambrosius Autpertus (8th century AD), which 'is new in the West and must derive in some way from the Greeks'. Travelling to reach Britain in the latter half of the first millenium AD, it is possible that the Lady went via southern Italy and Sicily, west to Marseilles and the Iberian peninsula, and round the western seaboard to England and northern France. Is it possible that the tradition of disappearance followed by apparition, the link with spring vegetation as well as with magical fertility, tree-splitting, and other forms of healing made the journey with her? Such a journey, unlikely as it sounds, seems to me less unlikely than other explanations.

This is as far as I can follow these miracle-working ladies. My intention has been to draw attention to the curious phenomenon of the Lady in the Tree Trunk and to raise some questions about her. As in any such enterprise, my conclusions are provisional; but I hope to leave the reader with a sense of the richness and diversity of human symbolic ideas, and the pleasure of inquiry into them. This may prompt more work on the subject which might prove my theories right or wrong.

Finally, is there an 'abiding human response' to natural features which creates such figures? If so, does it arise from humans or from the natural features? What part can such responses play in the dilemmas of Western culture in the 21st century? Do the tree-loving vegetation spirits pictured by the Greeks have anything to offer us today? These are questions for my last chapter.

Book References

Alexiou, Stylianos, 'Larnakes kai Angeia ek Taphou para to Gazi Herakleiou', in *Ephemeris Archaiologiki* (1972), 86–98, here 95–8

Apollonius of Rhodes, *Jason and the Argonauts*, trans. EV Rieu, Penguin Books, Harmondsworth, Middlesex, 1995 (first publ. 1959), 22–3

Athenaeus, *The Deipnosophists*, trans. CB Gulick. Vol. I, 1951, 362–2 (pomegranate); Vol. II, 1928, 428–9, 438–9 (shipboard shrines), Vol. IV, 1957, 286–7 (Aphrodite embarking), all publ. William Heinemann, London and Harvard University Press, Cambridge MA

Blake, William, 'The Marriage of Heaven and Hell' (etched c1793), in J Bronowski, ed, *William Blake: A Selection of Poems and Letters*, Penguin Books, Harmondsworth, Middlesex, 1973 (first publ. 1958), 93–109, here 96

Blue Guide, see Robin Barber, *Blue Guide: Greece*, A & C Black, London and WW Norton, New York, 1990, 443–457 (Delphi), here 450

Boetticher, Carl, *Der Baumkultus der Hellenen*, Weidmannsche Buchhandlung, Berlin, 1856

Buxton, Richard, *Imaginary Greece: The Contexts of Mythology*, Cambridge University Press, 1994, 108, 91–2

Castaneda, Carlos, *The Teachings of Don Juan: A Yaqui Way of Knowledge*, Penguin Books, Harmondsworth, Middlesex, 1987 (first publ. 1968), 142ff (first encounter with Mescalito)

—, *A Separate Reality*, Penguin Books, Harmondsworth, Middlesex, 1973, 50–63 especially 60–62; 67–74 especially 71–2 (all on Mescalito)

—, *The Fire from Within*, Black Swan, Transworld, London, Australia and New Zealand, 1985, 184–5 ('cocoon' of plants)

Clayton, Mary, *The Cult of the Virgin Mary in Anglo-Saxon England*, Cambridge University Press, 1990, 13–15, 21, 50–51 and *passim*

Coldstream, JN, *Geometric Greece*, Methuen, London, 1979, 329–331 (sanctuaries during 'dark age'), 330 (prehistoric Delphi), 355 ('crown of light')

Dakaris, Sotirios, *Dodona*, Archaeological Receipts Fund, Greece, 1993, 8, 9

Erysichthon, see the story in Callimachus, *Hymn to Demeter*, lines 23ff. For the earliest reference, by Hellanicus, see Crusius in Roscher's mythological dictionary *Lexicon der Mythologie* i. 1373. 56

Euripides, *Ion*, most accessible in Euripides, *The Bacchae and Other Plays*, trans. Philip Vellacott, Penguin Books, Harmondsworth, Middlesex, 1970 (first publ. 1954), 35–82

Evans, Arthur J, *The Mycenaean Tree and Pillar Cult and Its Mediterranean Relations*, Macmillan, London, 1901, 203

Farnell, Lewis Richard, *The Cults of the Greek States*, Clarendon Press, Oxford, 1896, Vol. I 428–432 (Artemis). Vol. II 14–15 (tree cults), 633–655 (Aphrodite)

Flint, Valerie, 'The Demonisation of Magic and Sorcery in Late Antiquity: Christian Redefinitions of Pagan Religions' in Valerie Flint, Richard Gordon, Georg Luck and Daniel Ogden, *Witchcraft and Magic in Europe: Ancient Greece and Rome*, The Athlone Press, London, 1999, 277–348, here 325 (energies absorbed), 334 (quoting Athanasius), 340 (quoting St Augustine and Constantine the Great), 338 (divination a loophole and quoting Origen), 339 (Christian compromise and reuse of pagan statues)

Frazer, James George, *Pausanias's Description of Greece*, Vol. IV, Macmillan, London, 1998, 227

Gordon, Richard, 'Imagining Greek and Roman Magic' in Valerie Flint, Richard Gordon, Georg Luck and Daniel Ogden, *Witchcraft and Magic in Europe: Ancient Greece and Rome*, The Athlone Press, London, 1999, 159–276, here 162 (decisions about religion being political), 228 (quoting Iamblichus)

Gortyn, see William Smith, ed, *Dictionary of Greek and Roman Geography*, Vol. I, Walton and Maberly and John Murray, London, 1854, 1005–6; Robert E Bell, *Place-Names in Classical Mythology: Greece*, ABC–CLIO, Santa Barbara, CA and Oxford, 1989, 138, and references cited in both books

Green, Miranda, *Celtic Goddesses: Warriors, Virgins and Mothers*, British Museum Press, London, 1995

Hamilton, Mary, *Greek Saints and Their Festivals*, William Blackwood and Sons, Edinburgh and London, 1910, 35 ('Phaneromeni'), 170 (Ithome), 202–5 (rags on trees)

Herodotus on Dodona, see, most accessibly, Herodotus, *The Histories*, trans. George Rawlinson, Everyman, JM Dent, London and Charles E Tuttle, Vermont, 1992 (first publ. 1910), Book 2, Paragraphs 52–57 on 146–148

Homeric Hymn to Apollo, lines 244–544; *Homeric Hymn to Demeter*, *passim*; both most accessible in *Hesiod, the Homeric Hymns and Homerica*, trans. HG Evelyn-White, Loeb Classical Library, Heinemann, London and Harvard University Press, MA, 1982 (first publ. 1914)

Le Rider, Georges, *Monnaies Crétoises du Ve au 1er Siecle av. J-C*, Librairie Orientaliste Paul Geuthner, Paris, 1966, 166 and *passim*

Nilsson, Martin P, *The Minoan-Mycenaean Religion and its Survival in Greek Religion*, CWK Gleerup, Lund, 1950 (first publ. 1927), 305–6 and 466–7 (prehistoric Delphi), 523–532 (Ariadne and Helen), 527 (death of Ariadne), 623–9 (sea journey to Elysium)

Parke, HW, *Greek Oracles*, Hutchinson University Library, London, 1967, 19, 21, 73–4, 75, 77, 80, 82, 84

—, *The Oracles of Zeus*, Basil Blackwell, Oxford, 1967

—, *Sibyls and Sibylline Prophecy in Classical Antiquity*, ed Brian C McGing, Routledge, London, 1988

Parke, HW and DE Wormell, *The Delphic Oracle*, Blackwell, Oxford, 1956

Pausanias, most accessible in the Loeb Classical Library Editions: *Pausanias: Description of Greece*, Vol. I (Books I and II), trans. WHS Jones, William Heinemann, London and GP Putnam's Sons, New York, 1918; Vol. II (Books III–V), trans. WHS Jones and HA Ormerod, William Heinemann, London and GP Putnam's Sons, New York, 1926; Vol. III (Books VI–VIII) trans. WHS Jones, Heinemann, London and Harvard University Press, MA, 1939; Vol. IV (Books VIII–X), trans. WHS Jones, Heinemann, London and Harvard University Press, MA, 1935. Relevant passages are as follows: Vol. I, Book II on Corinth, 15.2 (Nemea); Vol. II, Book III on Lakonia, 10.7 (Artemis and walnut tree), 16.7 (Artemis 'Upright'), 16.11 (Artemis in willow), 22.12 (Artemis, hare and myrtle), 24.8 – 9 (Artemis Daphnaea and Diktynna); Book V on Elis I, 13.7 (Aphrodite of living myrtle); Vol. IV, Book VIII on Arkadia, *passim*, especially 13.2 (Artemis in cedar tree), 23.4 (plane tree of Menelaus), 23.5 (list of oldest sacred trees), 23.6 (Kaphyae), 24.7 (Alkmaeon's tomb), 38.4 (Mount Lykaeus); Book IX on Boeotia, 3.1–9 (Hera and wooden image), 12–4 (Semele and Log), 22.2 (Hermes and strawberry), 25.1 (Menoekeus' tomb), 35.2, 40.11–12 (Agamemnon's sceptre); Book X on Phokis, Ozolian Lokri, 30.6 (Orpheus and tree), 30.8–9, 31.4 (myth in circulation in Greece), 32.9 (tree nymph Tithorea), 32.10 (grove of Athena)

Persson, AW, *The Religion of Greece in Prehistoric Times*, University of California Press, Berkeley and Los Angeles, 1942, 85 (boat of setting sun)

Psilakis, Nikos, *Monasteries and Byzantine Memories of Crete*, Editions Karmanor, Heraklion, 1994, 34–8 (Angarathos monastery)

Skutsch, Otto, 'Helen, her Name and Nature', *Journal of Hellenic Studies* 107 (1987), 188–193, here 189, 191, 190

Theocritus, 'Idyll XVIII', see *The Idylls of Theocritus*, edited with a translation and commentary by ASF Gow, Cambridge University Press, 1950

Warner, Marina, *Alone of All her Sex: The Myth and Cult of the Virgin Mary*, Vintage Press/Random House, London, 2000 (first publ. 1976), 262–8, 276, 307, 314–331, 390–2

Warren, Peter, 'Tree Cult in Contemporary Crete', in *Loibe: In Memory of Andrea G Kalokairinou*, Society of Historical Cretan Studies, Heraklion, 1994, 261–278, here 273–5

West, ML, *Immortal Helen*, Inaugural Lecture at Bedford College, London, 1975

—, 'Burkert (W.), *Structure and History in Greek Mythology and Ritual*' [review], in *Journal of Hellenic Studies* 104 (1984), 232–3, here 232

5

FORCES OF NATURE

I have told a story about holy trees linked to apparitions, miracles, oracles, healing and a female spirit. It gave glimpses of the lives, concerns and beliefs of people in the European countryside across the centuries. But apart from these glimpses of the past, does the story have any meaning for our lives in the 21st century? Can it offer guidance, inspiration or a model for living relevant to the world of late capitalism?

Some people – folklorists, neo-pagans, local historians, dancers, fun-lovers – use such stories as a basis for reviving or recreating vegetation rituals from the past. Sometimes in the background there seems to be an unexpressed hope that if only our culture could 'get back to nature' in a similar way, then our personal, social and environmental problems could be solved: we could become happier, freer, wiser, more 'natural', more liberated from social stereotypes, more authentic.

In this chapter I suggest that it is not so easy; that there is no 'nature' to get back to, only a series of ongoing and changing relationships between ourselves and everything around us. And that unless we as a culture change our attitudes to our bodies and our own natures, we cannot change our relationships with the natural world.

New Mythologies for Old

While I was writing this book, a series of experiences reminded me that it is possible to communicate with trees without necessarily becoming a wiser or better person. Some of the experiences were disturbing, others relatively trivial though unpleasant.

It was some years ago at the thriving May festival in Hastings that I talked to the central participants. The focus of the festival was the 'Jack-in-the-Green', a large leaf costume on a structure which looks like a walking bush. It has its own fascinating history appearing at seasonal celebrations in various parts of Europe. A green-painted motley-wearing crew of 'bogeymen'or 'green men' took turns carrying the Jack and jumping around it. They made a major contribution to the atmosphere of the event and were at the end of an exhausting few days which had involved rising early, dancing, drinking and providing a hub of vitality for the Morris Dance festival. They had seen the dawn in two days running, as a couple of the men described:

> 'When we dance the dawn up there's a reverence to who we are as human beings humbled by nature. You reaffirm your place in the universe.'

> 'I looked at the sun, smelt the air, looked at the sea and thought "Isn't this bloody wonderful!" and I gave a tree a great big hugging and came away with a great big grin on my face.'

Their sacramental approach to the natural world seemed a refreshing alternative. The bogeymen felt that it reflected a tradition far older than the history of the Jack itself: 'Before the 19th century the Jack didn't exist as such. But the cult of the green whatever has gone back forever.' I spoke to a woman in a green leafy costume who was carrying a tin of green face paint and a sponge to dab the faces of passers-by. Asked if it was a religion, she replied that it was 'from *before* religion really'.

In the throng I got separated from my companions as a long procession of morris dancers, giants and other costumed characters, together with the Jack, wound its way through the old town of Hastings – with many stops for dancing and drinking – and then set off for the old castle on the top of the cliff where the festival would eventually culminate in the dismembering of the Jack.

After arriving at the cliff-top, I sat down on a grassy slope with a green-stockinged bogeyman, who had been involved with the Jack for several years, and asked him about it. Beerily enthusiastic, he told me

'I get a big buzz out of it. I think that inside everyone there's the old spirit harking back. You're still connected to the land and everything.' The woman in green ran past and smeared some more paint on my face. Below us a troop of men clanked by in chain mail with horned helmets, doublets and hose, bells, skulls, tattoos and high boots. Crowds were gathering to picnic on the grass. My companion spoke about pagan ideas of death and rebirth and about how seriously he and his fellows took the ceremony of the Jack. They got up very early, before the dawn, and, he assured me, the green paint on his face was not the half of it: they painted themselves green everywhere – 'and I mean everywhere'. To prove his point, he stood up and stripped down his tights to show me naked green-painted flesh in private places, behind and then in front. I began to realise how much he must have drunk. 'You've either got it in your heart and mind or not and you've got to have the balls to let it go,' he declared and pointed to the sun. 'That's what I worship because I can see it, it's real. If you want to do something else, fine.'

Perhaps he felt he had exposed himself too much. Perhaps I had asked too many questions. Perhaps he was just excited about the possibility of a new convert. When we joined some of the other 'bogeymen' he suddenly declared that if I really wanted to take part, I should be painted green too. 'All over.' And he meant all over. The bogeymen gathered round. The green sponge came out and covered my legs and up and up, aiming (all in good fun, of course) for the same private places and I suddenly felt very alone on a public hillside. Fortunately, my skirt was in fact culottes so I was well protected, and the joke was over in a few moments; but it left a bad taste. I wondered what was 'alternative' about this, or was it just male bonding with leaves on?

As I washed the green paint off my legs in the pub later and tried to forget the incident, I remembered what an old man in Castleton had said to me at the Garland ceremony there one May: 'You make it mean what you want.' These bogeymen hugged trees and celebrated the May, but they made it mean what they wanted.

Then I read about how trees influenced the work of Marija Gimbutas. Gimbutas wrote several books proposing the existence of a 'Mother Goddess' religion in the earliest phases of European civilisation. Her ideas inspired many women to realise that the divine could be female. However, a number of archaeologists – some of them women and some of them feminists – have questioned the evidence that she presents. In the existing material from Crete, for example, there is no indisputable evidence for anthropomorphic religion – and not a single representation of a mother-and-child – before the Late Bronze Age.

Gimbutas worked in a house surrounded by an orchard of 60 trees, she told an interviewer from the *Los Angeles Times Magazine*. She explained that this proximity to nature was a necessity, for she believed she must be attuned to the natural world to understand the goddess cultures. "'I communicate with the trees around me," she said. "This is part of my work." Confident of her ideas prevailing, she predicted that "it will take maybe 10 more years or so for the goddess to be accepted by archaeologists".'

However, since this interview in 1989 some 20 years have passed and Gimbutas' interpretations are no more convincing to archaeologists now than they were then. Many feminist archaeologists still feel that, rather than constructing new ideological systems like 'the Goddess' to challenge the old male-dominated ones, their best contribution is to question received 'facts' and to bring a different self-reflectivity into the whole process of interpreting archaeological data. The goddess theory is still not accepted by archaeologists and in Crete, at least, no new evidence has come forward to validate it. Some archaeologists – such as Ruth Tringham and Margaret Conkey in *Ancient Goddesses* – suggest that the theory is prompted by modern needs rather than by an open-minded appraisal of the ancient material.

Yet again I was reminded that you can spend time 'tuning in to nature' without gaining access to any deeper source of knowledge in or outside yourself. An individual's own personality, conscious beliefs, unconscious attitudes, and the social context they operate in, mediate any contact they make with the natural world.

Ironically, this seems to be especially true when people attempt consciously to create new religious practices specifically focused on trees and plants. In recent decades, some movements – particularly in North America – tried to resurrect or reinvent alternative 'pagan' mythologies which are more appreciative of nature than mainstream Christianity. 'Nature spirits include real biological intelligences… They can be extremely powerful allies', writes Larry Cornett in an article on 'Nature Spirit Magic' in *Green Egg*, a US pagan magazine. He gives step-by-step instructions about how to hold ceremonies in the wild, including how to call nature spirits, channel love to them, and prepare and conduct a ritual. He emphasises a respectful attitude in choosing and using a natural site for such rituals, the importance of approaching the spirits as equals, and the need to thank them afterwards.

Interestingly, in other respects the suggestions in the article reproduce many of the elements of traditional religion, with a revered text, offerings, and a personified concept of divinity. A 'Book of the Law' replaces the Bible. Offerings can be made ('If it feels right, leave an offering of tobacco, or beer and honey poured on the ground'), and when he refers to calling the Elements, the Goddess and the Gods as well as local nature spirits, we seem to have a roll call of anthropomorphic divine personnel simply transferred to an outdoor setting. Moreover, he warns: 'If nature spirits are approached with disrespect by attempting to command them rather than listening to them and inviting them to work with you, they may flee, rebel or attack.' As an example, he describes how he once attended a ritual conducted by some 'pseudo-Crowleyites' which turned out badly: 'While the forest in general had loud insect and frog noises, the area at which the ritual took place got quiet immediately when the main ritualist declared that all spirits were subject unto him...' One participant became hysterical and another was attacked by bees.

Again, it seems that people may approach the natural world with unresolved issues, emotional needs, and predetermined attitudes which − instead of letting the soul open to the calm, beauty, creativity or power of nature − spew out humans' mess into the natural environment. Sometimes spiritual aspirations combined with a denial of physical and emotional problems can lead to a very sharp disjuncture in a person's being. A person may seem on the outside to be on a 'higher level', in mystical communication with trees and nature, while in private, in the human relationships of daily life, unaddressed human impulses are acted out in a pattern of unacceptable or even abusive behaviour with tragic consequences.

A friend sent me a book about the work of Allen Meredith, who spent years campaigning for the preservation of ancient yew trees in the United Kingdom. He made his connection with the trees through an experience close to traditional religious mysticism. In a powerful dream a circle of hooded figures pointed him to a yew, galvanising him into a response in waking life: 'You either listen to these things or you try to ignore them, but for me it was such an overwhelming experience I just had to take notice.' As a result he embarked on research which convinced botanists of the yews' great age, some of them up to 5000 years old. This meant that at some places they had been established before the adjacent church was built: they came first. At one time his organisation to protect yews received up to 20 letters a week from people who shared his feelings for the trees, describing changes in their lives as a result of living or working with yews, and giving accounts of experiences in which yew trees spoke to them. Allen Meredith came to terms with social prejudices against such intense involvement with trees: in a magazine interview on the publication of a book about his work, *The Sacred Yew*, he explained that 'I used to get embarrassed talking about it, but I don't care any more. I think I'm being used as a channel, that I'm representing the yew tree, and the yew tree has a power and a knowledge we don't yet understand.'

But there were other things Allen Meredith was not coming to terms with. Soon after the publication of his book, he was found guilty of sexually abusing young boys at the boarding school where he worked as a housemaster. As reported in 1997 in the local newspaper the *Watford Observer*, the contradiction was graphically expressed after the court case by the father of one of the abused boys: 'Just because he was a bloody expert on yew trees does not give him the divine right to bugger boys.'

Such a horrific case underlines for me the urgency to be aware of the unresolved human needs and internal conflicts which may be displaced on to the natural world. Talking to trees can cover a multitude of sins. After thousands of years of distancing itself, the dominant Western culture cannot simply 'return to nature'. There are problems and myths which stand in the way.

Symbolising Nature

Every society has its own way of constructing its view of 'nature', which usually serves not only to corroborate its organisation and values, but also to give its members guidelines about how to see and handle their own human nature. Everyday examples from the media show this process at work. 'Here we have an example of competitive advertising at its most intense,' said a television presenter standing in the middle of a sea of multi-coloured flowers. The intention was doubtless only to make the processes of flower reproduction seem accessible to the viewer. But talking about blossoms attracting insects in terms of marketing strategies is a clear example of the way we as humans tend to project on to nature ideas based on how our own societies work. It makes something unknown feel known, and it makes the known feel validated. In this case, the patterns of marketing and consumption in Western society are made to seem 'natural': the implication is that if flowers advertise, it must be innate in us to do so.

After a devastating earthquake hit a major city in the USA, I heard a TV newsreporter posing the question 'How one of the most technologically advanced cities of the world can protect itself against the simple forces of nature.' Here the use of the word 'simple' struck me and stayed with me. Talking about the complex and − literally − earth-shattering geophysical processes which cause an earthquake as 'simple' again suggested to me how unconsciously our culture projects on to nature, constructing a picture which suits it, in this case by priding itself on being cleverer and more complicated than 'nature'. It seemed to parallel the pressures in our culture for individuals to distance themselves from their own human nature and those 'simple' passions which threaten to erupt but which our superior controlling intelligence is meant to master.

Sometimes those passions are perceived as sinister and it is the baser aspects of human nature which are projected on to 'nature'. A newspaper article about Glasgow described a problem in one area of the city where a young girl had been murdered in neighbouring woodland. In response, 'some … residents demanded the cutting down of the trees where the girl's body had been dumped'. Here it is almost as if the trees were responsible for the young girl's death. Although the crimes which have caused most widespread human suffering have − historically − been committed by men in suits or uniforms with clever justifications for denying the responsibility of their link with humanity, it remains a truism for people to say 'that's human nature' to explain cruel behaviour. 'Human nature' is perceived as kin to what is wild or bestial in the natural world.

Myths about 'nature' are varied, but what they have in common is their function to reflect human needs. The natural world has been seen as a terrain of cruel struggle 'red in tooth and claw', and this picture has been used to justify the human casualties of *laissez-faire* capitalism as part of an inevitable process. Here the adjective 'natural' is used to legitimate our social structures and our values by suggesting that they are universal. Susan Griffin has explored fully in her books how the identification of 'woman' with 'nature' influences and seeks to justify the way women are treated in Western culture. At other times 'nature' has been seen as an area of random injustice and amoral disasters, or as an idealised haven of escape from modern problems.

It is ironic that moves towards a change of attitude to 'nature' – for example, in the environmental movement – seem to have led to a rephrasing of familiar dualities. In Western society, 'nature' – seen variously as a wild force to be tamed, a female sexual force, and a mystical repository for everything which a male-dominated society has denied – has for people with a growing ecological awareness often been identified with 'Earth'. In this role it has remained characterised as a female physical force, still mystified, still 'other', and now pictured as rising angrily to redress the wrongs done to her. 'Mother Nature' (or 'Mother Earth') is rephrased as the goddess 'Gaia' who has returned to claim her own. The holes in the ozone layer are sometimes presented in ecological writings as a revenge on 'man' for his violent ways. Now people campaign to save the rainforests; rather like a battered wife, 'Gaia' must be protected and better treated, and there is a moral resolve to make amends. But good intentions to be 'kind' fail to address the structures and premises of our society which underly the abuse of the environment. Raymond Williams has pointed out that the very use of the term 'nature' as a unified concept is the invention of a specific historical period, reflecting a denial of humans' sense of belonging in, and interaction with, their physical environment. As long as 'man' and male-dominated society maintain the illusion of separation from 'nature', that preconception will limit what is done and may preclude the fundamental changes that are needed.

In this, our attitude to our own bodies seems to me to be crucial: 'man' is separate from 'nature' (including his own nature) as long as 'mind' or 'soul' is separate from 'body'. Victor Seidler has written about 'the disgust and estrangement we are brought up to feel within a westernised Christian culture for our bodies...Our identities as "rational selves" have been so firmly set within a Cartesian/Kantian tradition as in opposition to nature, that we easily get lost when thinking about a different relationship to nature.' As long as this divide runs through our society's world view, it seems to me that new ecological mythologies cannot be more than cosmetic.

In attempting to return to past nature rituals, another stumbling-block lies in our culture's constructions of the past.

Symbolising the Past

At calendar festivals I often see jolly men with beards and silver tankards in bottom-smacking mood, who feel that they are recreating how things were in 'Merrie England'. I have met women dressed in robes who describe themselves as witches or priestesses of an old Celtic nature religion. Here projections on to nature and on to the past seem to be rolled together so that what is 'ancient' is also more authentic and 'natural'. The folklorist Georgina Boyes in her book *The Imagined Village* critiqued the myth of the 'ancient village' where the origin of many traditional customs is supposed to lie. In contrast to the complex, unstable, predominantly urban life of the contemporary West, the ancient village is pictured as happy, earthy, simple and frozen in time, eternally enacting its universal rituals. There is no sense of internal conflict within the community, nor of processes which might cause change over time. The notion of the 'ancient village' owes a lot to the work of Frazer who, by emphasising similarities between customs at different places and times, contributed to a picture of a homogeneous and static past. This imaginary village encapsulates what contemporary culture feels it has lost, and involves the recreation of 'natural' roots as well as national, racial and gender identities. As such it reveals Britons' favoured picture of their history and a romantic image of their own identity rather than a representation of any lived past.

Take, for example, the movement to revive 'Celtic mysteries'. Ronald Hutton examined and described the development over 200 years of a picture of traditional Celtic culture as 'archaic, emotional, mystical, creative and "feminine"'. He pointed out that it was originally French Romantic writers who 'evolved the concept of the imaginative, dashing, sensitive and cultured Celt, as opposed to the practical, dull, brutish Teuton'. They had nationalistic motives, siding themselves with the Celts against the 'Teutonic' Germans and English. He suggests that this fantasy 'turned Welsh and Gaelic culture into an intellectual holiday camp for English people jaded with their own civilisation' and gave separatist movements a sense of moral superiority. Since the 1960s a number of scholars, like Robert Graves with *The White Goddess*, have used poetic creativity and inaccurate research to reconstruct a mystical tradition 'out of old materials but suited to modern needs'. While working on this book, I found Hutton's querying of the stereotyped Celt/Anglo-Saxon divide supported by a number of links and parallels between the two cultures. Some recent studies of skeletal remains have suggested that the two races were more genetically mixed than had been thought. These are among the considerations which prompt scholars to refer to the 'Celts' in quotes.

Van Morrison sings a song about 'Haunts of Ancient Peace': the words refer to times when we need rest and harmony, when we need to find our feet, and suggest that we can find peace in the sunlit silent avenues of the past. With his rich, gravelly voice, the song is tender, calming and nostalgic. But when I listen to it I sometimes wonder whatever happened to ancient unease. Also, what about ancient pettiness, jealousy, disagreement, anger and incompetence? Do we assume that people in the past were too simple to have such experiences? Is our inability to create peace in our own world so overwhelming that we have to use a fiction of the past as a haven to visit to soothe our souls?

The contrary tendency, to drain the past of all emotional and spiritual content, provides an equally partial picture. The sceptical trend of some recent folklorists, as I mentioned in Chapter Three, is to challenge any romanticisation of the past and even to challenge how old the imagined 'past' is in the case of traditional customs. They recreate a world of social and economic transactions in the organisation of traditional rituals, without a glimmer of human relationship. In my own field of Aegean Bronze Age archaeology I see the same current tendency, with many archaeologists concentrating on evidence for wealth, status and social power (in keeping with contemporary values) and reluctant to think about the personal and emotional experience of those living in that past age. Archaeology – even more than history – used to be seen as based on incontrovertible 'facts', represented by the concrete evidence which was dug out of the ground. Now it is increasingly acknowledged that all versions of the past are based on an active and subjective 'reading' of whatever evidence is available, and that even those most committed to objectivity tend to reconstruct the past they need.

What of the preconceptions and predilections which come into play when we try to reconstitute the spiritual life of people of another era?

Symbolising the Spiritual

While I was working on this book I went to a Palm Sunday service in London at the Catholic church of Christ the King at Cockfosters. I had heard that they took vegetation very seriously.

The service had an overwhelming atmosphere of warmth and friendliness. The congregation held hands; there was singing with a band; we each kissed the cheek of the person next to us; the Passion was performed like a radio play; and members of the congregation went up to lead prayers. And, yes, they did hold boughs. A mass of laurel branches were provided which people shared and held aloft while they sang. I was reminded of the Minoan seal designs from the early stages of the Bronze Age, where people in bird or animal costume hold boughs. Apart from the bird heads, people I saw at Cockfosters looked rather like the figures on Figs. 3 and 4.

At the same time, I was aware that they were not only about 4000 years but also a world apart. At the modern service the boughs were an accessory, whereas in the early stages of the Bronze Age in Crete – as we saw in Chapter One – it seems that the tree or bough was itself the focus of attention. There is an underlying assumption in our contemporary approach to religion that divinity will take human form. This has resulted in a determined search by scholars and writers for anthropomorphic deities in prehistory, whether a 'Great Goddess' or the first Zeus, even where the evidence is inadequate to support it. It is noticeable that in this book I have looked at a period of history where there clearly were anthropomorphic divinities, from the Late Bronze Age onwards. Perhaps I was attracted to the familiar. My own life experience has not prepared me to study the worship of living wood, and may have led me to underplay how much such elements continued in the centuries after personified deities appeared.

Moreover, behind the person holding a branch at Cockfosters lay the powerful institution that the Church has become. It was presenting a benign face: I found the supportive hand offered by this remarkable service very appealing, and from my agnostic position was attracted momentarily by the possibility of being 'held' by a large organisation, the possibility of not having to make sense of the world afresh for myself each morning. In contrast we cannot assume that in Early Bronze Age Crete there was even a priestly class, and the social organisation of religious experience on the scale of the Christian Church is out of the question for that period. So there was no such institution providing a larger structure around the ritual experience; the small communities may have provided a holding framework of a different sort, but we cannot be sure of what it consisted. In the Late Bronze Age we know from Linear B texts that humanised deities had human officials who mediated between people and the divine, and religion had thus become open to being used as an instrument of social control legitimising hierarchy. However, the nature of the control and of the hierarchy, as well as the structure, organisation and ideology of the religion are lost to us. The role – for example – of the 'palace' or 'temple' (as some call it) of Knossos is still unclear. By the classical period, freethinkers in Greek culture were questioning the right of religion to reinforce the moral-political order. Socrates challenged the gods from a philosophical position, Aristophanes' comedies lampooned them, Euripides' tragedies showed their failings. Richard Gordon suggests that the development of civic religion in the Greco-Roman world reflected the classic tendency, pointed out by Weber, towards the monopolisation of 'legitimate religious capital' by a particular social group or interest. The changing attitudes to 'magic' in the ancient world are an example of how the spiritual experience of people became appropriated, defined and controlled, and this process continued within the Christian Church. Traditionally it has been hard for us to think of spiritual experiences outside the context of such an institution, and the context greatly affects the experience.

In reaction to the restrictions of conventional religions, there has been a movement recently to opt for the alternative of 'going it alone' in the spiritual life. While some people choose sects which reproduce a religious organisation in miniature, others choose aspects of world religions which suit them – from Buddhism to Celtic mysteries. Director of an organisation called Whole Life, Tim Gunns, interviewed in the *Observer* newspaper, commented that 'Americans are becoming more open to universal spiritual principles and the old religious structures are breaking down. In the nineties you can pray anywhere, you don't need to be in a place of worship to pay homage to whatever you believe in.' There are no confining beliefs or commandments beyond that to 'be yourself'. This 'cafeteria-spirituality', as sociologists have called it, is again light years from anything the Early Minoans would have known. The DIY attitude, individualism, geographical dislocation and consumeristic approach are the product of a particular moment in history, and would have been as alien to the members of those small farming communities in the Cretan countryside as Westminster Abbey or the Spanish Inquisition.

Moreover, most of our contemporary religions whether traditional or alternative rest on the assumption that the 'spiritual' is separate from, and superior to, the physical. In Bronze Age Crete, by contrast, the involvement of the body in religious activity, and the veneration of physical elements – whether animal, vegetable or mineral – suggest that the divine was perceived as immanent in the physical. At Cockfosters the congregation did not dance or move like the participants in the Minoan rituals (as on Figs. 5, 6, 8, 10, 14), whose bodies evidently played a key role in accessing the divine. Some of that sense of kinship with the natural world has survived, as we have seen, against the odds, through the ancient world and into the era of Christianity. But the dominant tradition of Western culture speaks of separation, and here too there is a long history. Since the beginning of the historical period in Greece, there is evidence of how a socially divided society has separated men from women, mind from body, and humans from the natural world. In *Moving Heaven and Earth* I traced a process in which attitudes to the body were central to the construction of a two-way world of splits and conflicts: superior versus inferior; good versus bad; reason battling to control baser urges; the spirit struggling to rise above the chains of the physical. In the classical period, with the dominant Olympian deities elevated above their plant and animal accessories, Plato's writings provided a philosophical rationale for the split between physical and divine. This way of thinking fed into Christian ideas during the early, formative centuries to become the prevailing ideology of Europe ever since.

This is our cultural baggage; we cannot simply put it down on the pavement and walk away.

With all these preconceptions and preconditionings colouring our view, it is not surprising that we cannot simply 'return' to nature, or to the past, or to traditional rituals. When a group of people come together to perform a ritual, it seems to me that a number of factors – the emotional, spiritual, social and economic – are involved simultaneously. When the ritual purports to be a recreation of a phenomenon from a past culture, which is mediated through the experience of contemporary culture, the experience can be even more complex – as emerged when we visited the strange ceremony of 'Bawming the Thorn' at Appleton in Cheshire.

Dancing Round the Hawthorn

The earliest hawthorn tree at Appleton was said to be an offshoot of the Glastonbury Thorn, and its ceremony brings the story of the holy tree up to the present. When we turned off the motorway and arrived at the village – which is also known as Appleton Thorn – there was little to see except a bleak crossroads with the tree, a church and a pub. The church was locked and we were told the vicar had gone to a wedding. This was consistent with other experiences we have had of such ceremonies, where the attitude of the Church can be uneasy or ambivalent. Some vicars find a role by blessing the activity, others interfere or protest; here the priest had something else to do. In the pub, lunch was a 'home-made' soup out of a tin, eaten at a heavily varnished wood table with a small vase of artificial flowers. At the bar burly men were discussing football. It seemed an unlikely setting for an authentic tree ritual, one of the very few still practised in the British Isles. We speculated about what had prompted the revival of the ritual in 1973. The programme-seller in the pub looked like a very solid church lady. Outside some boys on bikes were drumming up interest.

The tree was young and well-kept, with a fence and a placard which began 'This thorn tree is an offshoot from the famous Glastonbury Thorn in Somerset...' It told the story of how the original Appleton tree was planted on the spot by a Norman knight, Adam de Dutton. Returning from the Crusades, he made a pilgrimage to Glastonbury Abbey and brought back with him an offshoot of the Thorn to plant as a thanksgiving for his safe return. The date of 1178 AD was given for this planting, and the placard stated that a thorn tree had stood here ever since. The present tree was a gift from the Appleton Thorn Women's Institute in 1967. As to the custom of 'Bawming the Thorn', which we had come to witness, the placard was non-committal as to its date. It merely stated that the custom had grown up 'over the centuries', and involved decorating the tree with flowers and ribbons, and then the singing of the 'Bawming Song', after which village children dance round the tree. Inside the fence around the bottom of the tree, we could see a dozen flower arrangement exhibits, some blown over by the strong breeze, the work of local children for a competition.

After a short wait, a crowd started to gather. A makeshift public address system was set up, and before long there was a ripple of anticipation as we heard the first strains of the brass band accompanying the procession as it headed towards us from the school. Leading it was a boy dressed as a knight, in a cardboard visor and shield. At his side was a page with a sword and a hawthorn bough. There were 24 dancers following, the boys in white shirts with a red kerchief at the neck, the girls in white shirts and red skirts. They all carried posies. Behind them came a procession of children from the age of 10 down to about 3 in various forms of fancy dress. They included a strong man with weights, a wizard, a king, a shepherdess, several butterflies, a nurse, Noddy, Frankenstein, a Hawaiian grass-skirt costume, Worzel Gummidge, Little Bo-Peep, a fairy, the Tin Man from the *Wizard of Oz*, Minnie Mouse, a fireman, an American Indian, a pirate, Desperate Dan, a cowboy, a penguin, a boy in commando gear, a lion, Batman, Robin, Snow White, Captain Hook, a traffic light, a mouse, a bee, a devil, a garden gnome, a footballer with bandages, a skeleton and a tree.

When everyone had gathered round the hawthorn, the master of ceremonies introduced the speaker, who was an official from a local prison for young offenders. He spoke 'from my background in penology', stressing the importance of family life and how much the prison was part of the local community. He talked about a current project in which the young prisoners were creating a conservation area and preserving an endangered species of newt. My notes at this point read 'Very windy', which I think was a comment on the weather rather than his speech.

The next event in the ritual was a re-enactment of the planting of the first thorn. The small knight entered through a gate in the fence and stuck his hawthorn bough into the ground under the tree. The 'Bawming Song' was the unmemorable creation of a local gentleman in Victorian times, and the children's high voices were carried away by the gusty weather, but I remember clearly the dancers fixing their posies on the fence and then joining hands around the tree. This was a striking moment. Was it that I had seen old pictures of such dances, like the 17th-century painting of a May dance by Pieter Bruegel the Younger, or the 16th-century German woodcut of peasants dancing under a lime tree shown on Fig. 40? Was it, as some might say, a memory of such rituals stored in my bones? Was it the quality of the crowd's attention? Or was it the aesthetic satisfaction of watching the circle of children turning around the tree trunk? Whatever the reason, the dance – although brief and simple – was for me the high point of the day.

Afterwards, the procession made its way along the side road, past the new red-brick buildings of the young offenders' prison, back to the school, where there was a small fête in the playing field, including a tombola, needlework stall, turns at throwing tennis balls into buckets, plants for sale and a second-hand stall. On a large square of asphalt the fancy-dress costumes were paraded and appreciated, parents having decided against a competition and prizes. The tree was having a difficult time as his costume did not allow him to retaliate to the attacks of another small boy dressed as Batman. After the parade, the asphalt was used for morris dancing.

Before we left, we tried to learn about the recent break in the continuity of the ritual. No one seemed sure when it stopped, although they said that when it was started again in the 1960s or 1970s – by the local headmaster as well as the villagers – some of the older members of the community remembered it from when they were children. For further information we were directed to the archivist at Arley Hall, the centre of the big local manorial estate, although we were told that fire had destroyed some of the records held there and it turned out in any case to be closed. I learned from reading sometime later that the ceremony had been stopped in 1933, due to 'rowdyism'. Also that 'bawming' derives from a Middle English word meaning to 'embalm' or 'anoint' (I am reminded of Spenser's tree mentioned in Chapter Three, which was also anointed), and that the ceremony – now in July – used to be held in June.

Even a brief and straightforward ceremony such as this shows how many different strands of human experience are involved. There were the economic factors, such as trade for the pub, and the role played by the local school as a funded institution with the resources to support the ritual, which we have noticed elsewhere. Local prosperity is often a factor: the hosting village or establishment has to have enough spare time and confidence to organise the event. A chronological study of the fortunes of the ritual might reflect the fortunes of this part of Cheshire. But although there were economic factors shaping it, there was no economic motive for the event; none of it had money-making as a priority. Its raison d'être has to be sought elsewhere. If it is as old as is claimed, it may originally have had a political motive concerned with fostering loyalty under feudalism, but this is not clear. In the present, the ceremony evidently served a social role. As a community gathering which attracted outside visitors, it encouraged a sense of local identity. Having a speaker from the prison promoted social cohesion by connecting the ritual to the most dominant institution of the area.

Along with these considerations, there was also a moral dimension to the event. There were the traditional values, with references to the family, and an emphasis on the educational aspect of the occasion. It also embodied some of the newer values of ecology which have been entering public awareness more recently. The young offenders' conservation project, and indeed the whole ceremony focused on a tree, made a statement about good intentions towards the natural world. There has been a revival in 'tree-dressing' ceremonies in England not only in areas with a tradition of special trees, like the thorn I saw at Glastonbury, but also in areas where there is no existing local tradition, like the wintry tree I saw in the Abney Park Cemetery in Hackney, decorated with mobiles and silver streamers by a class from a local school.

It was also an occasion which provided an affirmation of a shared culture. The repertoire of fancy-dress costumes was like a survey of many of the predominant icons of contemporary European culture, drawing on the themes of fairy tales, nursery rhymes, books and comics, Hollywood movies, cartoons, TV shows, religion, circus traditions, popular sport culture and national stereotypes, as well as the natural world. Some of them, such as the commando costume, reflected popular fantasies totally at odds with the day's focus on the tree ('I do army' this child told me chillingly); but we could all rest in the knowledge that we knew what each child was meant to be. Side by side with this expression of present culture, there was also an affirmation of a real or imagined past: the Crusader knight planting the thorn, the morris dancing. Elements from different centuries rub shoulders, some surviving in traditional stories, some retrospectively recreated.

There was also what one could call a 'spiritual dimension' to the event. This is a difficult word: many people assume it refers to what you might feel in church, and dissociate themselves from it. Since it is an area of experience which – like sex – is very personal and lacks a shared verbal language, it is hard to reach any consensus about what it might mean for different people. Traditional religion has sought to define it in terms of attending services, subscribing to certain cosmological beliefs and following a certain moral code.

Without using any of those definitions, one could say that the ritual at Appleton – with its unusualness, its excitement, its costumes and its shared atmosphere – made a particular kind of impression. Alongside the economic, social, moral and cultural aspects of the event mentioned above, the central part of the ritual was couched in specific symbolism and had a particular impact. For me it had a quality which I would not associate with the time spent eating lunch in the pub beforehand, or driving home afterwards. If not exactly moving, it was touching; it fed the imagination. It held the attention like any good theatre, and as with any good theatre there was an exchange or chemistry between those present. The repetition of a ceremony – even if only over a few decades – gives it a certain dynamic, and those present seem to gain something from the sense of continuity. It is perhaps not a ritual's 'timeless' quality, but precisely its relationship with time, which makes this possible. We met a lady from Liverpool who had once happened to be in Appleton for the ritual, and now makes a point of driving down for it every year. She could not explain what compels her to do so. Later in this chapter, I give examples of the words some people have used to describe their sense of a spiritual experience associated with a tree. The deconstructing folklorists might deny that such a thing exists and, of course, it cannot be proved any more than the existence of an emotional experience. One can only approach first-hand accounts with an open mind, and try to find a way of understanding them – as with any good fieldwork.

What does any of this have to do with ancient tree cults? The event at Appleton Thorn serves a function in the present for the people who organise and attend it. However, for me a curiosity about its history inevitably arises. It was typical that the people participating in the event had only the scantiest information; what records survived were at the seat of the local gentry. Unlike many other rituals, it had a clear alleged starting date, at least for the planting of the tree, in 1178 AD. If this were correct, it would also help to place the Glastonbury Thorn, which the story suggests would be earlier than that time. However, there is no evidence beyond hearsay for the 1178 AD date, and no starting date at all is given for the 'bawming' ceremony itself.

While working on this book, I have frequently been struck by the complexity of the problem of understanding survival, revival and continuity. Why a ritual is dropped or picked up again, whether survival means continuity since a ceremony may mean something very different in a different context, are hard questions to answer. Whatever the pedigree of the Appleton ceremony, it is in itself suggestive of the many economic, social and cultural factors which mediate the 'spiritual' experience, in church or outside it. I would not wish to treat spirituality as something mystical and separate from society and history; but neither would I want to deny the special quality of human experience which spirituality can make possible.

The Appleton Thorn ceremony offers an interesting collective experience based on a real or invented tradition which uses a tree as a communication device to access a particular period of history associated with the origins of local and national identity. Although the Appleton tree's story is set in the Christian context of the Crusades, it diverges from the Old Testament use of the tree as an emblem of temptation, sexuality and sin in the Garden of Eden. With its planting motif, the Appleton tree carries a hint of the 'sprouting staff' story, but there is no sign of a 'Lady'. This raises the issue of diversity. I have been investigating trees associated with a healing female force, but it is important to acknowledge that this is only one variation of the many ways in which trees have been perceived.

It also seems worth considering how people have explained the sources of those perceptions about trees. Three schools of thought in particular come to mind. One approach proposes a static or 'archetypal' symbolism of trees. A second stresses social influences in shaping symbolic experiences. A third approaches the tree as a living organism and looks for a non-discursive reality in the interactions of humans with trees. Looking at each of these in turn may help to provide a context for understanding the symbolism of the Lady trees. I will start with the first two.

Symbolising Trees: 'Archetypal' or 'Social'?

The 'archetypal' approach to symbols is put forward in the work of Carl Gustav Jung. He believes that human imaginings originate from innate structures in the mind or from preformed symbolic templates – 'the archetypes' – which have an autonomous existence, influencing human society and behaviour. For example, he discusses at length the story of Attis, the son/lover of the goddess Cybele who, 'driven mad by his mother's insane love for him', castrated himself under a pine tree. In his cult a pine tree was annually decorated, hung with an effigy of Attis and then cut down. Cybele takes the pine tree into her cave to mourn. Jung takes this story as a basis for developing a universal tree symbolism: 'The tree obviously signifies the son . . . whom the mother takes back into her "cave", ie, the maternal womb . . . In that case the tree would have more of a phallic meaning. But since the tree is primarily significant of the mother, its felling has the significance of a mother-sacrifice.' He untangles these 'intricate overlappings of meaning' by concluding that the tree represents the libido of the incestuous love each feels for the other. The tree is seen as the key to a primal and universal psychological drama.

This sets the stage for an argument: what is the 'real' symbolism of the tree? Adrienne Rich affirms that 'The tree in leaf is not phallic; it is a female symbol' and follows Erich Neumann in seeing the conversion of the tree into a phallic-patriarchal symbol (in the form of post or pillar) as a distortion, an 'unnatural symbol'. Such arguments, and the evidence used to support them, can become loaded. Some feminist writers, for example, are convinced that the Pythia was the original prophetic figure associated with the tree at Delphi, subsequently overshadowed by Apollo and his male priests and overlooked by historians. Some scholars – even, or perhaps particularly, female scholars – want to distance themselves from this view and to put the Pythia back in her traditional place as a subordinate and late arrival. Tempers rise, because a symbol is a powerful ideological weapon, and an 'archetypal' symbol has a built-in political message about how it is 'natural' to live.

The sacred tree of Attis with its decorations (Fig. 11) looks rather like some of the decorated Lady trees (eg Fig. 31). Do we have to argue about which of the two is the 'natural' or 'true' symbolism? Or could we just say that the Attis story came from the near East and became popular in the Greco-Roman world in late antiquity, while the Lady trees have a different constituency and journey?

There are a huge variety of tree symbolisms that have developed in different cultural contexts. Some of these traditions carry a rich mythology, others a complex esoteric philosophy, like the mystical Hebrew tradition, the Qabalah, which uses the 'Tree of Life' as a symbolic map for all levels of experience. As Will Parfitt describes in *The New Living Qabalah*, 'From its structure a complete knowledge of the structure of life in all its aspects can be derived ... It encompasses the outer world, the inner world and the relationship between these two.' The Jungian approach would have difficulty in pressing all of these cultural phenomena – such as the variety of 'World Trees' – to conform to one 'archetypal' symbol. Even in my small study of the Lady tree, while I found mostly female entities associated with trees, there were also male examples and other variations. The Jungian scheme also conflicts with research such as that of Jurgen Beyer described in Chapter Two; he showed how the nature of religious visions could change dramatically in response to social pressures over the course of a generation in countries where Lutheranism had replaced Catholicism.

An opposing view is to stress social influences in shaping symbols, to the exclusion of all other factors. Trees have certainly been called to the support of a variety of social causes. Karel Čapek in *Letters from England* in 1925 found trees perhaps the most beautiful things he saw: '... splendidly broad-shouldered, ancient, generous, free, venerable, vast trees ... It is possible that these trees have a great influence on Toryism in England. I think they preserve the aristocratic instincts, the historical sense, Conservatism, ... golf, the House of Lords, and other odd and antique things ... sitting under an ancient oak tree in the park at Hampton Court I was seriously tempted to acknowledge ... the harmonious comprehensiveness of tradition ...'

How different from the role trees played after the French Revolution. 'Liberty Trees' became a widespread feature in the towns and villages of the French countryside; there were also many 'Fraternity Trees' and 'Equality Trees'. In his *L'Arbre et La Forêt en Normandie*, Jean Fournée describes how the worlds of peasant folklore and of political expression met as May trees metamorphosed into an incarnation of the principles of the French Revolution, living and growing at the heart of the settlement. He quotes an archive account of a series of such plantings at the village of Saint-Arnould, which variously involved processions with drum and flags, dancing, and decorating the trees with tricolour ribbons to cries of 'Long live the Republic! ... Peace to the hamlets! ... Death to the tyrants!' The local church was renamed the 'Temple of Reason' and one of the trees bore an inscription saying it was replacing 'superstition and fanaticism'.

Other trees have earned their revolutionary associations by being used as a meeting-place. In his book *Meetings with Remarkable Trees*, Thomas Pakenham describes a visit to 'Kett's Oak' at Wymondham, Norfolk. It is named after Robert Kett, the leader of a revolt of about 20,000 peasants against King Edward VI in 1549 to protest against the enclosure of common land. Kett was defeated, condemned for treason and hanged, but the 'Reformation Oak' under which his army assembled still stands, and has been a place of regular pilgrimage for radicals.

Another famous meeting-place, we went recently to see the sycamore tree whose branches are thought to have sheltered the founding of the first trade union in Britain. When in 1833 their wages were cut from nine shillings to seven shillings a week, six men met underneath this tree in the Dorset village of Tolpuddle to start a trade union with the aim of combating the exploitation of farm workers. In February 1834, they were arrested and after a hurried trial found guilty under an old 'Mutiny Act'. Sentenced to seven years transportation to work on chain gangs and government farms in Australia, they became known as the Tolpuddle Martyrs. In 1836, campaigners obtained a pardon for them, although the leader George Loveless did not return until 1837 and the others later. Their story is commemorated by a museum at the site and an annual trade union festival nearby. The 'Martyrs' Tree', as it is known, is visited by many with respect for the memories it carries. It is several centuries old and on the damp autumn Sunday when we visited, its leaves were dripping slightly. The huge trunk, held together with girders, encircles a hollow space inside open to the sky, its floor filled knee-deep with leaves and moist crunchy bits of bark – a perfect haven for small insects or animals or playing children. But to me the tree as a whole seemed tired. It would be easy to pursue the projection and add 'like the British trade union movement', and then perhaps mention a seedling planted in 1984 by the Trades Union Congress to commemorate the 150th anniversary as representing new life and a fresh start. Trees cannot answer back, it is easy to use them to symbolise whatever we wish or need.

Far from Jung's picture of an archetypal tree with unchanging intrinsic properties, we find a very fluid tree: a Conservative tree, a radical tree, a tree which can symbolise social values and foster cohesion in a social group. It is only recently that Christianity's view of women and nature as a source of sin, starting with the tree in the Garden of Eden, has been reconsidered in the text and structure of the services which reflect its values. Modern innovations, whether Victorian revivals of folklore ceremonies or 'new age' neo-pagan rituals, will equally be serving a world view and promoting symbols or values which have a meaning for those present.

But is that all trees are – cyphers for human projections? The journal *Re-Action* commented of the symbol of the Holy Grail that it 'can only be understood when it is viewed historically, that is to say as an unstable signifier of continuous becoming'. Is that also true of the tree: is it simply an ever-changing symbolic carrier of whatever meaning humans assign to it? Certainly trees have in many different ways been the carriers of human projections and unresolved conflicts, particularly about identity, gender and the body. But such an anthropocentric emphasis assumes that the natural world has nothing in and of itself to offer; it does not acknowledge the possibility that as well as symbolic relationships there could be physical relationships between people and trees. A third approach exists which recognises this possibility, that people do not just put things on to trees, but can engage in a dialogue. Unlike the Holy Grail, trees are living organisms. There are accounts written by people who have encountered them as such and the accounts are usually tinged with surprise.

Close Personal Encounters With Trees

While sending me information about 'hernia trees', Gillian Spraggs also sent me a personal anecdote from her childhood:

> This may well sound crazy, but when I was a child of about seven or eight, there was a particular tree on the edge of the junior school playground that I thought of quite seriously as a friend. From what I can remember of its trunk and leaves, it was probably a silver birch. I was a solitary child, rather a misfit, and for a while I spent most playtimes and lunch times leaning against the trunk of this tree and feeling a strong sense of – what? Warmth, empathy, protectiveness, recognition even, flowing to me from the tree. Now, this is all very well – I was an imaginative child – but two years later, when I had settled down a bit better with the other kids, and had almost

forgotten about the tree, I was wandering about one playtime and noticed my seven-year-old brother leaning against the same tree in the way that I remembered doing myself. I went up to him and asked him why he was leaning there like that. He didn't want to answer, but I pressed him to tell me, and in the end he said very fiercely, 'This tree is my friend.' The answer was what I expected, and at the same time it amazed me. Quite honestly, it still does.

Gillian Spraggs' story resonates with an experience of my own. Some years ago when I was living in Dalston there was an Italian Black Poplar tree (a 'Lombardy Poplar') outside the back of the row of houses. It was growing in a garden several doors down, but it filled the window of my room. It was huge, maybe about 60 feet tall. I watched it around the seasons, waiting for the leaves to appear on the bare branches in spring. It gave me a sense of calm, lightness and reassurance. I loved the way it moved: the magnificent stability of the trunk combined with the delicate, dancing, flexibility of the leaves gave me inspiration for living. In a strong wind it rippled like water and the whole tree seemed to shimmer in an ecstasy of silver and green. Then one day in August I came back from a weekend away and found that the landlord of that house had had it pruned. Did I say pruned? It was more like savaged. In the middle of its high summer glory, almost every leaf was suddenly gone. He had evidently paid cheap and somebody inexpert had done it in a hurry: they had ripped and hacked so that the ends of the branches were torn, hanging off or staring at strange angles into the sky. There was hardly a limb left. It hurt to look at it.

It was also clear that if it were left like that it would not recover. I knocked on doors and found that people in the adjacent flats and houses were willing to share the cost of tree surgeons to rescue the tree by doing the job properly. In an alienated city street, people rallied round the tree. The landlord agreed. The day they came I was allowed into the garden, and I could see the bottom of the tree and touch the tree trunk for the first time. They trimmed the giant branches off neatly, lowered bits down, and cut them into one-foot lengths to carry away. I asked to keep a segment. In two years the tree returned to its former splendour, and I have kept the bit of branch with me through two house moves. Every time I sit on it, I feel reconnected to the companionship of that beautiful poplar tree.

It is an idiosyncracy of our culture that belief in an invisible supreme supernatural being is a respectable part of religious experience, while communicating with trees may be taken as a sign of mental disorder. Many accounts of experiences with trees start with the caveat 'This may sound crazy, but...' Nevertheless, a number of people have given detailed descriptions of experiences with trees, branches, or even wood, which would be regarded as unusual in terms of our culture.

A letter from Brandon Astor Jones, an African American on death row in Georgia, reprinted in *New Internationalist* magazine, described coping strategies adopted by prisoners to maintain their sanity in conditions of extreme deprivation. He mentioned that one of his own was to look for a shred of 'good' in the worst of daily experiences and that this included trying to be in physical contact with wood, hard to lay hands on in prison. He recounts how once while he was sweeping with a cracked broom, a piece fell off it, which he kept after turning in the broom: 'I... went back to the cell. I picked up the small piece of wood, closed it tightly in my fist and sat down on the bunk. I saw myself in the mirror of my mind's eye and for a moment I felt like a crying infant whose parent had just shoved a pacifier into its mouth. That tiny piece of wood had brought a quiet calm over the storm that was raging within my wood-deprived soul.' The sense of comfort did not last, as within a week a routine cell search led to the confiscation of the wood. Jones then describes how three years later he was one day examining a spaghetti sauce ('You can never tell what you might find') when he came across a bay leaf. He took it away, washed it and put inside his heaviest book, where he kept it for several months. He wrote that although dry, flat and hard, the leaf 'does share a familial kinship (in a leafy fashion) with the tree of life that is rooted deeply in my soul'.

Sometimes the interactions recorded are very intense, and they may range from an experience of reassurance and calm to one of ecstasy. Stephanie Kaza, for example, recalled in the magazine *Turning Wheel* how she fell in love deeply for the first time in a grove of madrone trees in southern Oregon, and wondered retrospectively whether she fell more in love with the person or the trees: 'The love affair with madrones has lasted longer. Each meeting with a madrone rekindles my original passion for them. The leaning branches, the solid red trunk, the thin peeling bark... The smooth rippling limbs feel so like human skin – warm, firm, sensuous, evocative. I want to wrap my whole body around the trunk. I want to know this tree as lover.'

While spending a summer in the hills of coastal California, she also climbed many old oak trees ('venerables who welcomed me into their branches') and found one in particular which seemed to call her and her lover. During a kiss in the branches, 'In one inexplicable moment of tongues entwining, all barriers suddenly melted. We could not talk for the awe of it. What happened? Who made that story? I swear it was the oak, rising up to meet us and join in the ecstasy of mutual causality.' Trying to understand this experience afterwards, she wondered 'Why should the power of love be reserved only for the human heart? I am willing to investigate with body and soul the possibility that this capacity for love can be met in trees, animals, rivers, and mountains. It just may take a different form than love between human beings.'

Perhaps the faithful people visiting Lady trees for healing and consolation in past centuries, as described in Chapter Two, or the prehistoric Cretans shown ritually touching branches in Chapter One, experienced a similarly intense communication with trees. Usually the only language available to record the sense of communion with the natural world is the vocabulary of religious mysticism, infant bonding or falling in love – as Stephanie Kaza described it. But such experiences can also be understood as exchanges between the energy of the tree and the energy of the human. We tend to think of these as experiences induced by mind-altering drugs. On a 2002 TV documentary about hippies, a veteran of the 1960s recounted how under the influence of LSD 'a tree seems to come towards you and pick you up and take you away'. However, such experiences can also be accessed without chemical interference. This is how they are described in the esoteric discipline followed by Carlos Castaneda and others.

Thus during her training Taisha Abelar was instructed to spend time in a tree to restore herself after she had used up all her energy reserves in a demanding and unsuccessful venture. She was told that the tree could calm her mental disorder and reinforce her mental power. In her book *The Sorcerer's Crossing*, she describes how she cleared unresolved issues from her past through a long process of 'recapitulating' in a tree house, during which she felt a mood of lightness and clarity. After spending six months learning to climb and living in a grove of tall trees, she started to become aware of differences between them and to absorb their mood and insights. She reports sensing the younger trees' optimism and the older trees' greater experience; she avoided the very old ones where she felt her presence would be an intrusion. She recounts how she began to communicate with them through a sensation that came out from the inside of her body, often starting with a spontaneous spilling out of pure affection. She describes gaining a sense of the trees' experience: their roots reaching down into the earth, their seeking for water and light, their silence, their ability to feel pain, and the affection that they pour out once communication is engaged. Here her focused work on clearing away emotional debris seemed to allow a contact with the tree in which she responded to the tree as a living entity, rather than using it as a carrier of symbolic content.

I wonder whether those medieval people who – despite the best efforts of the Church – persisted in perceiving trees as inhabited by spirits were actually having similar experiences.

On one specific occasion during her apprenticeship Taisha Abelar performed an exercise where she leant against a tree and allowed a force that came out of the crown of her head to rise up the tree until it reached the top branches. The tree was there to support her in this expansion of her awareness. She had a momentary perception of the view from the top of the tree. She felt a deep sense of empathy for the tree, and afterwards felt something like a waterfall rushing back down into her body. She then wanted to embrace the tree, but was told by her companion that she should not stay merged with the tree for too long: she might sap it of vital energy which it needed, or she might leave some of her own energy behind by getting attached to the tree emotionally. Her instructions were that merging with something strong can enhance our energy, but she should stay away from things that are weak or ill. Such intense merging – even with a strong tree – was, in any case, described as a two-edged sword which should be used sparingly because outside energy is always different from our own.

Castaneda himself in one passage describes how he had a perception of a tree while in an altered state of consciousness. It was not a tree as a god or as a spirit but as a physical entity whose qualities he could sense in a new way. In *Tales of Power* he describes perceiving a tree as an experience of coming into contact with a spongy, bouncy feeling which was both part of him and outside him at the same time. He knew it was a tree by its smell, although it did not smell like any particular tree he knew. The smell was warm and friendly and Castaneda felt that it was enabling him to tap into the tree's essence. It invited him to merge with it in a bond that was neither exquisite nor displeasing.

Castaneda recounts being told other specific details about the subtle anatomy of trees. While other organic beings have their 'assemblage point' high on their luminous cocoon, he was taught that trees have it on the lower part. It is especially low on very big trees and very small plants. The low position of this point on the enormous luminous shell of trees enables them to be aware of the feelings of human beings. At another time, when his own 'assemblage point' had moved and he was capable of 'seeing' energy, Castaneda became aware of perceiving 'lines' of energy coming out from a tree which someone was climbing, drawing the climber like pulleys; the climber, on his part, used a series of lines coming from his mid-section to facilitate his movements.

On the other side of the Atlantic, the spiritual community at Findhorn in Scotland provided in its early days an interesting example of combining practical (and productive) gardening with developing a specific language of communication with plants. During the 1960s one of the founder members, Dorothy Maclean, described contacting – in meditation – the 'essence' of many different kinds of plant, from rhubarb to clematis. Not belonging to any tradition which could locate these experiences, she was uncertain whether to regard these forces as 'spirits' or 'angels', and opted to use the Sanskrit term 'devas'. She was able to translate her sense of the communications into sentences and paragraphs, which gave detailed – and often unorthodox – instructions about practical tasks like preparing the soil, making compost, watering, and thinning. While allegedly 'scientific' claims that plants feel and communicate (for example from Cleve Backster, an ex-CIA man using a lie detector on plants in the 1960s) have been discredited, the Findhorn experience showed conspicuous results. From her unusual 'communications' Dorothy received recommendations about the plants' needs and about humans' cooperation with the natural world which resulted in the creation of a garden of extraordinary productivity for a sandy patch in a northerly climate. Brussel sprouts grew over twice the size of those in a nearby garden; 64 different vegetables and 21 fruits were eventually planted, and the garden became a showplace for visitors.

Dorothy also described 'receiving' specific information about humans' interaction with trees. She wrote that the 'Landscape Angel' told her: 'there are no individual egos with us; when you love one beech tree, for example, you love all beech trees, you are connected with the whole genus of beech. Even though it may be one particular specimen that brings out the love in you, that specimen is incapable of taking your regard to itself, and thus you are automatically linked up with the spirit of that species. If the human kingdom could learn this quality, it would mean the end of war and rivalry, competition and strife.' Dorothy kept a record of the 'Pear Deva' encouraging her to be more friendly to a rather spindly specimen of pear tree growing in the garden: 'Come nearer and feel a oneness with the tree. Slip into its limbs and feel the same unity that the tree spirit feels with it.'

It is perhaps a legacy of Western culture's split way of thinking that work and activity are linked with being practical and rational as a 'right-sided' activity, while tuning in to plants is seen as a rather limp alternative: sensitive, intuitive and 'left-sided'. At Findhorn, however, the need to communicate with plants related to the economic survival of the founding group setting up in an unfriendly climate and dependent on their vegetable garden. The love about which the 'devas' communicated did not seem to be passive, wishy-washy or undifferentiated. Dorothy Maclean was told that: 'Gooey sentiment is not love and does not exist with us. When we step towards you, we do it energetically; you can do the same.' She described communications telling her that plants, being open and without the many skins that humans have, cannot help being affected by human vibrations which are specific and vary from person to person. It was suggested to her that some individuals have personal qualities which can be used by the forces of the natural world to stimulate plant growth; one member's 'forceful and purposeful' radiations were apparently described by the 'devas' as very useful to the plants. Others apparently 'have a depressing effect and even draw upon the plant forces. Happiness has an especially good effect on plants, as do children at play.'

All of these experiences fall outside our cultural norms of 'rational' behaviour. However, I recall Gillian Bennett's comment, quoted in Chapter Two, that good practice requires researchers to 'believe their informants, or at least not disbelieve them on the basis of their own beliefs'. If we dismiss evidence simply because it is new or unfamiliar, the boundaries of human knowledge will not be extended.

How do we account for their unusualness? Are there key factors which such experiences have in common? I am struck by two factors:

one is that the people involved were prepared to be surprised; another is they were able to pay attention. There was no agenda of human emotional preoccupations or religious aspirations, but a concern – expressed in various ways – to encounter the trees directly in a way that was mutually beneficial. Can similar interactions take place outside the confined focus of a personal and individual experience? It seems that in certain situations they can.

Encounters With Trees in the Public Domain

A few years ago I visited a group of protesters who had set up house in some very old oak trees in Windsor Great Park. The Duke of Edinburgh intended to have the trees chopped down, allegedly because they were unhealthy and out of line, but the presence of the demonstrators eventually saved most of the trees. 'Let us Live!' read a banner attached to the trees when I arrived, under which visitors and residents with painted faces picnicked and sang to a guitar. Concern about the trees reached across barriers of age and class: while I was there two older women in navy Sunday suits strolled by on a walk with a white terrier and stopped to chat. 'The Duke's a prat!' exclaimed one of the ladies, a Windsor resident. 'I think it's outrageous to cut them down,' said her friend. They joked about whether it was their age or their fear of the legendary headless ghost of Herne the Hunter, said to roam the park, which would put them off ever spending the night there.

Of the tree people living in the park, some were old campaigners but some had become active for the first time around the issue of saving these oaks. 'I've always loved trees,' a young woman told me, stroking the bark of one affectionately. 'They make me feel safe. Oaks feel protective.' Ropes and ladders led up to hammocks and platform houses in several of the trees. 'I have my own house at the top of a young oak. We're not leaving until we've saved these trees,' another young woman told a visitor's video camera. Alluding to Woody Guthrie's song, a typed leaflet summoning supporters declared: 'This land is your land. This land is my land. ACT NOW!!' It was signed 'Herne'.

This is but one example of a wave of tree protests that have sprung up in recent years, many of them directed against the building of roads, logging profits, or other developments. They are based on recognising and valuing the most fundamental physical process of symbiosis between humans and trees, whereby trees transform carbon dioxide into oxygen and thus enable humans to breathe. The tree demonstrations are political in that they are confronting vested interests in society, but they are also linked to a sense of justice in the wider, natural world, and express a basic human need – for fresh air. Recurrently, those involved also speak of the personal impact of spending time close to trees. 'There is no way to be in the presence of these ancient beings and not be affected,' said Julia 'Butterfly' Hill, after spending two years living high up in a 600-year-old giant redwood tree in northern California. On an eight-foot-square plywood platform with a tarpaulin she survived gales and helicopter harassment by the logging company, giving interviews on a mobile phone. As a result she saved her tree, which she named 'Luna', and all those within a 200-feet radius of it.

The effect on them of the age and physical presence of the trees was also stressed by protesters interviewed at Newbury in the English home counties when felling started to make way for a new bypass. 'We need to re-learn a humility in the face of nature . . . These trees put me in complete awe . . . They've seen everything since the Civil War,' one protester, Cat, told *Guardian* reporter Jay Griffiths. A few days previously, members of the Church of England had held a service on the site of the bypass asking God's forgiveness for the damage being done to the Earth and to the trees. Some security guards had changed sides after witnessing a felling. Griffiths describes this as a painful process which he felt through his body from the ugly cadence of the splintering, and the breathtaking winding of the fall, to the earth-jolting impact and the whiplash body anguish afterwards. He concluded: 'The axis of grief is horizontal; the felled trees lying flat, the horizontal lines of sadness in the human face, or in the human form knocked flat to the ground. Hope, by contrast, is vertical – in the standing tree, in the standing human figure. The only hope for the trees is that enough people will stand up for them, answering an ancient and universal call – Tree Respect.'

Tree respect was channelled into organisational activity in a small London group called 'Friends of the Ankerwycke Yew', dedicated to protecting the interests of a very old yew tree on an island in the River Thames. It is best known as the site of a key event in the early history of the British constitution: the signing of the Magna Carta in

1215 by King John. The group contributed to discussions about maintaining the tree, conserving the area, regulating tourism and preventing damaging developments. They held a small ceremony to celebrate the purchase of the site by the National Trust, noting that the new warden 'has a real appreciation of Ankerwycke as a very special place – and somewhere that has been special for thousands of years, from the time of its Neolithic earthworks, through its associations with the Magna Carta and its medieval nunnery, up to the present; with the Yew, throughout, a living witness.' An example like this typifies the way in which low-profile work through secular channels can be combined with a sacramental attitude to trees, and can make a difference in the external world.

To give a rather different example, a tree was the focus of a secular ritual of mourning and commemoration that we witnessed some years ago on the anniversary of the dropping of the atom bomb on Hiroshima. It was an innovative ceremony held around a Japanese cherry in a square in Bloomsbury in central London. This type of cherry tree was the first species to grow again in Hiroshima after the devastation. The tree itself, a flourishing 20-foot-high specimen, had been planted in London in the 1960s.

There was nothing spectacular about the occasion, but it made an impression. It was a sunny August day with a good crowd of people who had turned out to show their concern and involvement. We stood around the tree and listened to a variety of speakers, including a woman rabbi and a campaigning member of the Westminster parliament. Each placed a flower under the tree and we stood in silence to commemorate the dead. A long list was read of organisations who had sent delegates or messages of support to the occasion. Some people went to lean their back against the tree trunk. A smartly dressed Japanese woman who had been videoing the event had tears rolling down her cheeks when people sang a song in Japanese. It was difficult that there was no happy ending: the dead were dead, and the arms trade – as we were reminded – goes on. The tree, like the people present, stood both in its own right and as a symbol of hope for a better future; but it was a ritual about a real-life story and there was no consoling fiction. There was a knife-edge balance between the terrible sense of loss and the fragile possibility of some form of healing, which gave the event a particular poignancy.

While fundamentalist religions assemble people around an emotive re-statement of hard-core conservative values, a ceremony like this seemed to pose some kind of alternative. The tree was appreciated in its own right. The ceremony, like many of the ancient Greek festivals, and the traditional Portuguese saints' days we had attended, took place away from the home patch of those who attended it, in a special place visited just for the occasion. It did not rest in the bosom of conventional certainties, but went out on a limb to pose other possibilities. It had no power objects, no gods, just people and the natural world. It used a very simple form, and it had a tree as its focus.

Perhaps returning to the past is not the only way to reinvest trees with value, and life with the richness of rituals.

The 'Spiritual' and the Physical: Living With Trees

There have been times and places when humans believed that trees were divine. Pictures from prehistoric Greece suggest a culture which honoured the natural world, and rituals where humans participated in cycles of plant life. Evidence from northern Europe has suggested that here too trees were once sacred. In some small corners of the European countryside they are regarded as sacred now. It was a tenacious tradition and I have pointed to a few tattered shreds of evidence suggesting that in some places there may have been a direct line of continuity. The Lady tree – with a female spirit and healing properties – may be an example, albeit weathered by time and affected by changing fortunes, of such survival.

Ecological crisis has prompted a flurry of interest in old mythologies of nature. There has also been a proliferation of new myths, many of them based on ideas about trees and vegetation, and legitimised by reference to the distant past. These new mythologies have included a 'great nature goddess' at the beginning of history; a 'vegetation king' who must die yearly; an archetypal Jungian 'earth mother'; a 'green man' whose leafy vitality defies Christian ethics; and an ancient earth spirit, 'Gaia', seeking revenge for the ecological abuse inflicted on her.

Such symbols are often presented as valid for all time, inherited from the distant past and crucial for bringing about changes in individuals and society now. The 'green man' has been enjoying popularity among folklore enthusiasts and those searching for new images of manhood. 'Gaia' is presented as a rallying point to avert environmental disaster.

There has been growing interest in pre-Christian nature religions and traditional or pagan rituals of the countryside, which have been enthusiastically adopted by some groups both in Europe and North America. In the climate of 'self-assembly' religion, we see the recreation or renovation of deities, beliefs and ceremonies. While some writers, sensing the importance of nature rituals, have carefully tracked down records and documented survivals, others have participated actively in reviving and developing such rituals, and some have sought to turn them into a new religion. The struggle to define a new relationship with the natural world has been conducted in the realm of mythology. When this book was at final proof stage, I came across Ken Dowden's *European Paganism* and noted his comment that ultimately the function of myths and legendary associations can be to translate the brute religious importance of the tree into the language of anthropomorphic and heroic religion: '... We must beware the infiltration of personalities and god-language into raw ecology'. A 'raw ecology' was perhaps present in the early stages of Minoan religion and it seems to emerge in some of the above accounts of personal encounters with trees, though such experiences are rare and elusive in our culture.

It is tempting to believe that we could reverse the centuries which have witnessed a process of separation between 'man' and 'nature' in order to re-find an earlier and different view of the natural world. In this chapter I have discussed some of the problems with making such a 'return'. I have suggested that some spiritual reconstructions are the product of the same mindset which people are supposedly seeking to change. Looking at specifics on the ground, as I have done in this book, draws out certain realisations. One is the diversity of tree stories and rituals, and the other is the connection of those stories to the context from which they grew. Various formulations of the same theme at different places and times reflect changing historical situations and social needs. To imagine that we can change attitudes without changing our lives is to assume that beliefs are not connected with the societies which generate them. The social organisation and way of life of – say – prehistoric Greece were very different from ours, and it is not possible to uproot an idea or attitude from one culture and expect it to take root in another which has a very different social climate. Our attitude to trees is based on our society's economics, our means of survival, and the things we do every day.

What seemed urgent to me while writing this book was for the natural world to be restored in our culture to the level of importance which it held in some societies in the past. This involves structural change. It is not that people now should go back to believing in tree spirits, but that a practical respect between humans and the natural world needs to be embedded in the way we live our lives. It is not a question of returning to the past, but of learning from it. This involves change right through our world, from the macro level of global warming, pollution, the food chain and capitalism's misuse of natural resources (including human resources), through to local development and planning, food supplies and – on the micro level – the physical texture of daily life. This will include our relationship with individual trees. I would also suggest that such a reversal would mean drastically rethinking our attitude to, and our treatment of, our own bodies.

In Minoan Crete the evidence suggests that the sun, the sea, and the tree were revered in their own right. To honour the tree itself rather than a personified deity linked to the tree means to relocate the divine in the physical world. This implies acknowledging the divinity in our own physicality and its resonance with what is perceived as numinous in the natural world. It implies acknowledging a level of physical experience underlying – and coexistent with – the stories and symbols of religion: a physical experience which cannot be argued away and which can be investigated and understood. It implies acknowledging that the tree is not a god or an archetypal symbol or a carrier of human projections but a living organism like ourselves with all the miraculous qualities that implies. I am attracted to the idea that alongside the symbolic role they have played in human perceptions and religions, trees also have an energetic nature and a direct energetic relationship with people. This is a controversial view but it has been strongly argued in recent years. If we shift our model and accept it, a transformation of our understanding of our interactions with the natural world becomes possible.

American psychologist William James made an investigation of life-changing religious experiences. He found that most religious experiences occur out of doors amid mountains, sunshine and greenery: 'Religious awe is the same organic thrill we feel in a forest at twilight or in a mountain gorge.' What I find interesting is to pay closer attention to such experiences. Which forests? Which mountains? Why do certain trees recur in personal encounters and social rituals, carrying specific associations such as the ash for healing, the hazel for divining, the oak for wisdom? Do certain types of trees and plants have energetic qualities as specific as their medicinal qualities? Additionally, do certain sites where trees are located have a specific atmosphere or aura which affect humans in particular ways? And how are our bodies affected, specifically?

I have suggested that the alternative view of the body known as 'subtle anatomy' offers a useful vocabulary. This discipline, which is known under various names in the East and the Americas, has survived over centuries in the Western world despite attempts by the Church and the medical profession to suppress and discredit it. The system it describes places the human body within a living tapestry of physical transactions linking earth, trees and humans. Using the concept of a complex energy field in and around all living things, it brings a renewed perception to the present and the physical as a series of dynamic energy exchanges which function not only on the micro, personal, level but also on the macro level of the environment and social justice.

Underlying the movements to recreate ancient nature rituals there seems to be an urge to find the same certainty which was once supplied by conventional religions. I am suggesting a different process: one which involves new questions and a new way of reflecting on the texture of our physical experience. Reading about the detailed theory and practice of interaction with plants contained in some of the esoteric traditions I have mentioned excites in me the same curiosity as the Marian visions described earlier in the book. The tradition of the holy tree offers clues about how humans have reached a different kind of consciousness and a different quality of connection with the physical world in and around them. I wondered whether the Bronze Age Greeks in their tree rituals were really so 'primitive', or whether they had a system of belief and practice as coherent to them as the traditions I have described. The early Aegeans have sometimes been thought of as a fearful and superstitious people, their 'fertility cult' based on 'sympathetic magic'; but it is possible that they had access to skills, and subscribed to systems of knowledge, as detailed and as inclusive as the system of subtle anatomy.

Often marginalised in the past as 'magic', or mystified in the present by cults and gurus, this approach is part of a long-standing empirical and investigative tradition which does not subscribe to the separation of 'spirit' or energy from matter, and which sees dualism as only one among many principles. It has found a resonance in the recognition by physicists that it is not possible to distinguish between 'energy' and 'mass', since both describe energy vibrating at different frequencies, some of which give it the appearance of solid matter: actually the terms 'mass' and 'energy' are interchangeable. It offers one way to reintegrate the 'spiritual' with the 'practical', 'rational' and 'empirical'. We cannot put the clock back on the centuries of dualism but perhaps we can use them, acknowledging the strengths of a rational world view and rejoining reason and the body in a new way. We do not have to buy into the dilemma our culture has created, or make an either/or choice between 'science' and 'religion'. The process of investigation and open-minded search for understanding, which has been focused for several centuries on the physical fabric of our world through the 'natural sciences', can move its attention to new aspects of physical life, including those traditionally left in the domain of religion.

Our world is currently facing an ecological crisis. The ancient and medieval communities whose lives we have glimpsed in this book did not have the information we have about humans' relationship with the environment; but they knew that they were dependent on the natural world for survival. The current awareness that we are all part of a huge biological ecosystem might seem more worthy of spiritual attention than some of the man-centred religious systems which have been constructed. The biological relationship between humans and the plant world – not only our dependency on plants for food, clothing and the oxygen that we breathe but also the gifts of beauty or understanding which people acknowledge – can be embodied in the structure of our societies and honoured in new ways appropriate to new times.

While the ideology of classical Greece and of Christianity distinguished 'spirit' or 'soul' as superior to matter, and defined the flesh as weak, heavy, base or dangerous, the tradition of holy trees highlights the possibility of a different way of perceiving things. Challenging that dominant dualism involves an examination of our own day-to-day experience and a questioning of our attitudes to the world around us: how we treat our bodies and how we treat the world are not separable. I have suggested that real change cannot happen unless we re-evaluate our attitudes to the body, the 'nature' in us which we see reflected in the 'nature' around us. This means a fundamental renewing of our relationship to the physical world, one which is in the realm not of religion but of the practical. How we perceive things is shaped by how we act from day to day within our world. Unfamiliar behaviour – if disciplined and compassionate – shifts perception. This book is not laying down a system but offering a line of investigation which might allow us to approach the 'spiritual' through the physical. It has tried to demystify and to suggest the opportunities for personal and social change which open if – with William Blake – we acknowledge that 'Everything that lives is holy.'

Book References

Abelar, Taisha, *The Sorcerers' Crossing: A Woman's Journey*, Arkana, Penguin Books, Harmondsworth, Middlesex, 1993, 234–5, 243–5

Ankerwycke Yew, I quote Patrick Curry, *Friends of the Ankerwycke Yew Newsletter* (February 1998), London

Backster, Cleve, see Brett L Bolton, *The Secret Powers of Plants*, Abacus/Sphere, London, 1974, 13–19

Blake, William, 'The Marriage of Heaven and Hell' (etched c1793), in J Bronowski, ed, *William Blake: A Selection of Poems and Letters*, Penguin Books, Harmondsworth, Middlesex, 1973 (first publ. 1958), 93–109, here 109

Boyes, Georgina, *The Imagined Village: Culture, Ideology and the English Folk Revival*, Manchester University Press, 1993

Čapek, Karel, *Letters From England*, Geoffrey Bles, London, 1925, 15–16

Castaneda, Carlos, *Tales of Power*, Penguin Books, Harmondsworth, Middlesex, 1976, 162–8, 176, 177–179, 197

Cornett, Larry, 'Nature Spirit Magic', *Green Egg*, Vol. XXVI, No. 101 (1993), 8–9, 33

Dowden, Ken, *European Paganism. The Realities of Cult from Antiquity to the Middle Ages*, Routledge, London and New York, 2000, 68, 35

Findhorn, see The Findhorn Community, *The Findhorn Garden*, Turnstone Books/Wildwood House, London, 1975, 53–99, here 79, 80

Fournée, Jean, *L'Arbre et La Forêt en Normandie*, Vol. II, Le Pays Bas-Normand Société d'Art et d'Histoire, 1985, 161–7

Gimbutas, Marija, see Jacques Leslie, 'The Goddess Theory', *Los Angeles Times Magazine*, 11 June 1989, 26

Goodison, Lucy, *Moving Heaven and Earth: Sexuality, Spirituality and Social Change*, The Women's Press, London, 1990 (abridged, Pandora, 1993), 125–182 (dualism in early Greece)

Gordon, Richard, 'Imagining Greek and Roman Magic', in Valerie Flint, Richard Gordon, Georg Luck and Daniel Ogden, *Witchcraft and Magic in Europe: Ancient Greece and Rome*, The Athlone Press, London, 1999, 159–276, here 163

Griffin, Susan, *Made From This Earth: Selections from her Writing*, The Women's Press, London, 1982

Griffiths, Jay, 'The Dying Fall', *Guardian*, 14 February 1996, 4

Gunns, Tim, see Martin Wroe, 'DIY Spiritualists Challenge America's Old-time Religion', *Observer*, 2 April 1995, 18

Hill, Julia 'Butterfly', see Giles Whittell, '"Butterfly" Comes Down to Earth After Tree Triumph', *The Times*, 20 December 1999, and Associated Press, 'Protester Saves Tree That was her Home', *Daily Telegraph*, 20 December 1999

Hutton, Ronald, *The Pagan Religions of the Ancient British Isles*, Blackwell, Oxford, UK and Cambridge MA, USA, 1993, 142, 144

James, William, *The Varieties of Religious Experience*, Random House, New York, 1983

Jung, Carl Gustav, *Symbols of Transformation*, trans. RFC Hull, Routledge and Kegan Paul, London and Princeton University Press, NJ, 1956 (Vol. V of *Collected Works*), 423–4, see also 219–222

Jones, Brandon Astor, 'Thinking of you, Amelia', *New Internationalist* (February 1996), 35

Kaza, Stephanie, 'Erotic Ecology', *Turning Wheel* (Fall 1992), 10

LSD experience, in television documentary *When Hippies Ruled the World*, a BBC Manchester production for UK TV BBC-1, transmitted 10 April 2002

Meredith, Allen, see Peter Mason, 'At One with the Yew', *Green* (November 1993), 34–37, here 35; Anand Chetan and Diana Brueton, *The Sacred Yew: Rediscovering the Ancient Tree of Life through the Work of Allen Meredith*, Arkana, Penguin Books, Harmondsworth, Middlesex, 1994

Neumann, Erich, *The Great Mother: an Analysis of the Archetype*, trans. R Mannheim, Routledge and Kegan Paul, London, 1955

Pakenham, Thomas, *Meetings with Remarkable Trees*, Phoenix Illustrated, an imprint of Weidenfeld and Nicolson/Orion, London, 1997, 114–5

Parfitt, Will, *The New Living Qabalah: A Practical and Experiential Guide to Understanding the Tree of Life*, Element Books, Dorset, 1995 (first publ. 1988), 13

Re-Action, see 'The Grail Unveiled' in *Re-Action*, Newsletter of the Neoist Alliance, No. 2 (Summer Solstice 1995), London, 4

Rich, Adrienne, *Of Woman Born*, Virago, London, 1977, 100

Seidler, Victor J, *Recreating Sexual Politics*, Routledge, London and New York, 1991, 187, 257

Tringham, Ruth and Margaret Conkey, 'Rethinking Figurines: A Critical View from Archaeology of Gimbutas, the 'Goddess' and Popular Culture' in Lucy Goodison and Christine Morris, eds, *Ancient Goddesses: The Myths and the Evidence*, British Museum Press, 1998, University of Wisconsin Press, Madison, 1999, 22–45

Williams, Raymond, *Problems in Materialism and Culture: Selected Essays*, Verso/New Left Books, London, 1980, 67–85

EPILOGUE

This book has grown like a tree. Over years, different ideas and branches of research developed and grew away from the trunk. It was pruned to fit the requirements of publication. It suffered various natural catastrophes, like the take-over of its first publisher by a tabloid newspaper magnate, and the total demise of its second publisher weeks before publication date. It waited many years finally to blossom into publication. As one potential publisher wrote to me: 'this seems like a very intriguing project, part travel-narrative, part academic study and part ecological treatise . . . I'm afraid that this doesn't really strike me as the sort of book that I could work with.' The manuscript fell between the categories acceptable to mainstream publishing in the present climate. It dealt with a topic – holy trees – which many people in mainstream religions find discomfiting. At the same time it challenged the alternative orthodoxies of the 'new age' movement by rejecting Jungian/archetypal explanations in favour of examining the physical and material experiences of people. It did not promote authoritative historical 'truths', but spoke with a personal and perplexed voice. It attempted to make the materials of history accessible and the process of history-writing transparent, offering tentative conclusions as work in progress awaiting further investigations which – hopefully in a DIY spirit – the book may stimulate. For all of these reasons it has become an appropriate book to be published through Just Press.

The intervening years have brought forward much material that contributes to the thesis of the book. I am grateful to Geoff Parr, Jean Robson and Janet Wooder for bringing photographs from the region of Paphos showing contemporary trees decked with rags, reflecting a holy tree tradition in Cyprus. Also to Ana Robinson for drawing my attention to early European traditions of stained glass, particularly the motif which shows a tree trunk growing from the loin of Jesse, variously through the Virgin Mary as its stem to Christ as fruit in the branches. This theme appeared in the 12th century: monumentally in a window in Notre Dame Cathedral, Chartres, but also at St Denis, Paris, and there is a king in a Jesse tree at York Minster. It provides an iconographic parallel for some of the early 'Lady Tree' depictions.

As for the sprouting staff motif, I was continually coming across new material. Some of it confirmed that symbol as both very old and having non-Christian roots, like the passage in Sophocles' 5th-century BC tragedy *Electra* where Clytemnestra dreams that King Agamemnon plants his staff by the hearth and trees grow from it (lines 419–23). Some of the newly found examples showed again how it has been conceived of as a sign of divine approval and will, as with the Irish legend that the wooden altar steps burst into leaf when St Brigid became a nun. Some extended its geographical spread, like the stories of the sprouting staff in the West Country of England attached to St Benignus, St Newlina and St Congar, as described by AR Vickery.

Some material new to me put a different spin on the practice of healing by passing through plants: I found that in 1993 Christopher Faraone discussed a tradition of people in antiquity passing through severed parts of animals; this practice could be used as a purification rite or to seal an oath. It showed that in this area of ritual animals could fulfil the same function as plants.

Odd discoveries assailed me. I tried to imagine what beliefs had prompted people at Holme-next-the-Sea in Norfolk four thousand years ago to build a circle of 55 oak posts and then bury a large oak tree at the centre, upside down with its roots up. I read that William Blake's mother once beat him for running in saying that he had seen the Prophet Ezekiel under a tree in the fields; and that later, when he was still under ten, as he was walking one day on Peckham Rye, he saw 'a tree filled with angels, bright angelic wings bespangling every bough like stars'.

The theme popped up in the field of visual arts, from Gerolamo dai Libri's Renaissance painting of the Virgin under a tree, in the National Gallery in London, to the Columbian Fernando Botero's 20th-century 'Our Lady of Cajica' who sits massively on a tree trunk offering fruit to the infant in her arms. At the Preveli Monastery in south central Crete, a 19th-century icon screen depicts the Virgin with Christ in her lap, sitting in a grape vine. People directed me to films which featured or mentioned Marian visions in trees, including Luis Buñuel's *The Milky Way* and Federico Fellini's *La Dolce Vita*.

Repeatedly, new finds enriched the connections between the ancient and medieval worlds: I came across the story of Halirrhothios who was sent by Poseidon to cut down Athena's olive trees, but accidentally cut off his leg, and died. The story is dated – by his name – to the 6th or early 5th century BC, and the prohibition on cutting holy trees recurs centuries later, in medieval France and in England, as Chapter Three recounts. I continued to be dogged by the question as to how such themes could recur over such a long time span.

I was tempted to delve further into special trees in the UK, such as Herne's Oak at Windsor (site of pseudo-magical happenings in Shakespeare's *The Merry Wives of Windsor*), the 'Midsummer Tree' on the Downs behind Broadhurst in Sussex and an ancient yew tree at Fortingall in Perthshire associated, curiously, with Pontius Pilate.

There were also the many areas of tree cult which I had not even broached, such as the near-Eastern traditions from which ultimately ancient Greek and other Mediterranean tree cults may have derived. Moreover, reading about the famous apparitions of Our Lady of Guadalupe in Tepeyac, Mexico, in the 16th century, reminded me what a wealth of material lay on that continent in relatively recent times, which could be related to what was happening in Europe.

Further, there have been developments in the academic world since I completed the manuscript for the book. The study of folklore has moved away from the preoccupation with recording material details which I mentioned in Chapter Three. The pages of *Folklore* journal reflect a broadening of attitude to tackle more esoteric elements of the cultural record such as shamanism and charismatic healing; these are explored with discussion of their psychological, religious and social basis, although how they are physically experienced and whether they 'work' are questions which remain beyond the academic pale.

In recent years the questions raised in my text about scrutinising the process of history-making have been increasingly debated. The

investigation of how contemporary social structures, values and attitudes affect scholars' view of the past has grown as a whole area of
study in its own right (Reception Studies). I await impatiently the
time when scholars also acknowledge that our notions of 'common
sense' derive from a social consensus which is local and specific to us,
and that – as Naomi Janowitz reminds us – our 'notions of cause and
effect are culturally based'. When we can recognise that such notions
vary widely over time and space, then the miracles, apparitions, divination and healing phenomena so important in other cultures may
receive fuller and more respectful study in our own.

There have been books which friends suggested I should have
read, such as Geoffrey Ashe's *The Virgin* and Stephanie Kaza's exquisite book on conversations with trees, *The Attentive Heart*. There
have been several substantial new books about human experience of
trees and the natural world, such as Jay Griffiths' *Wild: An Elemental
Journey* and Roger Deakin's *Wildwood: A Journey Through Trees*; these
might have influenced what I wrote.

Despite all this new material, I decided against a major re-write of
the book, limiting myself to a few minor textual changes demanded
by the passage of time, for example if people mentioned had died.

However, the intervening years brought one major gift which I
will include in this epilogue. This was the find, in northern France,
of the remains of a centuries-old tree at the altar of a church which is
still in use. A chance meeting also brought to my attention a significant piece of new evidence for the icon/tree story existing in ancient
Greece. At the same time, the period of gestation has produced some
new ideas about the role of 'nature' in religion over the centuries.
These fresh thoughts about ritual, place and memory I will add here
as well, to make my work on holy trees as complete as can be.

In Chapter Two I mentioned reading about a chapel dedicated to
Notre Dame du Chêne (Our Lady of the Oak) in the middle of a wood
near Bar-sur-Seine in the region of Aube in north-east France. At the
time, a phone call to the town hall informed me that the chapel was
still the object of an autumn pilgrimage, but that there was now no
particular tree associated with the chapel. As often with holy trees,
official sources were ill informed. This could have been the end of
our investigations at Bar-sur-Seine, if we had not had the opportu-
nity to go there ourselves.

We were on holiday visiting family in France and discovered that we were near Domrémy, the birthplace of Joan of Arc. On a day trip we visited the monumental architecture which now enshrines her memory, and walked down a nearby grassy slope to see the site of the spring in which her inquisitors were so interested (as described in Chapter Two). We found a small built cairn topped by a statuette and bearing a plaque with the words: '"Have St Catherine and St Margaret spoken to you at the fountain near the tree?" "Yes, I have heard them".' A visitor was taking photographs. A pale young woman was also there taking the air, with her boyfriend. We had been told that people still came to the place for healing. Only a patch of brown earth marked the site of the tree, but the persistent tradition linking Joan's visionary experiences with that tree is still reflected in pictures circulated in the locality (see Fig. 41).

On the off-chance and out of curiosity, we also visited nearby Bar-sur-Seine. On a tree-covered hill outside the town we found the small but solidly built church of Our Lady of the Oak. Inside, from a souvenir manual for pilgrims written in 1936, we learned that it had a well-preserved tradition. Perhaps it should not have been such a surprise to discover that it was a version of the same story as that attached to other trees in Greece, Portugal, England and elsewhere in France. It told how a young shepherd found a small image of the Virgin in the cavity of an old oak. He took it away, but it returned to the place. The local clergy placed it in the parish church, but it disappeared and reappeared back in the oak tree, where it performed healing miracles and became the object of popular pilgrimage. The windows of the church recorded the story (Fig. 42a and b).

So Joan of Arc was not the only person in the area having visionary experiences at trees: one of the heretical activities of which she was accused was nothing more than part of local tradition.

The image of the Virgin could be seen in the church, a roughly worked wooden sculpture about 12 cm high. However, the most stunning find was not the story, nor the icon, but what we found at the altar. It was fenced in by a high, four-sided wooden screen with arches carved in Gothic style. This surround served to contain and support it, and was hung with crutches apparently left by the healed. Inside, old, brown, fragmentary and seemingly lifeless, were the crumbling but nonetheless recognisable remains of a very large oak. This was the original holy tree, on which the miracle story was based and around which the church had been built (Fig. 43a and b). This,

FILLE DE DIEU, ...VA !

Fig. 41 (above) 'Daughter of God
. . . Go!' A modern depiction of St
Joan at the tree near Domrémy.

Fig. 42 Stained glass windows at
Bar-sur-Seine
(a) (top right) The shepherd finds
the icon in the oak.
(b) (right) Pilgrims gather to
worship the icon.

Fig. 43a Crutches hang on the screen surrounding the remains of the holy oak at Bar-sur Seine.

Fig. 43b Altar built around the oak tree in Bar-sur-Seine church.

our last find, was also the most complete example of a tree taking pride of place at the heart of Christian worship. Our last piece of fieldwork sealed our researches with a result which stunned us.

The history, as usual, was vague. Records stated that an early shelter was decorated with garlands yearly on 1st May. In 1669 the application to build the first chapel there described the oak as over 300 years old, which would place the miracle in the 14th century or earlier. A strong tradition claims the site was visited by St Bernard, who died in 1153, but that could not be relied on. A local history book included a map centred on nearby Langres marking holy springs, stones and trees scattered over the landscape. The text described trees sacred to the Virgin and 'the fairies', but their earliest date remained elusive. As far as I knew, the earliest example of the story about the vision or icon found in the tree was still St Ecgwine in Worcestershire in the 8th century AD. Then, that same summer, I learned about an inscription which would make the story a thousand years older.

It was at a conference on divine epiphanies at Exeter University. I gave a talk about epiphanies in trees, and afterwards a kind classical scholar pressed into my hand a slip of paper with a list of references to pursue at the library.

The text they led to was a Greek inscription containing a reply from Delphi to the people of the town of Magnesia. They had consulted the oracle about a portent: 'when a plane tree at the town was broken by the wind, an effigy of Dionysos was found in it.' The Magnesians asked what this signified and what they should do. The oracle replied that they should set up temples and a cult of Dionysos. The recording of this exchange dates from the 1st century AD, but – from the response's style, and references in it – the original enquiry has been dated to the 4th or 3rd century BC. It showed that the theme of the discovery of an image in a tree prompting the establishment of a cult dated back at least three centuries before the birth of Christ.

This prompted me to look again at how scholars have tried to explain the recurrence of such elements over such huge swathes of time. Most of the familiar explanations seemed inadequate.

One approach has been to claim that certain features of human experience are universal and therefore crop up autonomously at different times and places. So people are bound to keep celebrating holy trees. I have discussed Jung's ideas about 'archetypes' governing human life, for which, as proof, he pulled in parallels from far-flung cultures. Archaeologists and historians would not draw on those ideas, which were based on Jung's background and experience in psychotherapy, and which lack any systematic evidence to support them. However, the desire to rely on 'universal truths' is strong, and some have drawn on the work of another advocate of universal patterns, Arnold van Gennep. He, like James Frazer, assembled reams of anthropological data and identified a 'wide degree of general similarity' amongst the ceremonies of different peoples. He drew up a series of categories for rites, but admitted that it can be 'difficult to determine' to which type a ritual belongs. His vision was restricted by prejudices of his time which, for example, saw altered states of consciousness such as hypnotic states as 'pathological phenomena', and saw 'modern societies' as superior to less 'advanced' cultures. However, in the past some archaeologists have applied van Gennep's schemata to cultures like prehistoric Greece, which he never studied, and where there was no evidence that the material fitted his categories. Other scholars did not even feel the need to cite writers like Jung or van Gennep, and felt it sufficient to generalise about 'human nature'.

The growing academic challenges to such assumptions have discredited those ideas. Recent decades have also seen a systematic critique of the theories of structuralists like Claude Lévi-Strauss who emphasised recurring patterns in ethnographic material rather than diversity. Scholars have become more aware of the danger of projecting our own thought systems – such as dualism – onto other cultures and then claiming them to be universal. Critics have pointed out that if you set out with pre-formed categories in mind, you can usually squeeze the material into them, and that we are far from seeing any convincing arguments for inevitable or universal patterns in human behaviour.

Another approach has been to claim continuity. Thus Lawson in his 1909 book *Modern Greek Folklore and Ancient Greek Religion* amassed a wide array of parallels suggesting that many church and popular festivals in Greece have remained unchanged for thousands of years. He proposed that the beliefs and customs of the modern Greek peasant may be 'a direct heritage from his classical forefathers'. Few now would agree with Lawson's thesis. Scholars point out that such telescoping of ancient and modern Greece is ahistorical and compromises modern Greek notions of identity and nationhood, as if present-day Greeks were no more than shadows of an imagined past.

There are many parallels between ancient and modern customs, but current thinking is aware that this does not entitle us to think in terms of straightforward continuity or about rituals being 'the same'. While the form of a practice may be preserved, meaning may change over time drastically: we may still drop coins into wells, but it does not carry the same significance as the ritual well offerings of prehistory. Practices can also disappear and be re-introduced from a different source, serving a different function. Questions have to be asked about how a tradition could have been transmitted across so many generations, and about what may have changed on the journey.

I continued to be puzzled about the similarities, and the possibilities of transmission of ideas and ritual practices from prehistoric and historic Aegean culture to medieval Europe. What particularly intrigued me was the continuation of tree-centred practices in the Mediterranean area after the advent of Christianity, an other-worldly faith which locates the divine in heaven and the hereafter, not in the physical phenomena of the natural world. The dancing figures of the Minoan engravings suggest an ecstatic and expressive embodiment which contrasts strongly with early Christianity's denial of the body.

I tried to read across the gap. In *Pagan and Christian in an Age of Anxiety*, ER Dodds charts the progressive withdrawal of divinity from the material world and the devaluation of ordinary human experience during the 3rd to 5th centuries AD. He paints a vivid picture of how the debate between the old gods and the new 'must . . . have been fought out, frequently and bitterly, in the council-chambers of Greek cities, in the market-places of North African villages, and in thousands of humble homes'. Some writers stress what remained the same: J Elsner and I Rutherford note that Christian pilgrimage continued an earlier, pagan, tradition of travelling to sacred places. Vasiliki Limberis points out that Marian cult, originating from the East, developed independent popular practices in areas where cults of Demeter and Rhea had been strong. But this does not account for the survival of those cults and the nature of those practices. Naomi Janowitz spells out how 'magic' as 'a placeholder for hostile imaginings' had long been a label applied to divination and healing.

Nevertheless, in the fields and hills of the first millennium AD, religious practices around trees – including divination and healing – were still found. For me the question remained: how could these traditions still be in evidence after the major social changes involved in the conversion of the ancient world to Christianity, and the collapse of the Roman Empire?

Without the idea of universality, or any way of understanding survival, are we left with chance as the only explanation? Is it a coincidence that at the present time holy trees are functioning in Crete in the same area where the Minoans held tree rituals?

To try a different way of accounting for the apparent longevity of the holy tree tradition, I turned to Fernand Braudel's concept of the *longue durée*. Braudel, from the French *Annales* school, divided historical time into three planes, on which change occurs at different rates. On the first plane he put the things history books usually write about: short-term political doings of individual kings, diplomats and rich men, battles and treaties. Such conspicuous events, he suggested, are mere surface disturbances on the tide of history. His second plane registers medium-term cycles: social history, economic systems, states and civilisations which change at a slower rate. Thirdly, he gave the name *longue durée* to what he described as geographical time: a submerged, silent history which has often escaped attention, 'a history whose passage is almost imperceptible, that of man in his relationship to the environment, a history in which all change is slow, a history of constant repetition, ever-recurring cycles'.

A mountain rarely moves. The sun rises and sets and makes its seasonal shift with reliable regularity over millennia. Geology and climate usually change slowly. Even a tree can last a thousand years. If part of humans' relationship with such elements of the environment and the natural world falls within what we would call religion, as in the case of a cult of trees, then perhaps it too will move with that slow, almost imperceptible, rate of change, consistent with the *longue durée*. According to this theory, we should perhaps not be surprised to find that such elements have a long duration.

Braudel's theory has aroused the interest of archaeologists, and can perhaps help with regard to holy trees. Karl Marx famously proposed that in any society there is an underlying economic base which influences and to some extent determines its superstructure of culture and social activity. Braudel has expanded this framework. Beneath the social superstructure and the economic base, Braudel has inserted another more deeply determining layer: the environment. In some ways this thought seems prophetic now, when the fragility of that environment, and its capacity to destroy the social structures built on it, have become clearer to us all.

Like any model, Braudel's has limitations. As he himself acknowledged, it is too neat to encompass the multiplicity and irregularity of life. For example, Braudel is sometimes taken as suggesting that the slower, persistent forces of change determine the more momentary. But this is too simple: influence works both ways, and his intention was to balance the two, as Bernard Knapp has pointed out. A political decision can change the face of a valley. A political decision can fell a holy tree, and indeed has done. Social forces also cause change and rupture in human relationships with the environment. There is evidence for the intense cultural negotiations which resulted in the appropriation of visions at holy trees by the Christian church. A peasant farmer working the land can change the face of a hillside or the course of a river; Braudel notes that 'human life responds to the commands of the environment, but also seeks to evade and overcome them'.

Moreover, the model of *longue durée* does not foreclose the study of gradual changes in human relationships to the natural world within the slow march of history. In terms of tree cult, we saw a shift from Aegean representations of figures hovering in the air beside trees (Figs. 14, 15, 17) or sitting under them (Fig. 16) to later representations – perhaps in response to Egyptian influence – of figures sitting in them (Figs. 21, 38). Braudel notes that 'on every plane there are . . . horizontal relationships and connections'.

However, Bernard Knapp has commented that *Annales* historians succeeded in substituting a model of continuity and discontinuity for a model based only on change, and 'the study of anonymous people for that of great men'. Prominent, wealthy individuals make history and tend to leave records, whereas country people locked into the slow cycles of life on the land may not. Those most involved with trees may not have the resources to record their lives in writing, and their ways of transmitting traditions may be different.

Alan Griffiths has put forward storytelling as a significant factor in the slowness of change and the long preservation of some cultural elements at folk level. He counters the argument that uncanny parallels between modern and ancient tales are simply the result of reintroduction. He discusses in detail story elements from a tale about the Paeonians in Herodotus' *Histories* which reappear in *The Decameron* to silence 'Anyone who doubts whether structural elements of an ancient story could survive so many centuries of oral transmission so as to reach late medieval in a still-recognizable form.' Perhaps if a story could survive, so could a tree cult.

We need to recognise that memory will operate differentially in various strata of society and periods of history. Memories linked to landscape will also operate differently depending on people's relations with the natural world, which vary from one culture to another. Another point: memory is traditionally thought of in terms of time only. But cultural geography, consistent with the ideas of Braudel, has encouraged us always to think in terms of space and time together. This brings in another factor which changes everything. A memory linked with place is a specific creature with its own lifespan. Again, memory is traditionally thought of as a mental activity. Challenging this, Yannis Hamilakis and others have pointed out how memory is carried through sensory experiences and physical practices, repeated rituals which become embedded in the body. This would help to explain the longevity of certain practices at trees.

Perhaps we should also consider the possibility that it is not only in the human body that memory survives. Hamilakis has suggested that 'the sensory horizon of memory can be dispersed in the sur-roundings, drawing together objects and places and, of course, other bodies'. I wondered what this might mean for – say – the site of Gortyn in central Crete, discussed in Chapter Four. Coins from 4th-century BC Gortyn show a female figure seated in a tree (Fig. 38). In the 1st century BC Varro mentions a special plane tree near Gortyn which kept its leaves. And today there is a non-leaf-shedding plane tree standing at Gortyn which is used by local people to assist conception. Rather than seeing memory as a purely human activity, perhaps here the site and the series of trees which grew on the spot over millennia are players too.

Nurit Bird-David has cited other cultures where the relations be-tween humans and nature are not seen as detached or oppositional – as in ours – but as mutual. Personal relations include close contact with animals and plants not as passive objects but active subjects: 'nature and humankind are "seen" within a "subject–subject" frame as inter-related in various forms of personal relatedness'. Perhaps the quality of focused attention involved in a ritual can make an impact not only on the humans involved, but on other living beings present, includ-ing trees. We do not fully understand the interactions between plants and people, or the basis of our physical experiences of response to the natural world. Nor have we seriously considered whether human relationships might be reciprocal not just in relation to animals but also in relation to plants. The memory of tree epiphanies was perhaps held not only in human mind and body, but in place and tree. Far from relegating them to a nebulous world of mysticism and superstition, I feel that a better understanding of the tree rituals and experiences discussed in this book may lie in an expanded sense of the miracle of biology.

This may sound strange. Academic discussions about religion often assume that talk will be about deities. Or, if the natural/physical world is important and there are no spirits or deities in evidence, people may turn to the Victorian concept of 'Nature worship', which reproduces the religious schemata familiar to us. It simply transfers to 'Nature' the unequal vertical relationship of submission and adoration felt by humans for a monolithic God in our contemporary dominant world religions. Perhaps we could be open to the possibility of different kinds of relationship. I began to feel a need to turn these assumptions around, so that we could start from the understanding that religious experience happens in a topography, whether it is a geographical location or the landscape of the human body.

Amidst the sparse British material on holy trees, I was curious about accounts of epiphanic experiences without the Virgin Mary, as when the tree/cross speaks directly to the author of the 8th-century AD poem *The Dream of the Rood*. Also about Marian apparition stories with no tree, like that at Walsingham dated by Mary Clayton to the early 12th century (Chapter Three); these raise the question of the many Marian apparitions all over Europe linked to other settings such as rocks, caves or springs. Trees have not been the only natural elements playing a role in visionary religious experiences, and my sense of the importance of this grew stronger through continuing archaeological work. Evidence from the Aegean Bronze Age increasingly convinced me that the special stones or *baetyls* shown on seal and ring engravings (such as Figs. 10 and 14) were not only the site but also the stimulus for rituals involving epiphany and divination. In a series of archaeological papers I have suggested that both touching the branches of a tree, and bending over to hug a *baetyl* (as on Fig. 10), enabled the ritual participant to make contact with powers perceived as supernatural, perhaps represented in the flying figures shown at the scenes. The Minoan scenes of dancing, too, that were juxtaposed

with those apparitions, could be seen as preparing the body as a landscape into which ecstatic or epiphanic experiences could enter.

In thinking about such religious practices, and about the later tree
cults discussed in this book, we should perhaps take as our starting
point the physical elements involved and the conjunction of the space/
time axis. In a paper presented at the World Archaeological Congress
in Dublin 2008, I proposed as a tentative model that we should think
in terms of topography as the root, basis or framework for religious
experience in such rituals, whether that topography might consist
of an ancient tree, a boulder, a cave, a special animal, a mountain, a
receptive human body, water, a special building, or the sun.

What happens, then, in the religious process, happens at the inter-
section of this topography with a special moment in time. Here we
need to be aware that our perception of time is different from some
other cultures. In Western culture electricity and urbanisation have
ironed out many of the irregularities in the texture of living (such
as light/dark or summer/winter) which the passage of time creates.
There were no accurate clocks until the 18th century, and earlier
people had different – often less linear – senses of time, indicated by
gradual or instantaneous events on a daily, monthly or annual cycle.
When those moments came round again, and were pinpointed on a
topographical backdrop, they became markers of meaningful events.

Thus we may find activities placed at a particular time in the yearly
cycle, whether spring or autumn or solstice festivals. Or there may be
occasions and ceremonies to mark times of weather change, harvest,
planting, sailing or remembering the dead. Our tree ceremonies were
often linked to May, or to spring or autumn equinoxes. Activities
may also be placed at a particular time in the daily cycle, as suggested
by the Minoans' interest in dawn. Jan Bremmer has identified noon
as a favoured time for visions. In such rituals it is the specific conjunction of place and time which makes a special experience possible.

And of what then does the special experience consist? Not necessarily meeting your God, but more likely some form of transaction.
Christine Morris and Alan Peatfield have pointed out that it can be
restrictive to assume that religion is concerned primarily with worship and/or supplication of a deity. Outside our culture's prevalent
norms, religious activity may involve not only song and prayer but
sacrifice, dance, special gesture, possession or ecstatic communion
with elements of the natural world. This may in turn lead to a spirit

journey or vision, which may achieve one of a number of purposes or transactions including healing, receiving knowledge or revelation, rites of passage or weather magic.

Here I have moved a long way from seeing tree cults simply in terms of devotion to the Virgin Mary, or to a goddess of the ancient world. It will be clear that I differ fundamentally from Geoffrey Ashe's belief in a primal 'Goddess-shaped yearning' which enabled Mary, suddenly and within a lifetime, to enter Christianity after 300 years without her, so that 'through her the numinosity of the Female re-asserted itself'. I sometimes feel that Western culture has become too preoccupied with humanising the non-human. Thus we look for reflections of ourselves – whether Female or Male – in religion, framing non-ordinary experiences in comfortable human terms. I have noted that the unknown is mediated through the known, and thus epiphanic visions tend to take the shape of familiar, culturally specific forms. For the Minoans, intense contact with trees may have involved the vision of a female or male anthropomorphic deity, as shown on the gold rings. In one part of Archaic Crete, it apparently involved the god Hermes. For some Christians, it has involved the apparition of the Virgin Mary. However, underlying those different culturally shaped representations or anthropomorphic projections, the crux of the matter is the engaged relationship between human and tree.

Can we imagine how that was experienced by people in other centuries and places? We do know that it would have been different from how nature is generally experienced in our culture. I have cited (in Chapter Five) Raymond Williams' point that the very concept of 'Nature' as one unified entity is historically specific. In other cultures, the natural world – rather than being seen as a monolithic unity – has been treated as dispersed: multifocal, polysemic and intermittently numinous. The material reviewed in this book suggests an interest in diverse elements – particular trees in different places – which are drawn into specific ritual or relationship with humans on specific occasions.

Chris Fowler has emphasised that when looking at the past we must allow for 'personal experiences of the world which were radically different to our own', with different relations between humans and animals and plants. He suggests that contemporary scholars over-emphasise the 'self' in addressing past bodies, and that early religion was concerned rather with creating connections across time and space and between different types of being. He is writing about prehistory, but some of that quality is apparent in the tree cults discussed in this book, with their emphasis on miraculous encounters in the natural world. The tree celebrations of different periods are often group experiences, opening channels of communion and participation not only between humans and trees but between humans and humans, rather than fitting within the format of approaching a superior deity.

This model I arrived at – the conjunction of topography, time and transaction – provides a new framework for thinking about the many examples of tree cults described in this book: the occasions at particular times of day or year when people have focused attention on trees and entered non-ordinary reality. Hearing or seeing non-ordinary phenomena, they have – from the accounts – associated encountering the tree with a special transaction: a divinatory experience of receiving advice/information/instruction, or an experience of healing.

Such a model accommodates possibilities different from the practice of transcendent religion which was confirmed with the advent of Christianity. Instead it allows for an immanent spirituality which locates the divine in the physical world around us, in human bodies and in everyday lives.

Book References

Ashe, Geoffrey, *The Virgin: Mary's Cult and the Re-emergence of the Goddess*, Arkana, London, 1988 (first publ. 1976), vii, 22, 146

Baetyls, see Lucy Goodison, "'Why All This about Oak or Stone?'": Trees and Boulders in Minoan Religion', in A. L. D'Agata and A. Van de Moortel, eds, *Archaeologies of Cult: Essays on Ritual and Cult in Crete in Honor of Geraldine C. Gesell*, The American School of Classical Studies at Athens, 2009, 233–42; also 'Gender, Body and the Minoans: Contemporary and Prehistoric Perceptions', in K Kopaka, ed, *Engendering Prehistoric 'Stratigraphies' in the Aegean and the Mediterranean (Aegaeum 30)*, Liège, 2009, 51–7

Bar-sur-Seine, see M le Chanoine Lavigne, *Manuel-Souvenir du Pèlerinage de Notre-Dame du Chêne*, Imprimerie Saint-Pierre, Langres, 1936; also local history book by Georges Drioux, *Cultes Indigènes des Lingons*, Auguste Picard, Paris and Imprimerie Champenoise, Langres, 1934, 172–6 and map

Bird-David, Nurit, 'Metaphorization of Human–Nature Relatedness', in Kay Milton, ed, *Environmentalism: The View from Anthropology*, Routledge, London and New York, 1993, 112–25, here 121; see also Nurit Bird-David, '"Animism" Revisited', *Current Anthropology*, 40, Supplement, 1999, S67–S91

Blake, see GE Bentley, *The Stranger from Paradise: A Biography of William Blake*, Yale University Press, New Haven and London, 2001, 19–20

Braudel, Fernand, *The Mediterranean and the Mediterranean World in the Age of Philip II*, Vol. I, transl. Siân Reynolds, Collins, London, 1972 (first publ. 1949), 16, 20–1, 260, 267

Bremmer, Jan, 'Paul on the Road to Damascus: The Construction of a Hellenistic Epiphany'. Paper given in Exeter 19 July 2004 at conference 'Theoi Epiphaneis: Confronting the Divine in the Ancient World'

Deakin, Roger, *Wildwood: A Journey Through Trees*, Hamish Hamilton, London, 2007

Dodds, ER, *Pagan and Christian in an Age of Anxiety: The Wiles Lectures given at the Queen's University Belfast, 1963*, Cambridge University Press, 1990 (first publ. 1965), 7, 10, 37, 82, 103

Elsner, J and I Rutherford, 'The Concept of Pilgrimage and Its Problems', in J Elsner and I Rutherford, eds, *Pilgrimage in Graeco-Roman and Early Christian Antiquity: Seeing the Gods*, Oxford University Press, Oxford, 2005, 1–9

Faraone, Christopher A, 'Molten Wax, Spilt Wine and Mutilated Animals', *Journal of Hellenic Studies*, 113, 1993, 60–80, here 71–2 and n 45

Fowler, Chris, 'Body Parts: Personhood and Materiality in the Earlier Manx Neolithic', in Yannis Hamilakis, Mark Pluciennik and Sarah Tarlow, eds, *Thinking through the Body: Archaeologies of Corporeality*, Kluwer Academic/Plenum Publishers, New York, 2002, 47–69, here 58, 63

Gennep, Arnold van, *The Rites of Passage*, transl. Monika B Vizedom and Gabrielle L Caffee, Routledge and Kegan Paul, London and Henley, 1977 (first publ. 1909), 2, 3, 9, 12, 184

Goodison, Lucy, '"Nature", Ecology and the Minoans', paper given in Dublin 30 June 2008 at Sixth World Archaeological Congress

Griffiths, Alan, 'Behind the Lines: The Genesis of Stories in Herodotus', in Felix Budelmann and Pantelis Michelakis, eds, *Homer, Tragedy and Beyond: Essays in Honour of P.E. Easterling*, Society for the Promotion of Hellenic Studies, London, 2001, 75–89, here 75, 84–5 and n 42

Griffiths, Jay, *Wild: An Elemental Journey*, Penguin, London, 2008 (first publ. 2006)

Guadalupe, see Johnston, Francis, *The Wonder of Guadalupe*, Tan Books, Rockford, 1981

Halirrhothios, see Emily Kearns, *The Heroes of Attica*, Bulletin Supplement 57, Institute of Classical Studies, London, 1989, 144–5; Wilhelm Mannhardt, *Wald- und Feldkulte*, Vol. II, Verlag von Gebrüder Borntraeger, Berlin, 1905, 29–30

Hamilakis, Yannis, 'The Past as Oral History: Towards an Archaeology of the Senses', in Yannis Hamilakis, Mark Pluciennik and Sarah Tarlow, eds, *Thinking through the Body: Archaeologies of Corporeality*, Kluwer Academic/Plenum Publishers, New York, 2002, 121–36, here 124

Janowitz, Naomi, *Magic in the Roman World: Pagans, Jews and Christians*, Routledge, London and New York, 2001, 6, 8

Kaza, Stephanie, *The Attentive Heart: Conversations with Trees*, Shambhala, Boston, 1996

Knapp, A Bernard, 'Archaeology and Annales', in A Bernard Knapp, ed, *Archaeology, Annales, and Ethnohistory*, Cambridge University Press, Cambridge, 1992, 1–21, here 6

Lawson, John Cuthbert, *Modern Greek Folklore and Ancient Greek Religion: A Study in Survivals*, University Books, New York, 1964 (first publ. 1909), 1

Limberis, Vasiliki, *Divine Heiress: The Virgin Mary and the Creation of Christian Constantinople*, Routledge, London and New York, 1994

MacMullen, Ramsay, *Christianity and Paganism in the Fourth to Eighth Centuries*, Yale University Press, New Haven and London, 1997, 13

Magnesians consulting Delphi, see HW Parke and DEW Wormell, *The Delphic Oracle*, Vol. I, Basil Blackwell, Oxford, 1956, 334–5; also Vol. II, 137–8

Morris, Christine and Alan Peatfield, 'Feeling through the Body: Gesture in Cretan Bronze Age Religion', in Yannis Hamilakis, Mark Pluciennik and Sarah Tarlow, eds, *Thinking through the Body: Archaeologies of Corporeality*, Kluwer Academic/Plenum Publishers, New York, 2002, 105–20, here 110

Vickery, AR, *Holy Thorn of Glastonbury*, Toucan Press, Guernsey, 1987, 12–13

Williams, Raymond, *Problems in Materialism and Culture: Selected Essays*, Verso Editions and NLB, London, 1980, 68–9

PICTURE SOURCE LIST

Fig. 1 Holy tree in south-central Crete. Photo by Carlos Guarita.

Fig. 2 Plaque from Psychro in Ashmolean Musem, Oxford, No. AE.617. Drawing after Martin P Nilsson, *The Minoan-Mycenaean Religion and its Survival in Greek Religion*, 1927,171 Fig. 72.

Fig. 3 Male figure with branch. Steatite three-sided prism bead seal in British Museum (GR/R) 1947. 9–26. 3. From *Corpus der Minoischen und Mykenischen Siegel,* Vol. VII No. 3.

Fig. 4 Two female figures with vegetation. Sealing from Phaistos in Heraklion Museum, HM No. 683. From *Corpus der Minoischen und Mykenischen Siegel*, Vol. II, 5 No. 323.

Fig. 5 Tree cult on gold ring from Aidonia in Nemea Museum. From *Corpus der Minoischen und Mykenischen Siegel,* Vol. VS. 1B No. 114.

Fig. 6 'Tree-shaking' on dark green steatite lentoid of LM IIIA date in Metropolitan Museum, New York. Drawing by Carlos Guarita after *Corpus der Minoischen und Mykenischen Siegel,* Vol. XII No. 264.

Fig. 7 'Genii' with plant on bead seal from central Crete in Ashmolean Museum, Oxford, No. 1938. 1043. From Arthur J Evans, *Palace of Minos IV*, Macmillan, London, 1935, 453 Fig. 377.

Fig. 8 Two figures with branches on haematite lentoid seal from Midea in National Archaeological Museum, Athens, No. 8771. From *Corpus der Minoischen und Mykenischen Siegel,* Vol. I No. 195.

Fig. 9 Female figure with altar and palm tree on lentoid seal allegedly from Knossos. From *Corpus der Minoischen und Mykenischen Siegel*, Vol. VS.1A No. 75.

Fig. 10 Scene of ritual on gold signet ring from Archanes Phourni in Heraklion Museum, HM No. 989. Rough drawing by Lucy Goodison after Y Sakellarakis in *Archaeology* (1967), 280 Fig. 13.

Fig. 11 Sacred tree of Attis, relief from an altar to Cybele. From Hugo Gressman, *Die Orientalischen Religionen im Hellenistisch-Römischen Zeitalter*, Gruyter, Berlin and Leipzig, 1930, 99 Fig. 41.

Fig. 12 Boat scene on gold ring from Mochlos burial, replica in Heraklion Museum HM No. 259. From Martin P Nilsson, *The Minoan-Mycenaean Religion and its Survival in Greek Religion*, 1927, 269, Fig. 136.

Fig. 13 Boat scene on gold ring from Crete in Ashmolean Museum, Oxford, No. 1938.1129. From Martin P Nilsson, *The Minoan-Mycenaean Religion and its Survival in Greek Religion*, 1927, Fig. 7.

Fig. 14 'Ring of Minos', apparently a chance find from 'Knossos, above the Temple Tomb', formerly in the Evans collection. From Arthur J Evans, *Palace of Minos IV*, 1935, 950 Fig. 917.

Fig. 15 Religious scene at tree on bronze ring allegedly from Kavousi, east Crete, in Heraklion Museum, Bronze No. 970. From *Corpus der Minoischen und Mykenischen Siegel*, Vol. II, 3 No. 305.

Fig. 16 The 'Great Gold Ring' from Acropolis of Mycenae, in National Archeological Museum, Athens, No. 992. From Martin P Nilsson, *The Minoan-Mycenaean Religion and its Survival in Greek Religion*, 1927, 347 Fig. 158.

Fig. 17 Hovering god on gold ring from Knossos in Ashmolean Museum, Oxford, No. K 250. 1938. 1127. From Martin P Nilsson, *The Minoan-Mycenaean Religion and its Survival in Greek Religion*, 1927, 256 Fig. 123.

Fig. 18 Female figure on funerary urn from Arkades in Heraklion Museum. Drawing by Carlos Guarita.

Fig. 19 Procession to seated female figure on Geometric bowl from the Kerameikos in National Archaeological Museum, Athens, No. 784. Graphic by Lucy Goodison and Carlos Guarita.

Fig. 20 Prothesis scene on fragment in National Archaeological Museum, Athens, No. 812. Drawing by Lucy Goodison after a photo by Carlos Guarita.

Fig. 21 'Hermes Dendrites' on bronze votive plaque from Kato Symi in Heraklion Museum No. A21. Drawing by Lucy Goodison.

Fig. 22 The goddess Nut in her sacred sycamore bestowing the bread and water of the next world. From JH Philpot, *The Sacred Tree*, 1897, after G Gaston Maspero, *Dawn of Civilisation: Egypt and Chaldfa*, transl. ML McLure, Society for Promotion of Christian Knowledge, London, 1894, 185.

Fig. 23 Nossa Senhora da Piedade da Merceana, engraving hanging in church vestry at Merceana, central Portugal.

Fig. 24 Nossa Senhora das Brotas. From a Portuguese original on a leaflet handed out at her church in Brotas.

Fig. 25 Nossa Senhora da Gaiola painted on church ceiling in Cortes de Leiria. After a photo by Carlos Guarita.

Fig. 26 Nossa Senhora do Sobreiro at Convent of Varatojo near Torres Vedras. Anonymous engraving of late (?)18th century. In Biblioteca Nacional de Lisboa.

Fig. 27 Apparition of the Virgin at Fatima. From a postcard sold at Fatima.

Fig. 28 'Ex-voto a Nossa Senhora da Conceição' oil on wood 1819 probably from Lisbon. Graphic by Carlos Guarita after original in National Archaeological and Ethnological Museum, Lisbon.

Fig. 29 Engraving of Allouville oak. From *Patrimoine Normand* 2 (1995), 33.

Fig. 30 'La Bonne Notre Dame de Bon Secour' (*sic*) by Picard-Guérin in Bibliothèque Municipale, Caen FNE 2491.

Fig. 31 'Notre Dame de Pitié . . . a Banelles'. From Hansmann and Vogeser, Munich.

Fig. 32 'Our Lady of Scherpenheuvel' in Limburg, Holland. From Jules Frere, *Volkskunde in Limburg*, Stichting, Mens en Kultuur, Gent, 1992, 169.

Fig. 33 'Il Passaggio', Campania, Italy, 1979. Photo by Marialba Russo.

Fig. 34 Dodona oak precinct, reconstructed drawing by B Charisis. From Sotirios Dakaris, *Dodona*, 1993, 15, Fig. 9.

Fig. 35 Stone votive relief in National Archaeological Museum, Athens, No. 1390. From Kynouria/Thyrea, part of Arkadia on the east coast of Peloponnese. After Carl Boetticher, *Der Baumkultus der Hellenen*, 1856, Fig. 48.

Fig. 36 Boat embarkation scene on vase from Thebes in British Museum, No. 1899. 2. 19.1. From E Buschor, *Greek Vase Painting*, 1921, Pl. XI, Fig. 2.

Fig. 37 Holy myrtle at Paliani near Venerato. Photo by Carlos Guarita.

Fig. 38 Coins from Gortyn. (a), (b) After Georges Le Rider, *Monnaies Crétoises*, 1966, Pl. XVII Nos. 3 and 12. (c) After Carl Boetticher, *Der Baumkultus der Hellenen*, 1856, Fig. 46.

Fig. 39 Drawing of Pompeiian wall-painting. From Carl Boetticher, *Der Baumkultus der Hellenen*, 1856, Fig. 36.

Fig. 40 Bauerntanz unter der Linde, woodcut by D Kandel. From H Bock, *Kräuterbuch*, Strasburg, 1546.

Fig. 41 Design on memento given out at Domrémy, birthplace of St Joan (no attribution).

Fig. 42 (a), (b) Stained glass windows in church of Notre Dame du Chêne in Bar-sur-Seine. Photos by Carlos Guarita.

Fig. 43 (a), (b) Interior of church of Notre Dame du Chêne in Bar-sur-Seine. Photos by Carlos Guarita.

INDEX

248 Index